NORTHERN SIKKIM

KELLAS

Prelude to Everest

Prelude to Everest

Alexander Kellas, Himalayan Mountaineer

IAN R MITCHELL AND GEORGE W RODWAY

Luath Press Limited
EDINBURGH
www.luath.co.uk

First published 2011

ISBN: 978-1-906817-74-9

The paper used in this book is sourced from renewable forestry
and is FSC credited material.

Printed and bound by
MPG Books Ltd., Cornwall

Maps pp.9–14 (excluding p.13) © Jim Lewis

Typeset in 11pt Sabon by
3btype.com

Northern Sikkim endpaper map is from *Geographical Journal*, 1912,
courtesy of RGS.

Mount Everest Expedition endpaper map is from *The Everest Reconnaissance*
(1922) by CK Howard-Bury, courtesy of RGS.

Appendix 'A Consideration of the Possibility of Ascending Mount Everest'
reproduced with permission of Mary Anne Liebert.

Every effort has been made to locate image copyright holders. Should there be
any omissions please contact the publisher.

This book is dedicated to Professor John B West MD, PhD – for bringing his pre-eminent knowledge of the history of high altitude physiology and medicine to bear on the resurrection of the reputation of the all-but-forgotten Himalayan mountaineer and scientist AM Kellas nearly a quarter of a century ago.

Acknowledgements

WE WOULD LIKE to thank Doug Scott for providing a foreword to this book, and also Liz Smith, Peter Drummond, Mike Dey and Alexander and Laura Mitchell for their help and support.

We also owe a big debt of gratitude to all members of the 2009 Anglo-Indian-American Sikkim (AIAS) expedition who most kindly assisted this project by providing many of the images found in this work.

Further we would like to thank the Royal Geographical Society for permission to use the many images by Alexander Kellas which are published, mostly for the first time, in the book, as well as the Scottish Mountaineering Club, University College London, the University of Durham (Bentley-Beetham Collection) and the estate of Frank Smythe for permission to use other images which appear in the book. Uncredited images are in the public domain.

A Note on Nomenclature

Himalayan nomenclature is a problematic issue. We have retained the original usage of place and mountain names by Kellas and others in the quoted text, but after first citation in the main text tried to utilise standard modern map usage, as far as was possible.

Contents

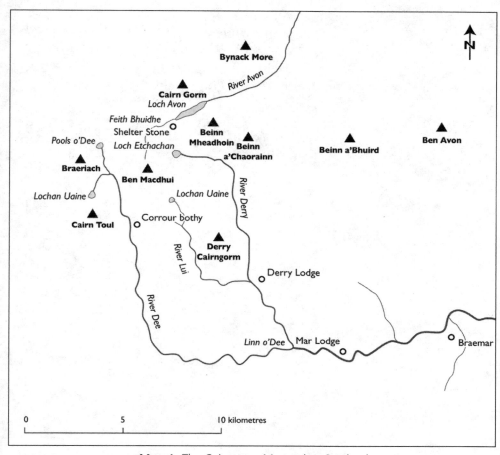

Map 1 The Cairngorm Mountains, Scotland

Bynack More

Cairn Gorm
Loch Avon

River Avon

Feith Bhuidhe
Shelter Stone

Beinn Mheadhoin

Beinn a'Chaorainn

Beinn a'Bhuird

Ben Avon

Pools o'Dee
Loch Etchachan

Braeriach

Lochan Uaine

Ben Macdhui

Lochan Uaine

River Derry

Cairn Toul

Corrour bothy

Derry Cairngorm

River Lui

Derry Lodge

River Dee

Linn o'Dee   Mar Lodge

Braemar

0   5   10 kilometres

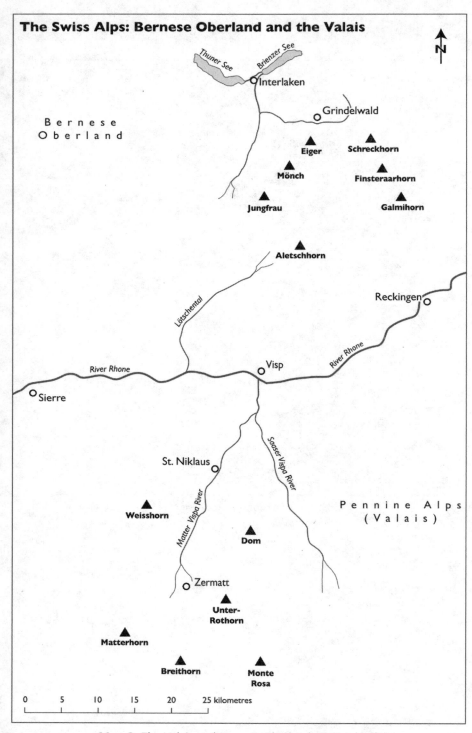

Map 2 The Valais and Bernese Oberland, Switzerland

The Sikkim Himalaya

TIBET

Chumiumo (AK)

Gyaogang

Sentinel Peak (AK)

Kangchenjhau (AK)

Thanggu

Pauhunri (AK)

Langbu Glacier

Jongsong Peak

Pangpema

Langpo Peak (AK)

Green Lake

Zemu Chu

NEPAL

Zemu Glacier

Lachen

Siniolchu

Kangchenjunga

Simvo

Jannu

Tista River

Kabru

SIKKIM

TIBET

Kokthang

Tulung Chu

Khangla Khang

Narsingh (AK)

Mangan

Dzongri

Yuksam

Gangtok

BHUTAN

INDIA

Kalimpong

| 0 | 5 | 10 | 15 | 20 | 25 kilometres |

(AK) = First ascent by Kellas

Map 3 Sikkim, India

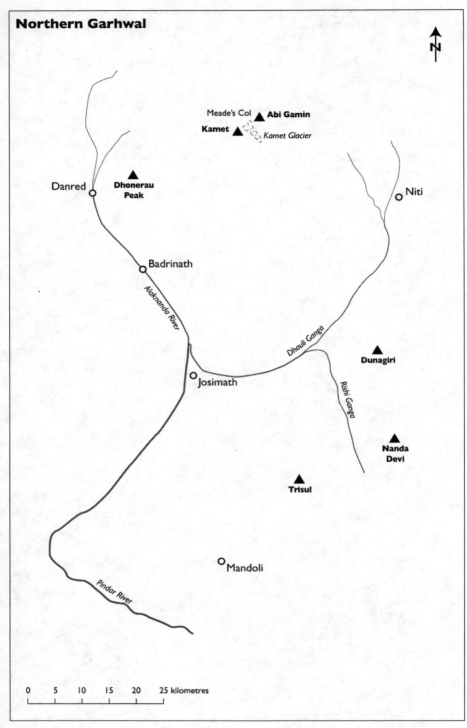

Map 4 Garhwal, India

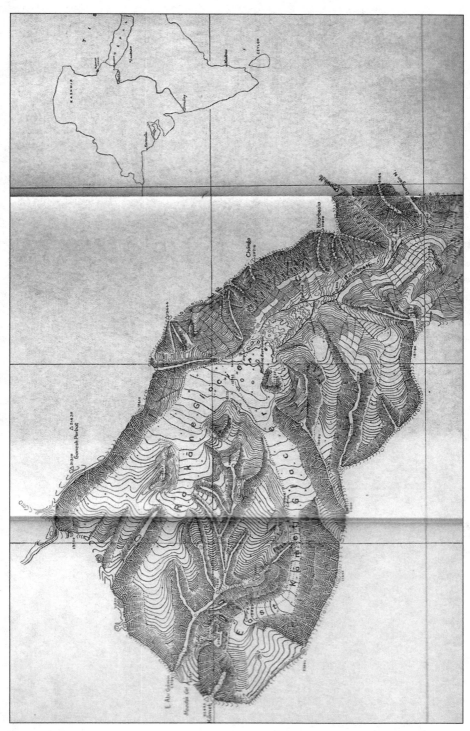

Map 5 The Kamet Glacier, 1920
(Laltan Khan)

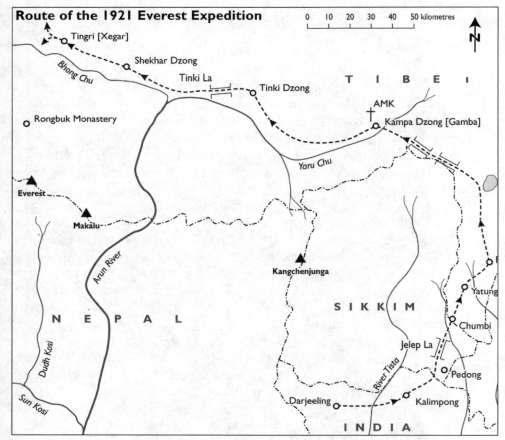

Map 6 Route of the Everest Expedition, 1921

The following labels appear on the map:

Route of the 1921 Everest Expedition

0 10 20 30 40 50 kilometres

N

Tingri [Xegar]

Shekhar Dzong

Bhong Chu

Tinki La

Tinki Dzong

T I B E T

AMK

Kampa Dzong [Gamba]

Rongbuk Monastery

Yaru Chu

Everest

Makalu

Arun River

Kangchenjunga

Yatung

Chumbi

S I K K I M

N E P A L

Jelep La

Dudh Kosi

River Tista

Pedong

Sun Kosi

Darjeeling

Kalimpong

I N D I A

Foreword

ALEXANDER KELLAS at his death in 1921, and for a considerable number of years afterwards, had an unrivalled reputation in the world of Himalayan Mountaineering.

This reputation was based upon the number of Himalayan climbs achieved, the lightweight style of his ascents and explorations, being the first to really champion the abilities of the Sherpa and his knowledge of high altitude physiology, which was second to none. For the latter reason alone he was such an important member of the 1921 Everest Reconnaissance Expedition during which he died.

Strangely, since the 1950s reference to Kellas in relevant mountaineering literature has diminished to the point where his achievements are all but unknown to the vast majority of mountaineers.

He did not write books of his exploits that perpetuated the memory of those contemporaries that did, such as Mummery, Collie, Younghusband, Longstaff and others to follow.

This book is therefore timely if not long overdue. In it the reader will discover all the climbs and explorations Kellas made, and it traces from early schoolboy days his journey from the Cairngorm Mountains to the remote Himalayan peaks of Sikkim and the Garhwal.

There is much more to this story than simply a list of events, for it is not only about his life but also about the times in which Kellas lived. It is good to be reminded just how fit our predecessors were before the motor car; in 1885 aged 17 he and his younger brother Henry walked the 35 miles from Ballater to the Shelter Stone in 12 hours, excluding an hour's rest. The latter part of the journey being over rough country into the heart of the Cairngorm Mountains.

Kellas had without doubt enormous stamina and was able to keep going with inadequate food, clothes, and shelter for days at a time when young, which characterised his later Himalayan explorations. There are many threads running through the narrative that help us understand Kellas' journey through life. It was a life that was extremely hard and often lonely since he appears to have been set apart from full social contact by inner voices leading to quite severe psychosis in later life.

It was only in the Himalaya, it seems, that he could find relief and be at peace with himself in the company of local people looking around the next corner or over that distant col. I had to read this book to write this foreword but once started I found it a compulsive and fascinating account of one of the great pioneers of Himalayan climbing.

Doug Scott
Kathmandu, April 2010

Introduction

EVERY BOOK HAS ITS own particular genesis, but the current volume's origin was possibly more particular than most, and involved a good deal of serendipity. Both of its authors had been independent admirers of Kellas for some time, but were unaware of each other's interest in the man and his achievement, or even of each other's existence.

To his shame Ian Mitchell had not heard of Alec Kellas until shortly before the celebrations of the 50th anniversary of the first ascent of Everest in 2003, when the mountaineer's name floated occasionally to the surface, though without there being any proper recognition of his real stature. It may be argued that few others were aware of the Scottish Himalayan pioneer either, but Ian was born and bred in Aberdeen, as was Kellas himself, and spent his mountaineering apprenticeship in the Cairngorm Mountains – as had Kellas himself. To rectify this neglect Ian wrote a popular piece outlining some of Kellas' main mountaineering achievements for the *Scots Magazine* in 2003, based largely on the obituaries published at his death in 1921. Pressure of other work prevented him then carrying this interest forward, as did his awareness that he lacked the scientific background to be able to contemplate undertaking a full biography of his fellow Aberdonian, who was both a mountaineer and a high-altitude physiologist.

George Rodway was fortunate in that his scientific and professional training brought him into contact with the eminent high-altitude physiologist John B West, whose admiration for Kellas had led him to the publishing of several articles on the neglected mountaineer, and also to the publishing of long-forgotten material by Kellas himself, from the 1980s onwards. George found a passion for Kellas was infectious and he too began to correct this historical oversight with the publication of various materials, mainly in scientific journals. Then in 2005 he wrote an article for the *Scottish Mountaineering Club Journal* on Kellas' preparatory work for the first Everest Expedition, including an assessment of his scientific high-altitude biology work on Kamet.

It was over three years later when circumstances allowed Ian's thoughts to return to Kellas, and when talking casually to Laura Mitchell (no relation) of the BBC in Aberdeen, with whom he was working on a totally different project, he mentioned that he was interested in the unsung mountaineer from the city. 'He was an ancestor of mine,' Laura informed him, and subsequently she sent Ian family materials of interest. Spurred on by this chance discovery, Ian wrote an initial letter to George inquiring as to the latter's further intentions regarding Kellas, and George replied by return with the offer of a joint project, confessing himself not equipped to deal with the Scottish background, and with no prospect of having the time to become so for many years.

It was a fortuitous fit. Ian knew the Scottish material, and could cover Kellas' period in London and also his Alpine experience, whilst George was not only a high altitude physiologist but also a Himalayan mountaineer, being familiar with Kellas' main area of exploration and ascents in Sikkim. Both were experienced in collaborative writing ventures. It is a collaboration which has taken George back to Sikkim, Ian to the Alps, and both of us to Kellas' beloved spot at the Shelter Stone in the Cairngorm mountains, where we survived a hurricane and the consumption of a bottle of malt whisky. Hopefully the appearance of this full-scale biography of Alexander Kellas will help to establish – or rather re-establish after three-quarters of a century of neglect – his reputation as a great Himalayan mountaineering pioneer, in the year of the centenary of his *annus mirabilis*, when Kellas not only climbed several virgin Himalayan peaks over 20,000ft, but also ascended – in Pauhunri – the highest summit then ascended by man. Tragically Kellas was unaware of this as measurements a century ago erroneously gave the height of Trisul, ascended by Longstaff in 1907, as being greater than that of Pauhunri. As with many other aspects of Kellas' achievement, this work aims to set the record straight.

Ian R Mitchell
George W Rodway
June 2011

CHAPTER ONE

The North East Scotland Background

Aberdeen and the Cairngorm Club

ALEXANDER MITCHELL KELLAS, arguably Scotland's greatest ever Himalayan mountaineer and one of the foremost in the world during his own lifetime, is today a largely neglected figure. He was born in Aberdeen in 1868 and there was little in his background or his early life that might have suggested that Kellas would become a leading pioneer in the Greater Ranges, exploring and climbing widely in the Sikkim and Garhwal areas, and dying on the initial Reconnaissance Expedition to Mount Everest itself in 1921. He thus became Everest's first 'martyr' and was commemorated in a memorial at the foot of the Rongbuk Glacier (unfortunately destroyed by souvenier hunters in recent years), which was also a *momento mori* for (in addition to the seven Sherpas who died in 1922 and the further two who perished two years later) the much more famous duo of Mallory and Irvine, who were killed in the subsequent 1924 Everest summit attempt.

The Kellas name is quite a common one in the North East of Scotland from whence Alexander and his forebears hailed, and is of some antiquity. Alexander's father, James Fowler Kellas, used to tell the tale that the triple sibling founders of the family had originally fled after some misadventures from Kellas in Morayshire, possibly during the civil and religious strife of the 17th century. The three fugitive brothers settled in the lands of Upper Donside – in Strathdon, Corgarff and Deskryside – and took the name Kellas from the land of their origins.[1] Today there are still many Kellases on Upper Donside. The family emerges from the mists of legend with Alexander Kellas (1738–1794), a tenant farmer at Newton in Glen Nochty on Donside, who was almost certainly an illicit distiller, as were all Glen Nochty men at that time. He was the great-grandfather of the mountaineer.

AM Kellas' actual grandfather, also called Alexander, was born in

1783 in Glen Nochty. But he moved sometime early in the 19th century from the delightful rolling hills and forests of the headwaters of the River Don, shifting about 30 miles eastwards to the lowland farming countryside around the village of Skene, about ten miles west of the rapidly growing city of Aberdeen. There at Crombie Cottage by Skene, Alexander Kellas and his wife, whose maiden name was possibly Fowler, farmed. According to family legend, Alexander had been kicked by a horse and was slightly lame. This probably compounded his difficulties at a time when farming in the North East of Scotland was undergoing rapid and painful transformations.

The middle to later 19th century was a time of crisis for the tenant farmers of Aberdeenshire, who were facing rising rents and falling prices for their produce. The movement towards the creation of larger farms squeezed the small farmer, who often had to give up hope of maintaining his economic independence, and was forced to take up a position as a farm labourer, or to migrate to the town of Aberdeen for industrial work. It was a time of social and economic agitation, both from tenant farmers' associations for lower rents, and from the emerging farm labourers' trades unions, for higher wages.[2]

Alexander Kellas, tenant farmer in Skene, appears to have been a victim of this economic process, since financial losses forced him to give up the lease on his farm and to take a croft. Crofting was a largely self-sufficient form of farming, leaving a small surplus of produce to be sold on the market, and a definite step down from being a tenant farmer. Alexander died in the town of Aberdeen in 1862, which might indicate that he eventually lost even his croft-holding. At Crombie Cottage in Skene in 1821 was born James Fowler Kellas, the only son born to the Kellases, who also had four daughters.

James Fowler Kellas, who would become the father of the later Himalayan explorer, would have had no thought of entering farming at a time of agricultural economic crisis, so instead of following in the path of his father Alexander, he went into business, moving into Aberdeen early in life. He was apparently involved in railway contracting at a time when the railways were still expanding from the earlier-constructed main line to Aberdeen from the south, into the branch lines being built throughout the North East of Scotland in the 1850s and '60s. But – again according to the family tradition – James lost all his money when his partner (an

Englishman) absconded with their joint capital. At some point James married Jeannie Nickleson, known as 'Bonny Jeannie'. Her face must have been her fortune, for her father was a journeyman blacksmith, a respectable but proletarian trade. The couple lived first in Marischal Street, a thoroughfare formerly consisting of grand 18th century town houses, though by the middle of the 19th century many of these buildings had become overcrowded city centre slums. Later the Kellases moved to Crown Street further from the city centre, this move in all likelihood indicating a rise in social status.

This slow rise up the social ladder was reflected in the fact that James Fowler Kellas could send his first son, also called James, to Bellvue Academy – a fee-paying school – and then to Kings College, Aberdeen University. But the precarious nature of the family's upward mobility was shown by the apprenticing of the second son William Clark Kellas as a ship's carpenter, a decidedly working-class occupation. This latter offspring subsequently died of an untreated chill at 19 years old.

James Fowler Kellas' first wife Jeannie herself died of complications during her third pregnancy. James married again, to Elizabeth, the sister of Jeannie Nickleson, naming the daughter of that issue Jeannie, and on his second wife dying, married for a third time to Mary Boyd Mitchell. She was to be the mother of the mountaineer Alexander – who was to be one of the nine children she bore James. By this time, the year 1868, the couple were living at 28 Regent Quay in Aberdeen. This is given on his birth certificate as Alexander Mitchell Kellas' place of birth, children at that time generally being born at home. Mary Mitchell hailed from Ballater, 40 miles west of Aberdeen, and the Kellases, including Alexander, were to maintain links with the Deeside town through family holidays. Ballater lay on the edge of the Cairngorm mountains, with the peak of Lochnagar being visible from the town, and visits to the village would likely have provided the young Alexander with his first views of mountain scenery as a boy. Ballater was reached by train from Aberdeen in the 1860s.

As well as bringing the Kellases relations in the countryside with whom to holiday, James' marriage to Mary would also have brought him economic advantages (the tradition of the wife's marriage dowry was still extant at this time), for her own family were prosperous farmers. Mary's brother Alexander farmed at *Sluivannichie* just outside Ballater, where he rented 90 acres from the Invercauld estate and ran a big farm employing four resident farm servants. He was also a horse dealer and hirer, and managed an extensive coaching business, taking tourists from the Ballater railhead to the various scenic attractions on Upper Deeside. This was an enterprise requiring substantial capital investment and indicates that the Mitchells were a family enjoying definite affluence. Just as the future Himalayan mountaineer's paternal grandparents had been victims of the economic change in the Aberdeenshire countryside, his maternal ones had clearly been its beneficiaries. The farm-house of *Sluivannichie* still stands, and remains within the Mitchell family, descendants of Alexander Mitchell being the present owners. The farm however was sold off and today its former land is largely occupied by Ballater Golf Course.

Regent Quay is right at the heart of Aberdeen's dock and harbour area, and cheek by jowl with what was the massively overcrowded slum city centre at that time.[3] It might thus at first seem that James Kellas' fortunes had taken another downturn, reflected in the residential move to No. 28, but the opposite was actually the case. The couple lived for some years at this address in a flat provided in the building above the offices of what was the Aberdeen Mercantile Marine Board. James Fowler Kellas had become Secretary to the Mercantile Marine Board at a time of Aberdeen's greatest economic expansion, involving the extension and almost complete remodelling of Aberdeen's docks and harbour, to deal with the economic boom at the time, and the massive increase in its maritime trade.[4] The Mercantile Marine Board was a quango, consisting of representatives from the Aberdeen shipowners and from the Board of Trade (a government department) and it was presided over by the city's Lord Provost, (the Scottish equivalent of a Mayor).

The tasks of the Mercantile Marine Board were various, including running the Royal Naval Reserve (consisting of merchant seaman who pledged to serve in the Royal Navy in wartime and were paid a retainer for the commitment), but mainly its work consisted in the examination and certification of marine engineers, navigators and seamen in their trades and crafts. It also ran a Merchant Seamen's Fund and Savings Bank, and would have overseen the implementation of legislation like the Merchant Shipping Act of 1875, intent on improving safety at sea. The residence at 28 Regent's Quay – now No. 49 – was above the Marine Board offices and the whole building was a substantial three storey granite-built merchant's house built in 1787, with fine, very striking, Venetian windows.

ABERDEEN HARBOUR IN 1875.
The scene a couple of hundred yards from the Kellas' house on Regent Quay,
where Alec lived at this time. Notice the dominance of sailing boats,
many working the China/India run. An exciting place to be a boy.

A side door into the building at No. 29 gave access to a ship's chandlers' business, and all around were the butchers, bakers and candlestick-makers supplying the needs of the local shipping fleet. Today the entire building has been renovated and turned into flatted dwellings.

The Kellases moved into Regent's Quay in 1867, and left in 1878 when Alec was ten years old. He thus grew up in an exciting place at an exciting time, and as a boy must have watched – even if only through the window of the house – the bustle of the dockside, and the coming and going of the ships, including the renowned 'clipper' ships like the world-famous *Thermopylae*, built in Aberdeen to carry tea back from the China run. His first decade on the harbour-side would have given the boy an idea of a wider world beyond the North East. Though the Kellas' house – and certain others around, in which in 1868 some of Aberdeen's elite still resided – were grand later 18th or early 19th century dwellings, the area behind Regent's Quay was a warren of lanes of slum housing and industrial and warehousing units.

We know little of Alec's first decade but it would appear unlikely that as a middle-class child he would have been permitted the freedom to roam these wynds and alleys, a freedom allowed to the local street urchins. We also do not know of his schooling at this time. The Education Act of 1872 introduced compulsory primary education for all over five years, but it stretches credibility somewhat to think that Alec would have gone to the local primary school. Parents educating their children at home were not obliged to send them to school, and one can surmise that Alec was home-educated at this time by a paid tutor, or in one of the several private elementary schools in the city. This practise was quite common amongst Aberdeen's middle class, expanding in numbers and wealth as the city industrialised.

Aberdeen's industrialisation in the 19th century was unique. Distant from the central belt of Scotland with the latter's coal and iron resources, industry in Aberdeen utilised local raw materials from the land (granite, flax, wool) and sea (fish) to develop a broadly based economy dominated by textiles, food processing and light industry. The population of Aberdeen grew from about 25,000 in 1801 to over 150,000 in 1901. At the time of Kellas' birth in 1868 it was approaching 100,000. Urbanisation in Aberdeen was also unique in that almost the entire population of the town, like the Kellases and the Mitchells themselves, were immigrants from the rural North East. This produced a town, or rather city, with a strong local identity and also a firmly provincial, some might say parochial, character. It also produced a town where many of the inhabitants still had strong family connections with the countryside. The Kellases were not unusual in this regard.

When Alexander Mitchell Kellas was born his father's career was on a rising curve, and this was reflected by the subsequent building of a family house in the new and expanding middle class residential area of the city's West End. Until the middle of the 19th century the Aberdonian middle class has generally lived geographically close to the working class, but increasing social segregation took place as the century passed, and by 1900 the social classes lived in broadly distinct areas. The residential pattern of Alexander Kellas' family fits neatly into this process of growing social differentiation. Now a successful administrator in the world of commerce, James Kellas would be reluctant to bring up his increasing progeny by the Aberdeen dockside, and so in 1878 the family moved to

48 Carden Place, to a house that would be in family hands well into the 20th century. (No. 48 was then one in a block of two with No. 50, both of which have now been turned into the conjoint offices of a commercial company.)

Carden Place was a typical example of a residential street to which the lawyers, doctors and other upper professionals of the local middle class increasingly were moving, separating themselves from the slum and industrial areas of the city, and house building commenced in the street from the 1850s. Now the Kellas' neighbours were not the colourful flotsam and jetsam of the harbour-side, carters, dockworkers and seamen, but people like clergymen, middling businessmen and a very large number of widows and spinsters living on annuities and investments. It must have been dull for the Kellas boys here after the delights of the dockside – even if those had been largely forbidden delights for them. The houses in Carden Place are solid middle class houses. These were too grand for the lower middle class, but they were also not the houses of the upper middle class, the granite palaces of the local plutocracy, which lay westwards towards Queens Road.

In the 1881 Census, it was noted that James F Kellas, who was then 62, had six children (and a nephew) living at No. 48, which was a large house of 11 rooms. Despite that, he had but one domestic servant and it thus appears that his wife – who was much younger than her husband at 36 – and the two teenage daughters would have assumed some of the domestic burdens of the large household. When JF Kellas died in 1905, apart from the Carden Place house itself, he left an estate of £1,102, 16s 5d. In modern terms this equates to between £75,000 and £100,000 – a substantial sum but not a great fortune. The Kellases were comfortably off, but they were not of the local bourgeois elite.

Middle class residential imperatives, then and now, are largely driven by two related motives; the desire for social separation from the working classes, and the search for good schooling. Carden Place lay very close, a brisk five minute walk, to Aberdeen Grammar School, which was the educational locus for the city's (male) elite in the 19th century – and somewhat into the 20th. Aberdeen Grammar school was one of the oldest such institutions in Scotland, and was noted for its rigid classical (hence 'grammar') curriculum, largely oriented towards gaining University entrance. Teaching had traditionally consisted of four hours work a day, three

PORTRAIT OF THE KELLAS CHILDREN.
Found in the Mitchell family album at *Sluivannichie*, and probably taken on a holiday
there in the late 1880s. It shows Alec, unmistakable to the left, as well as probably
Henry, John and Arthur, and the girls are possibly Helen and Margaret.
(Mitchell Family Collection)

of which were in Latin with English, History and Geography occupying
the other hour. It had formerly been located in the Schoolhill area of
Aberdeen and when there, one of its most famous alumni was the poet
Lord Byron.

In 1863 the school moved to a new larger building in the West End
of the city, allowing it to expand its curriculum to include a wider range
of subjects, the first of which was mathematics, with an hour a day
given to instruction in that discipline. But it was not until it was taken
over by the town council through the School Board in 1872 that the
institution began to develop towards teaching what we would recognise
as a modern syllabus, even though classics still dominated to an extent
hard to credit today. However, by the 1880s modern languages had been
introduced, as well as the teaching of science and physical education.
Luckily for Alexander Kellas it was just after these expansions and reforms
had taken place that he began to attend the Grammar School, otherwise

he would probably have undergone the fate of most of Aberdeen's previous middle class Grammar School and University graduates, that of becoming either a lawyer, a doctor, or a clergyman. Instead he was to become a research chemist who was to work with some of the leading figures of his day in the scientific field, including a Nobel Prize winner.

There is an indication even here in his Grammar School days that Alec was possibly a problematic youth, with a hint of the difficulties in his personality which would increase with time, culminating in severe psychosis many years later. The school had a six year secondary programme, which his brothers Henry and Arthur completed. But the *Aberdeen Grammar School Roll of Pupils 1795–1919*, shows that Alec attended the school from 1881–4, a mere three years. He joined late at 13, and left early, at 16. And his obituary in the *Aberdeen Grammar School Magazine* (XXIV, June 1921, No. 3, p.142–3) states that it was 'Some time after leaving school' that he entered Heriot Watt College in Edinburgh. Now Heriot Watt was a college, not a University and required lower entry qualifications, suggesting that Alec had failed to gain University entrance at the Grammar School. According to the Grammar School's former pupils' *Magazine*, after Heriot Watt, Alexander Kellas 'then entered University College London, where he graduated BSC'.

There are almost as many accounts of Alec Kellas' University training as there are obituaries of him. There is a letter written by Henry Kellas, Alec's brother, to Arthur Hinks at the Royal Geographical Society, in response to a request from the latter for material for an obituary, that might at first appear to provide accurate details. (Henry Kellas to Hinks, 17.6.1921 (RGS Archives)) Collie and Scott (the latter following Collie) have Kellas going to Aberdeen University before Edinburgh (see bibliography). That is definitely false and Henry Kellas makes no mention of Kellas at Aberdeen, where there are no records of any attendance by him. The *Cairngorm Club Journal* (CCJ) and *Scottish Mountaineering Club Journal* (SMCJ) obituaries have him attending Heriot Watt College and then Edinburgh University, and according to Henry he spent two years in Edinburgh attending classes at these two institutions. However, Henry gives Alec's dates at Edinburgh as 1889–91, and that would appear to be an error of memory. The academic records at UCL confirm that Kellas graduated from there in 1892, after enrolling in 1889. So it is likely that Kellas spent the year, or possibly two, previous to 1889 at Heriot Watt and Edinburgh University (though the latter institution is not mentioned in the Grammar School obituary, cited above), before transferring to UCL.

With its emphasis on science and technology Heriot Watt College especially was a good choice for Kellas, now intent on a scientific career. All this, however, means that his formal academic education – for whatever reason – was interrupted by almost three years, from 1884–7. Henry makes no mention of this and has Alec going directly from the Grammar School to his University studies. It is possible Henry was 'massaging' his brother's educational career a little. Or possibly his memory was just faulty. Later in the letter Henry notes that Alec and 'a younger companion' (who was Henry himself!) slept out under the Shelter Stone when Alec was 14. When Alec slept under the Shelter Stone in 1885 he was 17, and it was Henry who was 14. Similarly Henry has his brother studying in Germany for his PhD in 1895–6, whilst the other sources give the date as 1896–7. Henry appears to have shared his brother Alec's sloppiness regarding dates.

Outside the new Grammar School there stands a statue of its most famous student, Lord Byron. Though this statue was erected in the 1900s after Kellas had left the school, its erection was mooted long before and Byron was definitely the Grammar School's main claim to fame at that time. The schoolboy Kellas could not have been unaware of him. The libertine Byron of reality had by the later 19th century been re-habilitated and sanitised as a role model for youth. One of the things deemed respectable about Byron by this time was his love of nature and particularly his youthful explorations of the Cairngorm Mountains around Braemar. This supposed Byronic love for nature was reflected in some of his poetry, such as *Dark Lochnagar*, which celebrates the poet's purported ascent of the famous Cairngorm peak.[5] It is doubtful that Byron's sexual pecadillos were recounted to the pupils at the Grammar School.

It is interesting to speculate whether the young Grammarian Kellas pondered on Byron, and was inspired in some way by him. In the articles Kellas was later to compose about his mountain explorations, in contrast to many Victorian and Edwardian authors who were lavish with literary references in their writing, there is only one poetic reference. It is to Byron. And it was whilst at the Grammar School that the young Kellas made his first forays into the mountains. Could Alec have identified with the young Byron, who was himself an outcast, as a part-crippled

UNION STREET ABERDEEN 1880s.
Showing Union Street, Aberdeen's main thoroughfare, at the time Alec would have been attending the Grammar School, and his father's route to work in the docks, from Carden Place to the west.

child at the school, and have been attracted to the mountains because he, Kellas, was unsettled at school himself? Whatever the merits or otherwise of such a speculation, there was much more than the inspiration of Byron and his poetry driving a young man of the Aberdeen middle classes towards the mountains by the 1880s, the decade when Kellas discovered the Cairngorms.

Lying on the eastern fringe of the geological region created by the Highland Fault Line, the Cairngorm Mountains contain as their central core the highest land massif in Britain. There four summits reach more than 4,000ft, and around this heartland lies an area with many peaks of lesser height, such as Lochnagar. In a UK context it is a region with few roads and it contains large areas with almost no inhabitants. It is also, in winter, a sub-Arctic region and there is speculation that the last glaciers vanished only three or four centuries ago. Certainly in the 19th century there were still permanent snowfields, though these exist no more.

Nevertheless it was one of the regions of the Scottish Highlands to be first explored and opened up to outsiders. The terrain is not as rugged as it can be in the mountain regions to the westward, and the massif is penetrated by the River Dee, whose *strath* is fairly easily negotiable. In the 17th century an *Atlas Maior* of the world was produced in Amsterdam which contained many maps of Scotland. Of the areas covered in the *Atlas*, probably the best and most detailed mountain map is that which includes the Cairngorm Mountains or, as the wider area is often known, the Grampian Highlands.[6]

Even before the age of 'tourism' (a word coined in the early 19th century), a trickle of people had been attracted to the Highland area around Braemar for the most varied of reasons.[7] In the first century AD, Roman legions had actually crossed the eastern area of these mountains, even possibly giving the name 'Grampian' to them by calling the site of a battle they had with local tribes Mons Graupius – mis-transcribed later as 'Grampius'. One of the first definite ascents of a Cairngorm mountain was that of Mount Keen in 1618 by the eccentric English poet John Taylor, and later poachers, soldiers, bandits and others are recorded on the summits. After the 1745–6 rebellion, much of the area was investigated for its mineral and botanical resources by the Commissioners of Annexed or Forfeit Estates, who had taken over the lands of the Jacobite rebels. Working for them, James Robertson climbed Ben Avon and also probably Lochnagar in 1771. Improvement was also the motivation behind the journeys and ascents of the Rev George Keith who first ascended Ben MacDhui, Cairn Toul and Braeriach in 1810, publishing the next year his *General View of the Agriculture of Aberdeenshire* for the Board of Agriculture, a government body which encouraged farming improvements.

The region may have been penetrated but it was still not completely pacified. Until the middle of the 18th century the Deeside Highlands were a stronghold of Jacobitism with much support being given to the rebellions of 1715 and 1745–6, the first of these uprisings actually being launched in Braemar itself. Even after the crushing of the Jacobite threat, military garrisons remained at Braemar and Corgarff Castles to deal with the social banditry that was prevalent long afterwards. Armed conflicts with poachers and illicit distillers (both offences were punishable by death if 'taken in arms') continued till the early 1830s, when the troops were finally withdrawn from the area. Alexander Kellas's great-grandfather in Glen Nochty would have witnessed the tail-end of this colourful period.

As it receded this lost world took on an increasingly romantic hue, which was given the stamp of royal approval when Queen Victoria and her Consort, Albert, rented the castle at Balmoral on Deeside in 1848. The pair ascended Lochnagar almost as soon as they took up residence and over the years until Albert's death in 1861 they summitted on many of the Cairngorm mountains – though making only repeat, not first, ascents. But they were not alone. William MacGillivray, Professor of Natural History at Aberdeen University, had been wandering these mountains since before 1820, and the fruit of his lifetime's labours, his *Natural History of Deeside* was brought out in 1855, shortly after he died from the effects of a chill caught due to exposure on Lochnagar. In 1864 John Hill Burton produced the first actual tourist and walking guide to the area. His *The Cairngorm Mountains* takes us from tales of the 1820s when he wandered the hills alone, encountering poachers and distillers, to the present when he describes the growing trend for 'Alpine devotees' and 'Alpenstockists' as he designates them, to visit the upland district. It is clear from studying Burton's book that a definite mountain tourist industry, with transport, accommodation and guides was developing on Deeside at this time.

BALLATER c1900.
The Deeside village which was the home of the Mitchells and the holiday destination of the Kellas family. *Sluivannichie* farm lay beyond the trees at the upper left of the picture. This was the base for Alec's early mountain explorations.

Then in 1866 the railway line penetrated far into Deeside, and brought the romance of the vanished world of the Highland clans within the day-trip reach of the Aberdonian urban middle classes. Even though the railway line ended just beyond Ballater (due to opposition from Queen Victoria to its going all the way to Braemar and disturbing the peace of Balmoral), carriages quickly connected the rail passenger with points further, and the increasing trickle of individuals who had previously ventured into the mountains became a flood. The coaching business of Alexander Kellas' uncle in Ballater was largely based on this demand.

People wanted to read about the romantic Highlands, including the Cairngorms, and there were those willing to supply the want. In 1868 appeared, from the pen of Victoria herself, the book *Leaves from the Journal of our Life in the Highlands*, which became a modest bestseller, the first 10,000 copies quickly needing a supplementary printing. As well as describing local Highland customs the book included accounts of her mountaineering expeditions, and undoubtedly encouraged others to follow. It was not only books which covered mountaineering, newspapers – and periodicals – quickly realised there was a great demand for fireside Alpinism, and responded to the need.

During the 1870s an Aberdeen newspaper printed several articles by Alexander Copland, a prominent local businessman and long-time mountain rambler, under the pseudonym Dryas Octopetala (the name of a flower found in the Cairngorms). These were so popular they were brought out in book form with his co-author Thomas Twayblade as *Two Days and a Night in the Wilderness* (1878) and *Our Tour* (1880). These are books full of handy information, such as the train timetables for Ballater, and recommendations such as the use of 'those excellent and wonderfully cheap maps furnished by the Ordnance Survey. These maps, on the one inch to the mile scale [show] every road and path the tourist need take.' But the writings of Copland indicate that a serpent had entered this Cairngorm Garden of Eden, in the form of the problem of mountain access.

Prior to the later Victorian period there were few concerns about access to the Scottish mountains, and those who had reason to wandered at will over land that was effectively worthless economically. The changes which took place in the Highland economy between, very roughly, the 1790s and the 1850s, resulted in the large scale replacement of people by sheep over much of this terrain. In the Cairngorms it was different, and land usage was not given over to sheep farming but to the hunting of deer and other animals. This resulted in the desire of proprietors to limit access to the hills, especially – but not only – during the actual shooting season itself. From the 1840s onwards walkers were often confronted and even molested by threatening – and armed – gamekeepers. Originally mainly a Central Highlands problem, the access issue spread to the Western Highlands as sheep-runs became steadily less profitable there, and were increasingly replaced by deer-forests.[8]

Like other walkers, Alexander Copland had had, and had recounted in print, his conflicts with the guardians of deer hunting, and he attacked

> Our native Mumbo Jumbos who molest the traveller in Glen Derry, Glen Lui and other wilds (and attempt) selfishly, out of excessive relish for shooting deer... to prevent the inhabitants of this country from visiting its finest scenery, and turn back in disgust those who know no better. It is intolerable that this should be permitted.[9]

He denounced those who would 'shut up every hill and glen in Scotland' and asked fellow walkers to 'treat such molestation with the contempt it deserves.' For Copland this was not just an access issue, but a political one.

Copland, or Dryas Octopetala, to give him his botanical name, was a representative of the Liberal political interest which dominated the town of Aberdeen throughout the 19th century. Fighting for access fused with fighting against the landed interest as a whole. This landed interest was represented in the Conservative (later Conservative and Unionist) Party for Copland – and for many of his fellow mountaineers. When these early ramblers came together to form an association to promote mountaineering and mountaineering culture, access to the mountains themselves was to be one of its central objectives.

The Cairngorm Club, founded in 1887, was the first Scottish mountaineering club to have more than an ephemeral existence, and despite a patchy record of activity and publication at certain times, it still exists.[10] Its pre-history (sketched above) and the club's early years give us the framework of mountaineering in Aberdeen when the young Alexander made his first forays into the hills. The club had a foundation that must be *sui generis*. Alexander Copland, accompanied by five other stout pedestrians including the equally redoubtable Alexander Inkson McConnochie[11] had climbed Ben MacDhui to set off fireworks to commemorate the

Golden Jubilee of Queen Victoria on 22 June 1887. There the group enthusiastically startled every man and beast for a radius of 20 miles with their pyrotechnics.

They then descended the mountain to spend the night under the Shelter Stone, or in Gaelic *Clach Dian*, below the mountain by Loch Avon. This was a huge natural gite, formed by a cluster of massive boulders, which had been used as shelter by cattle drovers in former times, and before that, by bands of *caterans*, outlaws preying on travellers through the mountain passes, including reputedly the notorious Wolf of Badenoch back in the 14th century. The first representation of *Clach Dian* I am aware of is by Thomas Dick Lauder, showing a couple of Highlanders resting outside the gite, which is called by Lauder *The Shelter Stone*. It dates from July 1816. It is clear that this refuge was used by pedestrians very early in the 19th century, and I am glad to say that it is still being used by mountaineers 200 years later. It was to become a favourite haunt of Alec Kellas.

After what was admitted to be an uncomfortable night, our six splendid fellows, in the words of one of their member,

> Spontaneously and unanimously agreed to form ourselves into the Cairngorm Club, the name being naturally suggested by the monarch mountain so full in view in the foreground, [*Cairngorm, Authors' Note*] and calmly looking down on our meeting. Office bearers were elected by acclamation and with that generous and genial absence of exclusive selfishness which has always characterised our society, we resolved to open our ranks to the admission of men and women of heroic spirit, and possessed of souls open to the influences of enjoyment of nature pure and simple as displayed among our loftiest mountains.[12]

Fine words, but it took 18 months for the first meeting to be called and a Constitution drawn up. This has been lost alas, but the amended *Rules* of 1895 indicate that as well as encouraging mountain climbing, research into mountains and the spread of what we would now call 'mountain culture', and the publication of a *Journal* (first issued in 1894), the Club would 'consider the right of access to Scottish mountains and adopt such measures in regard thereto as the Club may deem advisable'. This commitment to access was underlined by the appointment of James Bryce as the Club's first President, a position he was to retain till 1922. (Bryce was also President of the Alpine Club 1899–1901.)

Bryce was the Liberal MP for Aberdeen South (the Liberal MP for Aberdeen North, Vernon Pirie, also joined the Club). Bryce – later Viscount Bryce – was a strong mountaineer, though not really a technical climber and his book *Memories of Travel* (1923) recounts his explorations and summit ascents worldwide. These included Hekla in Iceland, Ararat in Turkey and the Vignemale in the Pyrenees. Though born in Belfast, Bryce had been an enthusiastic walker in Scotland since his youth. But more than that he was an active campaigner for access rights. Bryce introduced on more than one occasion an *Access to Moors and Mountains Bill* to Parliament which would have legally enshrined the right of access to mountain land, but the bill was always defeated.

The Cairngorm Club's first Excursion was in July 1889, when about 30 people took a special train from Aberdeen to Nethy Bridge on Speyside. They then climbed Cairngorm, and subsequently made an ascent of Ben

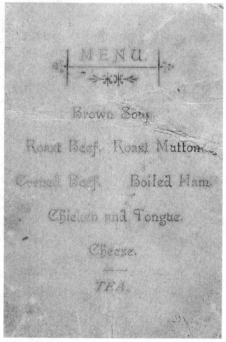

MOUNT KEEN INVITE.
The invitation to the record-breaking ascent of Mount Keen by the Cairngorm Club in 1890. The solid fare on offer afterwards might have compensated for the horror of the lack of cushions on the train outwards.
(Cairngorm Club)

MacDhui. This was followed in September by an ascent of Lochnagar. The party, 70 strong this time, took reserved carriages 'naturally first class' to Ballater and then 'wagonettes and brakes' up Glen Muick to where the ascent began. On the summit their right of access was re-stated by Alexander Copland, who also reminded them (this was a time of some-times violent labour unrest and 'outrages' in Ireland), that the Club did not wish,

> ... to interfere with or usurp the rights of the proprietors of this or any other country. We are not Revolutionists, but loyal and law-abiding subjects: we are not enemies of game or legitimate sports... There need be no friction between us and the proprietors of the land, on the contrary, the interchange of kindly, considerate feeling and good offices.[13]

The last outing of significance during Alexander Kellas' time in Aberdeen was that of the Club to Mount Keen, in May 1890. This outing reads as a wonderfully bizarre event to modern eyes, and it still probably ranks as the largest mass ascent of a Scottish mountain on record. On the occasion 162 people, of whom 45 were ladies, departed Aberdeen for Aboyne in reserved carriages. However, things were not well with the tran-sport. Some of the carriages were without cushions, and three quarters of those travelling did so third class to show their disapproval of the 'discourtesy shown by the Railway Company'. The excursion had been advertised in the local press as 'An Easy Day for a Lady' – but, no cushions! That's taking things a bit far. From Aboyne carriages whisked them to Glentanar House, home of Sir William Cunliffe-Brooks, where tea was served in the ballroom, and then another seven miles were passed in the carriages till the start point.

The entire party reached the summit in just over an hour and a half from there, and, as the ascent of one 3,000ft mountain was then the criteria for membership, several people were admitted to the Club by the ceremony of 'douping' (sitting them on the summit cairn against their will. *Doup* = local vernacular for bottom.) A wonderful summit photograph was then taken of all 162 summiteers, showing the men dressed as if going to the office, in bowler hats and top hats, with many a shirt and tie in evidence, and the ladies, resplendent in plumed hats and even the occasional veil. The enormous logistical problems involved in this outing led to the Club soon deciding to stiffen entrance qualifications to include the ascent of at least one of the Cairngorm 4,000-ers. This had the desired effect of reducing numbers at subsequent outings. But let us leave this wonderful world of Victorian sociability, and return to the more isolated world of Alexander Kellas himself, though there are connections between the two.

NOTES

1   The account given here of the Kellas family is largely based on the *Manuscript Book* complied by Mary Elsie J Kellas. She was the daughter of Alexander Kellas' half-brother James NF Kellas. A typescript of this *Manuscript Book* contains material, in several hands, and of several dates – the latest having a provenance of 1950. Although at times confusing and difficult to follow, it is an invaluable source. Much of it is rather speculative regarding the origins of the Kellases back to the 15th century, but the material is sounder from the 19th century onwards. The *Manuscript Book* was held latterly by Henry Ronald Kellas, a GP in Swindon, who died in 1986. He was Alexander Kellas' nephew, and one of the sons of his brother Henry. Another of Henry's sons, Arthur, became Ambassador to Nepal 1966–70, and a friend of Sir Edmund Hillary, with whom he went walking.

2   For an excellent account of the economic forces to which Alexander Kellas' grandfather apparently fell victim, see *Farm Life in Northeast Scotland 1840–1914*, Ian Carter (1979).

3   The economic and social development of Aberdeen is comprehensively covered in *Aberdeen 1800–2000: A New History*, ed. W Hamish Fraser and Clive H Lee (2000).

4   See 'Aberdeen Harbour – The Taming of the Dee' by John S Smith, in *Aberdeen in the Nineteenth Century* (1988) ed. John S Smith and David Stevenson.

5   Actually, despite Byron's fulsome praise of Lochnagar, and contempt for 'Albion's plain', once he left Aberdeen and Scotland, the poet never returned.

6   Blaeu's *Atlas Maior* was published in Amsterdam in 1654 and contained several maps of Scotland largely executed by and attributed to Timothy Pont. That of the North-East, *Aberdonia & Banfia*, is however by Robert Gordon of Straloch in Aberdeenshire. It shows us many Cairngorm

summits, such as Cairngorm itself, Bheinn a' Bhuird and Mount Keen, though all are spelled rather differently.

7   See the section 'The Cairngorms before the Climbers' in *Scotland's Mountains before the Mountaineers*, Ian R Mitchell (1998) for explorations there from c.1000–c.1850.

8   The access issue, and its historical context, is dealt with in Ian R Mitchell, *supra*. The same author's *On the Trail of Queen Victoria*, (2001) deals with the phenomenon of 'Balmorality'.

9   *Two Days and a Night in the Wilderness*, Dryas Octopetala and Thomas Twyablade (1878). p.7.

10   The history of the club is sketched in *The Cairngorm Club 1887–1987*, Sheila Murray (1987). A more detailed account can be had from a study of the volumes of the *Cairngorm Club Journal*, published from 1894.

11   Inkson McConnochie had already published his book *Ben Muich Dhui and his Neighbours; a guide to the Cairngorm Mountains* in 1885, and many articles on his explorations of the Cairngorms.

12   Quoted in Murray, Op.Cit., p.2.

13   Loc.Cit., pp.13–14.

CHAPTER TWO

Exploring the Cairngorm Mountains

Mountaineering Apprenticeship

ACCOUNTS OF KELLAS' early years, for example in the several obituaries after his death or in the relevant *Oxford Dictionary of National Biography* (*ODNB*) entry, tend to talk in rather general terms of him wandering the mountains of Scotland as a youth at every possible opportunity and gaining a thorough knowledge of them. And this view is echoed in those more recent mountaineering histories which make mention of Kellas.[1] From the records which are extant, such as his application to join the Scottish Mountaineering Club and the later application to join the Alpine Club, as well as from a long typewritten essay written as a schoolboy, which fortuitously remained in family hands[2] and from other more fragmentary sources we can try and piece together Kellas' early mountaineering experiences a little more accurately.

Kellas applied to join the Scottish Mountaineering Club (SMC) in November 1897, at which time he was working as an assistant to Professor Ramsay at the Gower Street chemical laboratories of the University College London (UCL). He was proposed for club membership by John Norman Collie, who was at that time becoming one of the most renowned mountaineers of the day and who also worked with Ramsay at UCL. Kellas was actually doubly seconded. The first of these seconders was Morris Travers, a further co-worker at Ramsay's UCL laboratories, and the other was Colin Phillip, an artist friend of Collie's (Phillip's father, also a painter and rather more famous in that regard than his son, was interestingly originally from Aberdeen though he had subsequently moved to London). As well as being proposed and seconded by existing club members, SMC applicants had to append a list of their climbs to date, in Scotland and elsewhere. Thus Kellas' application form allows us to assess the progress in mountaineering he had made by 1897, when he was nearing 30 years old.

Kellas lists almost 30 personal ascents of summits in Scotland over 3,000ft, far in excess of the 12 such climbs, spread over three or more years, that were the club's entry qualifications at that time (See *SMCJ* Vol. 4, No. 1, p.69 for the original entry requirements). These 3,000ft Scottish hills were already becoming known as Munros after the name of the man, Sir Hugh Munro, who had attempted to make the first complete list of them all in 1891. A hugely creditable effort, Munro's list has been subsequently partly revised by more accurate measurements. The SMC also asked that membership applicants have a minimum of two snow climbs in Scotland, and Kellas lists the requisite duo including a 'Snow climb up gully with Prof. Collie' on Ben Nevis in 1894. This would have been either No. 3 or No. 4 gullies, both of which were regular trade routes of ascent (and descent) by this time. (It is almost certain that the climb with Collie was in 1895, not 1894, since Kellas was not in attendance on Nevis with Collie's party on the earlier date, see below.) Kellas was admitted as a member of the SMC the year following his application, that is in 1898.

The first recorded mountain ascent on the application form is given as our old friend Mount Keen, and the date recorded as 1883 when Kellas was 15. It is fairly safe to assume that Alexander, or Alec as he was always known to the family, climbed this hill from the residence of his mother's relatives in Ballater, the farm of *Sluivannichie*. This supposition is strengthened by a consideration of his next mountaineering expedition, a full two years later, which certainly was launched from the family farm in the Deeside railway terminus town. Written at the age of 17 and carried out in the company of his two-years younger brother Henry, Alec's account of the 1885 expedition is one of the longest records of his mountaineering that survive, alongside one or two of his later Himalayan articles. This extended narrative at first looks like it might have been a schoolboy's essay, but the references in it to family matters makes it appear rather to have been written for domestic consumption. Anyway, by the time he wrote it Alec had dropped out of the Grammar School, so it was in all probability not written as an example of the classic 'What I did on my holidays' essay.

One can possibly read too much into innocent statements, but in this account Alec says that in 1884 – the very summer his education at the

Grammar School came to a premature end, – 'we were unfortunately prevented from making any ascents at all, as we spent our holidays Harry at Ballater and myself at Old Deer.' Why, in the year he drops out of school, is Alec not with the family at Ballater? And why is he making no mountaineering trips? Some kind of an emotional-physical crisis could be the reason for this interlude. It has not been possible to trace any relatives of the Kellases at Old Deer, nor at that time did any kind of hospital or sanatorium exist in the small Aberdeenshire town. But in the 1880s the sons of the middle classes did not simply drop out of school to experience the wider world, or take gap years from education. Something serious had happened. It could be that Alec's health was in some way compromised, but the fact that by 1885 he was capable of undertaking large walking trips tends to put a question mark over this. In the light of what we know about Alec's later mental heath problems, it is not unreasonable to suggest that he underwent in 1884–5 an adolescent harbinger of the emotional difficulties he was later to experience. By 1885 he was recovered enough to be able to resume his mountaineering activities, though not yet his formal education. That would have to wait till 1887.

The young Kellas' first intention was to climb Lochnagar from Ballater on their 1885 summer holiday, but Alexander tells us that 'we noticed a new guide to the Cairngorms by Alex. I. McConnachie' which book contained a map of the country to the west of Braemar. Armed with this guide, the boys decided to head for the Shelter Stone and Ben Muick Dhui [sic] instead. Wet weather delayed their expedition and they spent the first week of their holidays at Ballater, though on the somewhat more clement days they climbed the local lesser summit of Morven (which had also been climbed by Byron), and in addition made a longer trip and ascended the Munro of Ben Avon. (It is surprising that in his SMC application Kellas claims this latter summit to have been ascended by him only in 1893 but, as we shall see, sloppiness regarding dates was to be a feature of Kellas' writings.) The brothers finally set out after a week in Ballater with high hopes but with some trepidation as 'it was already past the 12th of August and we anticipated some trouble... and were only afraid that our progress to the Cairngorms might be stopped by keepers who were in some of the glens near to the Linn of Dee.' As it turned out, they were to encounter no access problems on this occasion.

Although regular horse-drawn coaches ran from Ballater to Braemar, indeed such were run by their own uncle, Alexander and his brother decided to walk that stretch of the journey. They were lightly burdened with one bag and a 'very light and thin' coat each, and no food. They intended to purchase provisions in Braemar to thus avoid the initial load-carrying burden. They took with them McConnochie's guide, but no OS map, despite the fact that one was available for the Braemar region by 1885. They left Ballater at 7.45am, arriving at Braemar at midday. It is 17 miles between the Deeside towns, so they maintained a very creditable pace of four miles an hour on the metalled road between the two villages. This appears to the modern reader as a cracking pace, but Victorian walkers seem to have been able to maintain such rates much more easily than we can today. Kellas was later to work with the great physiologist JS Haldane. In 1887 Haldane set off from Ballater station and completed a walk through the Grampian mountains of 103 miles in 31 hours (including rests), triumphantly recording, 'no blisters'. Such pedestrianism was commonplace at that time.

In Braemar the Kellas brothers were forced to wait an hour in order to purchase a loaf of bread, which was thus presumably fresh from the oven. (Or possibly the shop was closed for lunch). To this purchase they added a packet of biscuits (and as becomes clear later, also a bottle of lemonade) and then set off again with this 'very insubstantial fare' in the words of the account. Soon the pair of lads passed through the village of Inverey to the Linn o' Dee, by then a tourist hot-spot, partly due to Queen Victoria's visits to the area, then the brothers walked further to Derry Lodge in Glen Lui. Kellas along the way makes observations on the countryside and any fauna, such as deer, that the pair encounter. A little beyond Derry Lodge the boys get 'a magnificent view of Ben Muick Dhui himself, which appeared to rise away to the north in a steep peak with snow near the top.' (Possibly it is worth recording here that snow on top of MacDhui is a very, very rare occurrence in mid summer these days.) Derry Lodge by the Linn o' Dee is fully 12 miles from Braemar, and this leg was covered in three hours, thus maintaining the lads' cracking initial pace of four miles per hour. But even they slowed down a little on the next stage of their journey.

They headed north up Glen Derry, through the thinning Scotch pine forest and then struck up westwards to Corrie Etchachan. 'The night

INVEREY c1900.
Alec and Henry passed through this Upper Deeside village on their Cairngorm explorations. At that time Inverey was still mainly a Gaelic-speaking crofting settlement. The rather well-dressed peasant is posing beside his peat-barrow.

appeared to be closing in, but we got a good view of Corrie Etchachan as we toiled up it, the black precipices fringed with snow... which confine it and give it a very wild appearance,' Alec wrote. By the time they reached Loch Etchachan it was getting really dark and so they immediately headed downhill northwards towards Loch Avon, 'the most beautiful loch in Scotland of the wild type.' They descended about 600ft to the lochside and in the night began looking for the Shelter Stone, which to the non-cognoscenti can be a problem even in the daylight, amongst the huge jumble of great boulders which lie there. But the pair found it. They had reached their destination, after walking a total distance of 35 miles from Ballater that morning. They would appear to have arrived just before nine in the evening. Excluding the hour's rest at Braemar, they had done the distance in 12 hours.

It is worth quoting a little more than the odd sentence from Kellas' account of the night under the Shelter Stone. Apart from showing us that it was widely used as a refuge (the references to the numerous bottles, candles and the soap left indicate this), it is also possible to detect between the lines that the *wee loons* might have been *a bittie feart* in this vast wilderness.

> We were glad enough to get inside and take a seat for by this time it was quite dark. The stillness was something awful apart from the sullen roar of the cataracts that come down from Ben Muick Dhui and Cairngorm and from the Feith Bhuide burn.
>
> When we got inside we lighted about eight different candles that we found there besides the two we had carried with us and then went out over the boulders to the Feith Bhidhe burn for water. (For besides the bottle which we had purchased at Braemar we washed out one of the numerous bottles which we found under the stone.)... It was now past nine and we determined to have supper and then try and get some sleep. On examining our provisions we were a little disappointed to find that we had only taken about half of what we ought to have taken with us... after supper we found that all we had left for the next day was part of a dry loaf.
>
> After supper we extinguished the candles and lying down in our greatcoats tried to get some sleep (it was now past eleven). It was a hopeless task and after lying for nearly an hour quite still we gave up and rising lighted a fire in a small fireplace of stones built on the floor. It was not the intense cold alone which prevented us from sleeping. It was the awful silence broken only by the sullen roar of the Feith Buidhe cataract...We fed the fire from the heather with which the floor of the stone seemed to be deeply spread, but even with this fire the intense cold of the early morning (from 1 to 5 o'clock on the 19th August) was very severely felt.
>
> After a frugal breakfast of bread and water we took a piece of soap we found under the stone and went down to the loch and washed ourselves. The water was bitterly cold but the wash refreshed us... It was now nearly 5 o'clock so we started to ascend Ben Muick Dhui taking the route by the Feith Bhuide (it being the way we had selected while looking over the guide in the early morning).

The route up the Feith Buidhe burn is rough and loose, though possibly not quite as precipitous as is made out in the young Alec Kellas' account, and soon the pair were making good progress toward their target, which lay in the vicinity of the point of the burn's initial rise. Here Kellas inserts a short note 'The only glacier in Britain (IHB)' This shows us that the

LOCH AVON.
From the howff under the Shelter Stone Crag, Alec and Henry ascended
Ben MacDhui by the Feith Buidhe burn which lies beneath the snowfields in the
middle right of the picture, beyond which lies the summit plateau.

youngster has read more than McConnochie's guidebook, for IHB is one
Hill-Burton, whom Kellas refers to again soon afterwards in this
account of the 1885 trip. North East patriotism was hurt when accurate
measurements in the mid 19th century definitively replaced Ben MacDhui
with Ben Nevis as Britain's highest mountain. The idea that its then permanent snowfield at the Feith Bhuide's source was a glacier was a widely
held replacement myth at the time. Proceeding ever upwards, soon the
proud duo 'were at the top of Ben Muick Dhui 4,296ft above the level
of the sea.'

Kellas continues, 'It was bitterly cold. The view was grand, although
the morning haze still overspread the sky a little...' And he then proceeds
to give us an extensive description of the view – quoted verbatim from
Hill-Burton's *The Cairngorm Mountains*. Possibly the young Kellas could
not identify all he saw or could potentially see, or forgot what he saw
when back home and was engaged in composing the account of the trip, so
used the more experienced eyes of Hill-Burton to flesh out his description

when writing it up. It is even possible that Hill-Burton's accounts in his book of his own boyhood rambles in the Cairngorms back in the 1820s and 30s were the original inspiration for Kellas' own 1885 trip. The boys rested awhile on the summit and it may here be a suitable place for us to rest from our narrative and consider another matter.

There are many references to Alec and his brother Henry having an encounter with *Fearlas Mor*, or the Grey Man of Ben Macdhui on their ascent of the peak, which have been widely disseminated in varying forms. As Alec was to be subject to aural (though not apparently to visual) hallucinations in later life, there may be some substance to the various stories. The spookiest version is the one that states that Kellas wrote to Collie about their supposed joint experiences with the Grey Man in the mid 1920s – by which time Kellas was in his grave! But it should be noted that in this narrative of the 1885 trip from Kellas' own hand there is no reference to the appearance of such an apparition, which most authorities regard as a local variant of the Brocken Spectre phenomenon. Nor is there any written comment from either Alec or Henry at any time in their lives of such an encounter having taken place.

The main source for these stories would appear to be the work by Affleck Gray, *The Big Grey Man of Ben MacDui*, which is a compendium of tales concerning *Fearlas Mor*. One version he gives with no source and no date is that Alec saw the phenomenon and Henry did not. Another version, attributed to a letter written to the Aberdeen *Press and Journal* in 1925 by one WG Robertson claims that Henry, who had been a friend of his, had stated that both he and Alec saw the Grey Man in the form of a giant figure descending from the cairn.[3] (For devotees of such matters there are many more unattributed, unsourced often second and third hand accounts of the phenomenon in Gray's book.) But let us return to the 'chiels that winna ding', the hard facts of the case.

The boys wandered about the summit for a while and they tried to seek shelter from the cold wind in the ruins of the triangulation station set up by the Ordnance Survey men back in the 1840s, but finding it gave little protection, they decided to descend the rough western side of Mac-Dhui to the Pools of Dee in the famous Lairg Ghru pass. Kellas writes, 'We were now in a place which IH Burton characterizes as the grandest in Scotland.' – and again he quotes from his mentor's *The Cairngorm Mountains*, a passage containing words to the effect that the Lairig Ghru

BEN MACDHUI.

The summit ridge of what was thought Britain's highest mountain until downgraded to second place by Ben Nevis. Climbed on several occasions by Kellas, and later by Norman Collie, who claims to have encountered *Fearlas Mor* on his descent.

at this point is grander than Glencoe, which many would consider as possibly another example of local North East mountaineering patriotism overriding a more objective judgement. Anyway, so inspired were they by the scene that Alexander and Henry decided to climb the peak of Cairntoul at the western side of the pass.

Their progress went well across Garrachory and by Lochan Uaine, but then they ran into difficulties,

> We had progressed up to within about 200ft of the top, when we reached a ridge of snow which completely blocked the way. The position in which the snow was situated made it quite perpendicular and therefore further ascent was impossible. We began to climb over the precipitous rocks at the side of the path and although we might have succeeded in reaching the top in that direction… a single slip might have precipitated us into Lochan Uaine, a fall of more than 1,000ft… we therefore returned as quickly as possible to the foot of Cairn Toul…
>
> Between Glens Garrachory and Guesachan there is a small hut and as we came opposite it we met with a gamekeeper who accompanied us a short distance and showed us a ford across the Dee. The shadow of the Devil's Point projected far over Glen Dee to Cairn a Mhaim and warned us that it was getting late, for the sun was already sinking behind the mountains.

This 'small hut' was the Corrour Bothy. It was built in 1877 by the Mar Estate, which was then owned by the Duke of Fife. It functioned as a deerwatcher's hut, and was occupied during the summer months and shooting season by a gamekeeper. It had a bed, furniture and a fireplace. The resident's tasks were to watch the deer and indicate to the shooting parties where they might be found, and to keep an eye out for poachers. A further task was to frighten away hillwalkers especially during the shooting season, as the latter were in turn deemed likely to frighten off the deer. Most gamekeepers however, though officious in their duties when the gentry were around, were quite friendly to walkers and climbers at other times – as Kellas found on this occasion. The hut at Corrour was disused from the 1920s and occupied thereafter as a mountain shelter. It is now maintained by the Mountain Bothies Association, and is Listed as a Historical Monument. But we digress, (though hopefully not uninterestingly). Back to our bold lads...

Leaving the gamekeeper for dead (the latter stopped for a rest) the pair then ran most of the way down to Derry Lodge, but baulked at crossing the Duke of Fife's private Bridge at Mar Lodge, and took the longer way back to Braemar by the Linn of Dee, adding three or four more miles to their journey. The Kellas boys were unprepared to challenge proprietorial rights by crossing the private bridge, it appears, even if this meant extra footslogging. Past Braemar, and once more on the metalled road, Kellas says they were still making four miles an hour, but after one rest the pair headed back in the wrong direction towards Braemar for a while, before realising their mistake! Thereupon the totally exhausted and hungry lads crashed out in a forest between Braemar and Balmoral for a few hours' sleep. Next morning they continued towards Ballater and managed to get some food and drink at the Coil a' Creach Inn, some 'biscuits and ginger ale, which we enjoyed immensely, being so terribly hungry.' Finally they arrived at Church Square in Ballater and after a hearty breakfast, slept for six or seven hours, and then returned to *Sluivannichie*. Kellas concluded, 'Thus ended this great expedition as successfully as could have been expected under the circumstances.' An objective reader might conclude that the pair were fortunate not to have been killed by an accident or by hypothermia due to inadequate food and clothing. Nevertheless this trip shows a remarkable stamina and determination on the part of the boys, characteristics which were to mark Kellas' later Himalayan mountaineering.

LOCHNAGAR.

The impressive cliffs of Lochnagar in the 1880s, a time when Alec ascended the mountain from Ballater. He would not have gone by the cliffs, but over a popular pedestrian route which skirted along their summits from the left of the picture.

If Kellas' application to join the SMC is a full account of his youthful mountaineering, it was to be almost another two years before he climbed his third Munro. This was Lochnagar in June 1887 and it was probably, as with his other hills, ascended from Ballater, which is the most conven-ient staring point. In the same year (though it is not clear whether it was in the same month of June) Kellas spent another three nights under the Shelter Stone, on this occasion climbing another 4,000-er, Cairngorm.

Regrettably, Kellas filled out his SMC application form rather sloppily. He gives the year of his various ascents, but only on occasion the month as well, as is requested on the form. Additionally there is at least one clear mistake. On the SMC application sheet he states that he climbed Braeriach and Cairn Toul, from a base at the Shelter Stone in 1887, adding, under *Remarks*, '(*see note in Cairngorm Club Journal*)'. This note, entitled *Camping out among the Cairngorms*, by Alexander and his brother Henry, is found in the *CCJ*, Vol. 1, No. 3, for July 1894 on pp.176–7, and in this short piece he records that the described events took place in 1889, when Kellas has the brothers walking from Ballater to Glen Lui on Monday 29 July. This is no misprint in the published *CCJ* note, as *Whitaker's Almanack* confirms that 29 July was a Monday in 1889, but *not* in 1887.

The Shelter Stone would not today be considered to be the best starting point for Braeraich and Cairn Toul but in the 1880s there were few other places in the Cairngorm mountains offering any shelter in poor weather. Corrour Bothy might have been available in an emergency but not at that time as a place for walkers to routinely occupy overnight. Although Mummery had invented a light-weight silk tent in the 1880s it apparently had not reached Aberdeen, as the lads took hammocks and rugs to sleep outside with in good weather, retreating to the Shelter Stone when conditions deteriorated. Anyway, it would seem clear that Alec had a special affection for *Clach Dian*. In his application in 1911 (*infra*) to join the Alpine Club Kellas comments that between 1883 and 1889 he 'spent in all about a month under the Shelter Stone at the head of Loch Avon on Ben Muick Dhui (2,550ft)' Evidently, even as a youth, Kellas was a person who could put up with a considerable degree of discomfort, as well as one having good physical stamina.

On the 1889 occasion, learning from past mistakes, the brothers took 'provisions for about a week.' They were able to sleep out on two nights when the weather was favourable, spending another five under the Shelter Stone. They climbed Cairn Toul (avenging the setback of 1885) and Braeriach on the same day, Friday 2 August, camping out in the edge of the Rothiemurchus forest that night. After the first fine evening when they slung their hammocks in Glen Derry, the brothers experienced much bad weather on this trip, and cold conditions, with high ('*hurricane*') winds. They were soon heading back to *Clach Dian* for shelter, after aborting their attempt to sleep in Rothiemurchus, due to the cold.

(As) sleep was a failure, we wandered about for two or three hours to keep ourselves warm, watching the sun-glow circle the horizon. The night was not to be called disagreeable, but it was very cold and a drizzly rain fell at intervals. After a false start in the darkness we were well into the Pass by 4am rain not adding to our comfort. The col was leisurely reached by 6.0 then turning down sharply to the left, we held direct to the Shelter Stone… lured by an apparent improvement we emerged from beneath Clach Dian and, again, started for Ben Muich Dhui. But the threatening black clouds, having got us at a height of over 4,000ft, burst forth into a deluge. We made a hurried retreat Stone-wards, leaving the sole of a boot behind us, and thus putting a compulsory end to our mountaineering[4].

From the Shelter Stone the next day they walked all the way back to Ballater, almost 40 miles, most of it in the rain.

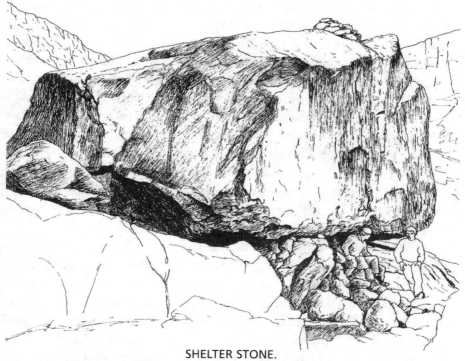

SHELTER STONE.
The most famous gite in Scotland, if not in Europe, which has had a continuous usage for almost half a millennium. Alec spent much time under it, using it as a base for his Cairngorm explorations.
(Illustrator: Ewan MacArthur)

Although the Kellas brothers were tramping the Cairngorms together, and Henry was to join the Cairngorm Club in 1895, Alec himself appears to have had tenuous connections with the organisation rather than otherwise. Another CC member in the 1890s was James F Kellas Johnstone (*Manuscript Book* p.12). He was the son of one of the (unnamed) daughters of Alec's Skene grandparents, who had married a Mr Johnstone. He was therefore Alec's cousin, and in a close knit town like Aberdeen he too would have been 'family'. So Alexander Kellas certainly knew people who were active in the Cairngorm Club. The fact that Alec himself wrote something for the *Cairngorm Club Journal* (see above) in 1894 indicates that he must have been at least marginally involved in the Club's activities at this time. His brother Henry, on the other hand, remained a lifelong member, never holding office in the Club, though he contributed the occasional brief article to its *Journal*. Henry also played a support role in the early exploration of Bheinn a' Bhuird's climbing potential, by providing a top rope for Parker and Drummond when they explored the Mitre Ridge in 1921. (We are grateful to Greg Strange for providing us with this information.) Alec's engagement with the organisation – which was to mirror his life-engagements in general – was more marginal than his brother's.

It is also worth remarking that after joining the SMC itself in 1898 Kellas appears not to have been on any club meets or outings, or taken part in any of the other club activities, such as the annual dinner, for all of which club activities the SMCJ religiously listed those members attending. The largely isolated nature of his mountaineering, which was to be a mark of his later Himalayan explorations, appears to have been established in Alexander's early wanderings in his native Cairngorm hills, and subsequent forays further into the Scottish mountains.

In 1889, Kellas's SMC application form records the ascent of another couple of Cairngorm Munros, those of Derry Cairngorm and Bheinn Mheadhoin, a pair of relatively easy hills near Derry Lodge. And a further two years later in 1891 another brace of 3,000ft Cairngorm hills, Beinn a' Chaorainn and Ben Bynack (usually known as Bynack Mor) were also climbed, each being pretty straightforward day outings. Whilst living in Aberdeen, Alexander Kellas' mountaineering had fitted in pretty well with the mindset of the other members of the North East hillwalking community, in being centred on the Cairngorm mountains, and in consisting of extensive hill walking rather than of any technical mountaineering. On leaving the city his outlook towards mountaineering was to undergo a gradual rather than a dramatic change, a change which would eventually lead him to the Himalaya.

Interestingly, though he appears to have played a marginal role in the Cairngorm Club's activities, the organisation itself kept tabs on the local lad as he rose to later Himalayan fame. In July 1912 their *Journal* (Vol. 7, No. 39), outlined the contents of a lecture Kellas had given that year to the Royal Geographical Society in London. Under the heading 'An Aberdeen Climber in the Himalayas', details of his expeditions to Sikkim and Garhwal were given and his ascent of Powhunri [*sic*] at 23,180ft was noted with pride. A breakdown in health forced Kellas to return to Aberdeen in 1919, and he recuperated at Carden Place until April 1920. At the Club's Annual Dinner in December of the latter year, a slide show of his Himalayan exploits was given – although by a Mr Parker, since Alec himself had – at least apparently – recovered his health and was back in Sikkim by late 1920. The *Journal* for January 1921 noted,

> The 'after dinner' proceedings were more varied than usual. A number of very striking photographs of the very grand scenery of the Himalayas were thrown on the screen. They were taken by Dr A.M. Kellas (brother of Mr Henry Kellas, a member of the club), who has made many journeys of exploration in these excessively high altitudes, and they included views of Kinchinjunga, K2 and Mount Everest.[5]

On Alec's death a fulsome obituary was contributed to the CCJ (Vol. 10, No. 57, pp.128–130.), and subsequently in 1922 the same publication informed its readers (CCJ Vol.10, No. 58) that a memorial to Kellas had been erected at Kampa Dzong, the place of his death, and it published an illustration of that memorial. The *Journal* also recorded in the same issue that the Club (which had a membership of over 170 people) had raised a contribution towards the proposed Everest 1922 expedition. This amounted to £8 13s 6d. Not exactly a massive amount from 170 people, but then this was Aberdeen, a town renowned for its parsimony. One might have thought Alec Kellas' memory, and his role in the whole Everest saga had merited a little more loosening of the purse strings in the mountaineering fraternity of the town of his birth, than £8 13s and 6d. The citizens of the town did turn out in force when George Mallory visited Aberdeen in the same year and gave a talk in the Music Hall on 7

February 1922, on the Everest expedition of 1921. Then the hall was 'completely filled', according to the reporter from the *Aberdeen Journal*, who described the famous mountaineer as 'quite boyish'. In his talk Mallory made mention of Kellas as follows, according to the reporter present,

> Dr Kellas, Mr Mallory told the audience, was taken ill on the march and was carried day by day in a litter rigged up for the occasion by his own faithful coolies... In him we had lost, he added, not only a delightful and helpful companion but a very experienced mountaineer of rare enthusiasm and one whose services could not possibly be replaced in the party (applause).[6]

But Alexander Kellas was soon to all but vanish from the memory of the town altogether. In the 1960s the name of Tom Patey was renowned in Aberdeen, partly because of his Karakoram exploits in the 1950s, but hardly anyone in mountaineering or other circles had heard of Alec Kellas, a situation which remained unchanged therafter.

NOTES

[1] Eg, 'During the next few years he came to know most of the highlands...' 'Alexander Mitchell Kellas' by Doug Scott, DNB (31) 2004, p.93. 'Later he visited many other mountain districts in Scotland.' 'Alexander Mitchell Kellas', by Norman Collie, *Alpine Journal* Vol. 34, No. 223, p.145. Based on Collie's obituary notice a more recent outline of Kellas' career portrays things in like vein as follows, 'By the time he went to Heidelberg [*Kellas gained his PhD at Heidelberg in 1897, Authors' Note*] he knew all the mountains of Scotland and Wales intimately and had climbed extensively in Switzerland also.' *Fallen Giants; A History of Himalayan Mountaineering*, Maurice Isserman and Stewart Weaver, (2008) p.78. These comments however tend to exaggerate Kellas' Scottish experience, especially at a time when any such detailed knowledge of the Scottish mountains was the possession of only a few intrepid peak baggers, like Hugh Munro himself, and the Rev. AE Robertson. Isserman and Weaver also magnify the Swiss CV, which in Kellas' own words in his application to join the Alpine Club in 1911, consisted by 1899, of 'a few minor summits'.

[2] *Our Tour To The Cairngorm Mountains* by Alec Kellas exists in a typewritten form. It is extremely unlikely that a 17 year old boy in 1885 would have the skill to operate the recently invented typewriter, even if the family possessed such a machine, so we have to assume the script was

hand-written and typed out some time later by someone else's hands. The typing of *John* Hill Burton's first initial as *I* would be an easy mistake to make when working from a script to the typewritten page, and supports this view of the involvement of a second person in the typing. *Our Tour...* might have the look of a schoolboy's essay, but it was composed after his leaving of the Grammar School, possibly as a Victorian evening's entertainment, when the young Alec would have recounted his adventures to an admiring middle class Victorian family *soiree*.

3 *The Big Grey Man of Ben MacDhui*, Affleck Gray, (1974), p.25.
4 *CCJ*, Vol. 1, No. 3, p.177.
5 *CCJ*, Vol. 10, No. 56, p.81.
6 *Aberdeen Journal*, (8 February 1922), p.4.

CHAPTER THREE

Scotland, London, The Alps

Scientist and Mountaineer

AFTER SOME TIME in Edinburgh attending classes at Heriot Watt College, and possibly also at Edinburgh University, Alec Kellas transferred to London to complete his scientific studies at University College, and he graduated there in 1892 as BSc in chemistry. Subsequently he began to work with Professor William Ramsay in the Department of Chemistry at UCL. Ramsay had apparently been impressed by the young Aberdonian when the latter was an undergraduate and was keen to have him on his team. Ramsay himself was only the latest in a long line of distinguished professors of chemistry at UCL who had – like the Glaswegian Ramsay – been born and educated in Scotland. Indeed UCL was in many ways a Scottish export to England, founded in 1829 though the initiatives of two Scots – the Glasgow poet Thomas Campbell and the Edinburgh philosopher Henry Brougham. UCL was largely based upon the Enlightenment model of Edinburgh University – even to the point of its neo-classical architecture. It was aimed at breaking the then near-monopoly of higher education in England by the High Church, High Tory, classical and ecclesiastically-oriented Universities of Oxford and Cambridge. No theology was taught at UCL and opponents described it as a pagan university in a pagan building.

Ramsay had taken over the professorial post in chemistry in 1887 and had arranged for his scientific associate Norman Collie to join him as his chief experimental assistant. Although Ramsay was the pre-eminent scientist of the two, and the overall director of research, Collie's own stature was recognised in 1890 by the UCL conferring upon him the title of Assistant Professor, and he was made a Fellow of the Royal Society in 1896. This was a period of great advance in chemistry, especially in organic chemistry. Ramsay's research was, at this juncture, directed towards filling in gaps that existed in the Periodic Table of the Elements, recently formulated by Mendeleeff. This work was taking place at a time just after the new north wing at UCL had been built, with the basement being given over to the new chemical laboratories, with the classrooms being on the ground floor. Possibly surprisingly, the rest of the building was occupied by the Slade Art School. The image of the shy, awkward Alec entering the same portals as the Slade Bohemians – of both sexes – is an interesting one.

Over the years subsequent to 1887 Ramsay and his team were to discover and isolate many of the so-called inert (also designated rare or noble) gases such as argon, helium and neon. These new-found elements had the unique property of very limited reactivity with other elements in chemical reactions. For this work Ramsay was awarded the Nobel Prize in 1904 and subsequently knighted[1]. Investigation into the inert gases is a good example of the pursuit of apparently pure, and to the layman utterly obscure and pointless research, which was however to have profound practical implications later, for example in neon lighting, refrigeration, lasers and air transport.

On this formidable team Kellas was employed as an assistant, or a 'demonstrator.' This was a supportive post consisting of maintaining the apparatus, preparing samples of chemicals for experiments, and of carrying out specific experiments as directed, rather than working as independent researcher on his own behalf. It is most probable that Kellas taught under-graduate students as well, since Ramsay was a firm believer in mixing his under- and post-graduate students in the labs and lecture halls. As well as being a scientific giant Ramsay was an excellent teacher and experimenter. Working with such a team was a very good career start for a recently graduated young chemist. Kellas was working on the inert gases project when argon was isolated in August 1894. This was the first such 'rare' gas to be identified and collected.

Ramsay had heated a form of the uranium ore – pitchblende – in order to attempt to isolate argon, and in the gas subsequently obtained was discovered the spectra of argon as hoped for, and also that of another unknown gas which was subsequently to be identified as helium. The second gas had not been expected by the researchers, and sent them off on a new quest. This must have been an exciting time for Kellas, as part of a team at the forefront of scientific discovery, and one which was soon joined by another member, Morris Travers, in October of that year of 1894. Travers had been an undergraduate in Ramsay's department at

UCL CHEMISTRY DEPARTMENT 1899.
Alec, easily spotted on the extreme right, with his colleagues at UCL in 1899.
Ramsay is the patriarch in the centre of a department which he had expanded
and whose reputation was growing. Note the female students.
(UCL Collections)

the same time as had Kellas himself. From the discovered argon, the attention of the UCL chemists switched to the helium investigation.

Morris Travers appears to have been everything Alec Kellas was not. He came from an upper middle class family of London physicians and legal people, with a home in Kensington. Whereas Kellas was always described as shy, and he spoke with a strong Aberdeen-Scots accent, which would have marked him out in metropolitan society as a 'provincial', Travers exuded self confidence. After leaving UCL the latter man became instrumental in attaining university status for Bristol College and subsequently became an important educational administrator in India. (See *ODNB* Vol. 55, pp.235–6). Whether Travers was a better scientist than Kellas is unascertainable; but he appears to have been altogether pushier. Travers soon established himself as on a par with Collie – if not quite with Ramsay himself – in the inert gases research team as a whole. On the other hand Kellas was relegated to the somewhat more routine working-out of the implications of the argon discovery, and was not involved in the cutting-edge search for helium. As Travers puts it,

> Kellas did not actually take part in the work of helium, but took up an investigation on argon. He was a very reliable worker, but perhaps too slow to work with Ramsay.[2]

Reliable, but slow is not exactly fulsome praise. Elsewhere Travers describes the work Kellas was doing as 'unexciting.' A fuller account of Kellas' role at this time is given in Travers' biography of Ramsay, where he states,

> Kellas had already begun research into the possible argon content of animal and vegetable matter. Obtaining 350 c.cs. of nitrogen from peas and 550 c.cs. from mice by the Dumas method, he found that in neither case did the gas contain more than 0.04 per cent of argon. The experiment was therefore negative, as it was expected to be, within the bounds of experimental error. Then he undertook the determination of the argon content of dry, CO_2-free air. His value, 0.937 per cent, agrees closely with the accepted value. In that he did not take part in the work on helium, Kellas may seem to have occupied a place in the background...

before praising his experimental skills as a kind of back handed compliment, and Kellas himself for having taken on 'the most difficult and exacting task' of this rather routine experimentation.[3]

Ramsay appears to have been very supportive of his scientific charges, and he conveyed to the Royal Society two short accounts of Kellas' work on argon. These were published in the *Proceedings of the Royal Society* and later used as supplementary documentation for Kellas' award of the degree of DSc in chemistry in 1918 from the University of London. They are evidently papers based on the research that Travers mentions Kellas as undertaking in 1894–5. The papers are in PRS, Vol. 57, pp.490–2 and Vol. 59, pp.67–8, and are respectively entitled *Is Argon contained in Vegetable or Animal Substances?* (with George W MacDonald), and *On the Percentage of Argon in atmospheric and in respired Air*. In the latter article Kellas is described as 'Assistant in the Chemical Department.'

Though the former was to leave the other somewhat behind, initially both Travers and Kellas appear to have been equal dogsbodies, as for example when their Professor, bathed in glory, presented his findings to a meeting of the Royal Society in May 1895. By this time helium itself has been successfully identified and isolated, as well as the original argon. Ramsay commented that, 'Kellas and Travers were kept hard at it the whole evening, and must have shown the spectra to 2,000 people.'[4]

But soon Travers was to assume a much more central role in the whole noble gases story, a position which Kellas did not achieve. Writing of himself in the third person, Travers sums up his own contribution as follows,

> During the next five years the writer of this book was to be very closely associated with Ramsay in his scientific work...
>
> Morris W Travers was to be associated with Ramsay in the researches which led to the discovery and isolation of neon, krypton and xenon...
>
> The work on helium was a happy opening to Travers' later years of service at University College. Whatever may have been the weaknesses in the team which started the work on helium in April, 1895, when Ramsay and Travers published their final paper in November 1900, no serious attempt had been made by others to enter the field.[5]

Victorians (and even when writing his biography of Ramsey in 1956, Travers had a Victorian mind set, and wrote stylistically as if it was still the 19th century) were gentlemen. They did not criticise openly. But reading between the lines, by 'weaknesses in the team' Travers probably meant Collie as well as Kellas, describing the former as 'a very clever experimentalist and a most enthusiastic researcher.' One can be damned by faint praise. Travers' view of his own importance in the discovery of the inert gases is probably not an excessively exaggerated one. He more or less claimed for himself the discovery of xenon, with a very high probability that he merits the credit. Collie on the other hand made the unjustified claim – several times verbally, but never in writing – that he personally discovered neon. The fact is however, that Collie had left Ramsay's laboratory when the discovery of neon was made. Travers must have been aware of this claim, but simply ignores it in his account of Ramsay's life. However, such a claim by Collie must have rankled with Travers.

Christine Mill in her account of Collie's work with Ramsay tends to overestimate Collie's contribution to the discovery of the inert gases, and does not acknowledge that of Travers to any great degree. But by any reckoning, Travers is a more important figure in the inert gases story than is Collie. Mill also tends to let Collie off the hook on his unsubstantiated neon discovery claims, arguing,

> Probably the answer will never be known, but considering Collie's total lack of self-advertisement, and the circumstantial evidence, his involvement with the discovery of neon must have some element of truth.[6]

But if Collie had a justifiable claim with 'some element of truth' in it, he could have made it, for example when in 1927 he wrote *A Century of Chemistry at University College*, privately printed by UCL. He made no claim there, as there was none to make, and Collie correctly in that work credited Ramsay with the discovery of neon. Further, that little pamphlet, *contra* Christine Mill, *is* full of self-advertisement by Collie, not only concerning his own scientific achievements, but also about his mountaineering exploits, which one might have thought out of place in such a publication!

KELLAS PORTRAIT.
The most familiar portrait of Alexander Kellas, from the late 1890s. His gaucheness and awkward body language are evident in this image, as in the previous one, and also in his early family portrait.

In these gentlemanly assertions of status and pecking order, Alec Kellas must have been aware that he was not able to compete with any degree of success. Whilst Travers was becoming Ramsay's *wunderkind* (the great scientist sent a letter to his wife, quoted proudly by Travers in his *Life...*, stating simply 'Travers is trumps!'), Kellas was doing routine experimentation on the argon contained in peas and mice. There is a photograph, originally printed in Travers' *Discovery of the Rare Gases*, which is reproduced in Christine Mill's biography of Collie (though the image does not include Collie personally, who left the department before the image was taken) of the team at the UCL laboratories in 1896. Ramsay lounges confidently, the alpha male looking at the camera, and Travers cocks his head assuredly so as to be in the frame. Kellas has his back to the photographer, as if he almost wanted to be elsewhere. This shy young man must have already been contemplating the possibility that he was not going to emerge into the ranks of the forerunners in scientific research, at least not with Ramsay. And Collie too had his dissatisfactions at this time.

The latter was frustrated at not being a full professor, and Ramsay was almost certainly never going to leave UCL and thus create a vacant post, so Collie applied for and obtained a professorship at the Pharmaceutical Society, which post he gained in November 1896. Collie stayed there for six years, returning to UCL in 1902 as Professor of Organic Chemistry, a then newly created position. By that time Kellas had left UCL and was working at the Middlesex College Hospital. There is a footnote to Kellas' obituary in the *Middlesex Hospital Journal*[7] which confirms that he took up his post as lecturer in Chemistry at the Middlesex Hospital School in 1900.

Christine Mill states that Kellas left UCL in 1896 at the same time as Collie. She comments that, (taking the information from Travers' un-published biography), 'At the same time [*as Collie leaving, Authors' Note*] Kellas also left Ramsay to become a lecturer in Middlesex Hospital Medical School.'[8] However, as noted, Kellas did not start work at his Middlesex Hospital post, subsequent to leaving UCL, till 1900, and there is a further extant photograph of the Chemistry Department at UCL in 1898 which contains Alec, shy and on the fringes as usual. What had actually happened?

It seems likely that the time line was as follows.

Kellas, realising he was possibly going nowhere with Ramsay as things stood in 1896, left UCL as Travers states. He then went to Heidelberg for a year where he gained his PhD in 1897. In those days a scientific doctorate at a German University was a one-year project with the degree awarded for the carrying out of a piece of original research; Collie for example had obtained his PhD at Wurzburg in 1882–3. In his submissions for the DSC which he was awarded by the University of London in 1918, is included a paper Kellas had had published in the *Zeitschrift fur Physikalischen Chemie*, XXIV, 2, pp.221–252, based on his German studies. This is rather cumbersomely entitled *Uber die Esterifizierungsgeschwindichkeit der monosubstituierten Benzoesauren und die Verseifungsgeschwindichkeit ihrer Ester*. This work allowed Kellas to become a member of the Deutsche

Chemische Gesellschaft, one of several organisations he joined in his life but appears to have played little or no part in (Source: *Open University, Biographical Database of British Chemists*). The fact that both Collie and Kellas could master German sufficiently to gain their PhDs in that country is testimony to their language skills, and also reflects that fact that German had at least equal status with English as the *lingua franca* of science at this time.

After gaining his doctorate, Alexander Kellas subsequently returned to work at UCL, not on the research on inert gases, but to his old job as an Assistant in what was a fast expanding department. Confirmation of this is given in his SMC application form, where he records that he was still working at UCL in November 1897, and in the photograph from 1898 mentioned above. But it seems that Kellas was never made up to a full lecturer in the Chemistry Department, which must have been frustrating even to one so unassuming. The OU database cited in the previous paragraph lists him as being an Assistant at UCL from 1893–99, and this is no oversight, as the UCL Chemistry Department website does not include Kellas in its alphabetical list of lecturers from 1826 till now.

So after a couple of years at UCL after returning from Germany, Alec moved to what he judged would be a better career opportunity, that is to the teaching of chemistry to medical students at the Middlesex College Hospital, which institution lay a short distance from UCL. This would mean that Kellas was still working in the chemistry department at UCL under Ramsay in 1898 when the latter, with Travers very much now acting as his right hand man, discovered neon. But Kellas would appear not to have been involved in these researches, as Travers never mentions him in connection with them. Alec Kellas may have been retiring, but he was not actually invisible. Had he been involved in the neon work Travers would have mentioned the fact. Kellas did gain a bit of a profile at this time however, when he became president of the Chemical-Physical Society in 1897–98. This was a social/debating organisation linking the two scientific departments at UCL, and Alec occupying this position indicates that whilst he may have been shy and retiring, he was not at this time a total recluse.

Whilst Kellas' appointment as an Assistant at UCL in 1892 involved the major change from being an undergraduate student to being a scientific researcher, it was accompanied by no great change in his mountaineering habits. Initially this may seem rather surprising since Norman Collie, with whom he was working, was soon to become of the greatest international mountaineers of the day. However Collie – although 32 years old when Kellas joined the staff at UCL – had actually not done a very great deal of mountaineering himself at this juncture, apart from a bit of adventurous scrambling on Skye and in the Lake District. But in 1892 an enterprising Easter of activity in Lakeland, followed by the first traverse of the Aiguille de Grepon in the Alps with AF Mummery and others in August that same year, signalled Collie's *annus mirabilis*. The traverse of the Grepon was followed by two more seasons in the Alps where Collie and Mummery, with Cecil Slingsby, virtually invented guideless Alpine climbing. This emergence of his senior colleague as a mountaineer of international standing appears to have made little initial change in the mountaineering habits of Alexander Kellas, though he does start wandering on occasion further afield from his native Cairngorms.

In 1893, presumably during his long University summer holidays, Kellas continued to explore the Scottish mountains on foot, according to his SMC application form. He made an enterprising foray to Ben Alder, which required a long walk through rough country. The gamekeeper at Ben Alder cottage was accustomed to giving mountaineers bed and board, and Kellas possibly overnighted there. Kellas also climbed Sgurr a' Mhaim, in the Mamores, which is an invigorating scramble, and the mountain would have been reached by him via the West Highland Railway. And in the same year he recorded five more Munros in the Greater Cairngorm area, Glas Tulaichean, Glas Maol, Carn nan Gabhar (Kellas gives this as Beinn Gobhar) of Beinn a' Ghlo and Ben Avon and its neighbour Bheinn a' Bhuird. All of these are straightforward walking outlings, of no technical difficulty. Beinn a' Ghlo and Ben Avon are recorded as having been the object of the July and September meets of the Cairngorm Club that year and it seems therefore probable that Kellas joined these expeditions whilst on holiday at home in Aberdeen. (CCJ, Vol. 1, No. 2, p.96, 99).

In March and April 1894 Norman Collie undertook a trip which is often seen as marking the beginnings of Scottish technical mountaineering. Kellas is not recorded as having been on any of the climbs made by Collie in 1894, such as the epochal first ascent of Tower Ridge on Ben Nevis. Graded today (in summer) as *Difficult*, this 2,000ft climb, possibly the longest in Britain, is quite another proposition in winter. Nor is Alec mentioned as an accompanying member of the small party of Collie, Geoffrey Solly and Joseph Collier who undertook this pioneering expedition. Collie had originally arrived at the SMC Easter meet at Inveroran, somewhat to the south of Glencoe, and then taken off with these two others. Kellas is not recorded as a guest at Inveroran and it is not credible that he was an invisible accompanist to the trio of Collie, Solly and Collier in 1894.

However, the three UCL chemists did undertake a trip north to Scotland the next year, when in April 1895, Travers and Kellas accompanied Collie as guests, within a wider party of mainly SMC stalwarts, to Ben Nevis. It was on *this* occasion that Kellas climbed Ben Nevis with Collie by a snow gully, probably No. 3 or No. 4, and *not* in 1894 as Kellas records on his SMC application. Once again, Kellas' sloppiness with dates creates nightmares for his biographer. There appears to have been only one Collie, Kellas, Travers Scottish outing, that of 1895. And just as Travers had occupied a more central space at the UCL laboratories, so he was to show himself a better – or at least a pushier – mountaineer on this trip.

About 20 members and guests met at the Alexandra Hotel in Fort William, arriving by the newly-completed Glasgow to Fort William West Highland Railway. From that base, in winter conditions, Collie, with Travers and two others, ascended Castle Ridge on Ben Nevis. Castle Ridge is only graded *Moderate* now in summer, but would have been a demanding climb to pioneer then in winter conditions. It was subsequently described as follows,

> A new ridge leading to the top of Carn Dearg, and since christened the Castle Ridge, after the huge castellated rock mass which towers over it, was discovered and climbed by three parties, who were unanimous in reporting that, although rather short, it afforded about 1,000ft of excellent sport. (*SMCJ*, Vol. 3, No.5, 1895)

Three further parties followed Collie and party's first ascent of Castle Ridge, but Kellas was not recorded as having been on any of them. Though he was present on this historic trip, Alec did not appear to take or to desire to engage in the technical climbing that was on offer.

On the other hand, Travers had not only taken part in the ascent of Castle Ridge with Collie, but on this outing undertook further climbs with him, though not all were actually recorded. They appear to have

BEN NEVIS (WINTER).
The mighty cliffs of Ben Nevis, 2,000ft high, in winter. Similar conditions were met on the 1895 SMC Meet Alec attended. No. 3 gully – which may have been the one he ascended with Collie – is just visible on the extreme right.
(AE Robertson, SMC Collection)

consisted in ascents under snow conditions on hills in the vicinity of Ben Nevis. In 1898, looking backwards in an article for the SMCJ (Vol. 5 No. 3, p.97) entitled, *Reverie*, Collie talks of an incident which almost certainly took place on the 1895 trip [*Aonach Mhor is just east of Ben Nevis, Authors' Note*];

> Now I am hacking my way through a cornice apparently hundreds of feet high, on Aonach Mhor, my companion Travers meanwhile freezing slowly on the brink of an absolutely perpendicular ice slope, the daylight waning and our retreat cut off.

Travers joined the SMC the following year, and as previously mentioned, seconded Kellas' own subsequent application. Morris Travers went on to climb in the Alps with Aleister Crowley, subsequently the Great Beast 666, and together they did some challenging ascents, including the first guideless traverse of The Monch in August 1895, but Travers gave up mountaineering soon afterwards.

However, Alec Kellas did do some impressive mountaineering on this April 1895 trip. I have mentioned at various points his sloppiness with dates; Travers however was rather more precise and through the *latter's* SMC application form we can date precisely several Munros Alec climbed that are not given dates in his own SMC application. Travers mentions Ladhar Bheinn and Sgurr na Ciche in the remote Knoydart area as being climbed on that Easter 1895 meet, as well as hills in Lochaber such as Stob Coire an Easain Mhor and Stob Coire Claurigh. Kellas gives *exactly* the same hills – not specifically dated – but as having been ascended sometime between the years of 1894 and 1897, and it is logical to assume that the two men (possibly, or not, with Collie) climbed these mountains together in 1895, from the obvious base of Fort William. The two Knoydart hills in particular are remote, hard and – in winter – of some technical difficulty, though not actual rock or ice climbs. Whilst not attracted by technical mountaineering, on this historic meet Kellas showed he had good stamina and he would have strengthened his overall mountaineering skills such as navigation and the use of the ice-axe, and possibly also had some practise in rope-work.

Ramsay, incidentally, appears to have been frustrated by the mountaineering interests of his three main co-workers. He had always been slightly critical of the way Collie fled to the mountains from the laboratory, or in Ramsay's words, 'bolted when the session was done.' (Another colleague more uncharitably described Collie as 'A chemist in his spare time.') For a brief period in the mid 1890s, the future Nobel Prize winner had three such mountain fanatics, and he is recorded by Travers as pressurising them to cut short their Easter holidays in 1895, at the height of the helium work,

> It was now the end of term and before the laboratory closed Ramsay asked Collie, Travers and Kellas, who were going to Scotland on a walking and climbing holiday, to return early, and to join him in working out the preparation of helium.[9]

SMC MEET 1895 GLEN NEVIS.
A fine portrait of some of the doughty gentlemen who participated in the
1895 Meet, illustrating the clothing and equipment of the times.
But Alexander Kellas is not one of them, he is The Man Not In The Picture.
(SMC Collections)

Further delays were to occur later on in 1895 when Collie was late back
from the Himalaya after a summer trip which ended in tragedy with the
death of his companion Mummery, and Ramsay was forced to take on
some of Collie's teaching load, as Travers noted,

> At the conclusion of the work on helium, Dr Collie had gone to
> India on a climbing expedition, and owing to an accident to one of
> his party, he was not back at college till some time after the commence-
> ment of the session, so that Ramsay, Kellas and I had to share his
> work, and there was little or no time for research.[10]

Mountaineering has often contributed to scientific advance, though
Ramsay must have felt on this occasion that the activity was holding
scientific development back.

The Himalayan trip which Travers refers to was an epochal event in the history of mountaineering, being one of the first serious attempts to climb an 8,000m Himalayan giant. With his former Alpine companion Mummery, who was to be killed on the expedition, Collie made an attempt on Nanga Parbat, which mountain the pair had greatly underestimated, and whose scale defeated them. Mummery in particular had not appreciated the effect of altitude on the performance of the human body, expecting to be able to climb at Alpine standards and speeds, even though at Himalayan heights. Collie himself noted this problem as being one of the main lessons of the trip and undoubtedly Kellas would have been made aware of the issue by his senior colleague in conversations at the UCL once Collie had returned from Nanga Parbat. But whilst it would be convenient if this adventure could be shown to have been the spark which inspired Kellas' later Himalayan trips, it is well over a decade – in fact 1907 – before Alec himself was to head for Sikkim on his first such foray. If Kellas was dreaming of greater things at this time, he was surely keeping such dreams to himself whilst he continued tramping around the Scottish hills.

Through most of the rest of the 1890s, Kellas' SMC application records him as faithfully ascending more Munros. (All these ascents were done between 1894 and 1897, but Kellas does not always specify the actual date of ascent for several of the hills.) We can however see a development in that he makes several forays into country remoter and wilder than his beloved Cairngorms, ascending Ben Lui and Ben More in central Perthshire, and Ben Cruachan in far Argyll. Both these hills could by the 1890s be accessed by railway transport.

But if we can see a progress in Kellas' mountaineering in the later 1890s, it is noteworthy that few, if indeed any, of his ascents were done with Norman Collie. In her biography of Collie, Christine Mill writes that,

> Kellas and Collie had been drawn together from the first by their mutual love of the mountains. Kellas, like John Collie, came from Aberdeen and had spent his early years wandering over the Scottish hills. Collie later introduced him to the possibilities of the Himalayas...[11]

It would appear that this overstates the actual relationship. True in 1897 Collie was to propose Kellas for SMC membership, but they were hardly drawn together as stated, since no record exists of them mountaineering as a unit apart from the one gully climb on Ben Nevis in 1895. An intensive investigation of the Visitors' Books at the Sligachan Hotel, Collie's main base for his pre-1914 explorations and ascents in Skye, was made by the authors of this book in September 2010. Collie's name cropped up almost yearly, as did that of his various climbing companions on Skye. That of Alec Kellas does not occur once, though his brother Henry did pay the Misty Island a visit in August 1909. The Kellas-Collie Himalayan connection is also rather tenuous and Collie's Aberdeen connections were not really as strong as often stated. Granted, his father was originally from the city but apart from a few years in his teens spent at Glassel outside Aberdeen after the family business fortunes in Manchester had failed, Collie spent his entire life elsewhere. Collie may have been an *inspiration* for Kellas, but in no real way can he be seen as a mountain-eering *mentor*. Collie was to be full of praise for Kellas' later Himalayan achievements, and the men kept in personal touch and corresponded over the years. But they were never strongly connected in the actual mountains themselves, where Kellas was a figure ploughing his own furrow, or as they might have said in his native Aberdeen *ganging his ain gate*.

The solitary nature of Alec Kellas' mountaineering at this time is further illustrated by considering the comment made in his application of 1911 to join the Alpine Club that his 'numerous ascents' in Britain included (apart from those of the Grampians, already discussed above) the 'chief summits' of the 'Lake District and Wales'. Collie was a frequent visitor in the 1890s to Wasdale in the Lake District, the birthplace of British rock climbing a decade before, a development outlined in Alan Hankinson's delightful book *The First Tigers* (1972). But there is no record of Kellas being at Wasdale with Collie, or being there in any of the other groups which assembled in that last decade of the 19th century. In the absence of any evidence to the contrary we have to assume that Alexander Kellas' mountaineering in the Lakes and Wales – as in his native Scotland – was done largely, if not entirely, on his own, especially after he left UCL for the Middlesex College Hospital. Again, by contrast, Morris Travers' SMC application records that he was at Wasdale with Collie in December 1895 and climbed Napes Needle, a plum route at that period.

Middlesex Hospital Medical School, where Kellas had moved to

COLLIE IN 1921.
An unfamiliar portrait of the chemist and mountaineer, in his laboratory at UCL in 1921 (the year of Kellas' death), just prior to his retirement as Professor of Organic Chemistry. He was then President of the Alpine Club (1920–1922) and a member of the Everest Committee.
(UCL Collections)

after his UCL years, was founded in 1835 as a teaching hospital. Kellas would appear to have found a slightly more congenial role here than he did in the UCL laboratory. The Kellas obituary in the hospital *Journal*, mentioned above, is actually by Collie, and he observes of Kellas that while at the Hospital, 'his bent in those days lay more towards teaching than research, and he always would be ready to assist backward students, spending all his time helping them over their difficulties.'[12] Confirmation of this bent towards teaching is that while in his teaching post, Kellas wrote three textbooks which were published from 1909–10. *Introduction to Practical Chemistry* (1909) was followed by *Introduction to Practical Organic Chemistry* (1910), and in the same year appeared *A Manual of Practical Inorganic Chemistry: Including preparations and qualitative analysis with the rudiments of gas analysis.* Its sub-heading noted that it was 'specially adapted' to cover preliminary and intermediate university courses and the syllabus for the Board of Education [*ie. teacher-training, Authors' Note*]. This book, and the other textbooks he wrote, must have been a steady income-generator and possibly helped fund Alec's subsequent Himalayan trips.

More information is given on Kellas' time at the Hospital in an anonymous note appended to the above obituary, which states that he retired due to ill health early in 1920[13], – although this illness had actually forced him to return to convalesce in Aberdeen in 1919. The note records that Kellas enjoyed 'success as a teacher', and that, after being appointed as a lecturer in Chemistry in 1900, 'Four years later a separate Department for the teaching of Physics was established under his charge.' Clearly specialisation had less of an academic hold in those days, for by 1904 the chemist Kellas had become a physics departmental head, indicating progress on the career ladder – and an increasing income. By the time of his application to join the Alpine Club in 1911 he was living in the prestigious Regent's Park district, at 2 St Mark's Square. This is a very large house, indeed almost a mansion. He appears not to have had an apartment here however, as his will, written in 1907, refers to his 'room' in St Mark's Square. He could walk to work at the hospital from here, through Regent's Park, in about 15 minutes. The St Mark's Square address was given as his London residence at the time of his death in 1921.

Kellas appears, for someone who can sometimes seem almost like an inert gas, not reacting with those around him, to have been reasonably well integrated into College life. He wrote a paper for the Hospital Journal in 1908 entitled 'A glance at the development of Medicine as a Science', and was a member of the Council of the Medical School for 'several years.' He also gave the *Introductory Address* at the Prize-giving of the Medical School on 1 October 1908, where Rudyard Kipling distributed the actual prizes. Most surprisingly it is stated that 'He was a zealous member of the Middlesex Hospital Masonic Lodge.' The word 'zealous' does not strike one as applying aptly to Alec, but it was presumably used advisedly to convey that he was an enthusiastic, not just a fellow-travelling, mason. Was there something about freemasonry that allowed his shy character to break out of his social reserve and into organised rituals which gave him emotional outlets denied in certain other areas of his life?

The fact that Alec was hardly burning the midnight oil as a London batchelor is shown by the fact that he appears to have spent much time at the London home of his half-brother James FN Kellas, who at this period was a stockbroker's accountant in London. James' daughter Mary noted that, 'A place at our dining room, supper at our London home was always ready for him.' Alec passed Sunday evenings there, as well as ceremonial occasions such as Christmas, and visited his relatives after his Himalayan trips, bringing them small gifts from India and Tibet.

But before he went out to the Himalayas, Alec was to widen his mountaineering experience in the Alps. It was whilst he was still working at the UCL that he had his first Alpine experiences. Kellas' leap across the channel was similar to Collie's Alpine initiation in that the transition from

British hills to continental mountains took place for both men in their early 30s – but the similarity ends there. It had taken Alec more than 15 years from his first mountain walks to get to the Alps; Collie arrived there within little more than a couple of years of adopting the sport of mountaineering. And whilst Collie in a few seasons – with his allies – practically revolutionised Alpine climbing, Kellas was content to proceed with caution in acquiring new skills when he first went mountaineering abroad.

Kellas' Alpine Club application indicates that before 1899 he had 'Ascended a few minor summits in Switzerland, eg Pilatus, Brevent, Unter-Rothorn.' No precise dates are given but as these appear mentioned at the end of a list of ascents dated from 1883–99, we can assume they were in the later 1890s. These are indeed minor peaks, though the Unter-Rothorn, at 3,100m would have been Alec's first 'three thousander' and doubtless given him some quiet pride. In 1899, Kellas' mountaineering took a leap forward when he ascended his first Alpine 4,000-er, the Breithorn. The ascent of the Breithorn (4,159m, 13,685ft) is regarded (at *Peu Difficile*) as one of the easier climbs of a 4,000m peak, perhaps even the easiest, though in Kellas' era there would have been no cablecar and he would have faced a much longer walk from the Zermatt valley base to engage in the climb.

Today in summer hundreds of people a day climb this peak, or at least the last 1,500ft of it. Kellas was evidently starting carefully, and he was doubly-careful in not trusting to his own devices, indicating on his AC application form that he took a guide. This guide was identified as Friedrich Imboden one of the clan of guides of that name from the town of St Niklaus which lay down-valley in the Matterthal from Zermatt. There were various dynastic clans of guides based at St Niklaus, and their daily bread and butter by this time was guiding on the Breithorn's neighbouring peak, the Matterhorn[14]. It is worth noting that another of the Imboden clan, Joseph, had been with W Graham in 1883 to Sikkim on a trip which resulted in an attempt to circumnavigate Kangchenjunga. It is possible the fluent German-speaking Kellas discussed this Himalayan expedition with his guide Friedrich. Graham's trips to Sikkim were already famous – or possibly infamous – ones, since he made claims to ascents, including that of Kabru (24,258ft), which many doubted. Was it possibly on this trip to the Alps that Kellas began to develop ideas of the Himalaya? Interestingly, Kellas would actually attempt to climb Kabru itself in 1920.

ZERMATT & MATTERHORN.
Zermatt around 1900, tiny in comparison with today's mega-resort. Many came to climb the Matterhorn, as did AE Robertson, but Kellas' ambitions for the Breithorn were more modest. It lies to the left (east) of Zermatt, and out of the picture.
(AE Robertson, SMC Collections)

The next year, in 1900, Alec was back in the Alps, this time in the eastern Bernese Oberland. He lists several 3,000m peaks he climbed including the Galminhorn at 3,486m, but the biggest scalp to come his way that year was the Finsteraarhorn, the highest summit – at 4,273m – in the whole of the Oberland. Highest, but not hardest when one considers it is situated in the near company of the fearsome duo of the Monsch and the Eiger. Nevertheless at PD it is a tougher peak than the Breithorn, and the standard guide to the Alpine 4,000m peaks describes it as follows, 'To Hugisattel a glacier climb with snow to 35 degrees. On the North west ridge of the summit block there is exposed climbing to II... objectively a very safe climb.'[15] The mountain was first climbed in August 1829 by the geologist Professor Hugi with two guides. Hugi stopped short of the summit, the guides – J Leuthold and J Wahren, climbed to the top. We would very much doubt that Alec failed to accompany his guide to the summit.

One wonders if Kellas was aware that the Finsteraarhorn had played a similar catalytic role in the formation of the Alpine Club, which he was later to join, as the Shelter Stone had done in the formation of the Cairngorm Club (which he never joined). The first British climbers ascended the peak in August 1857, and subsequently, inspired by their experience, formed the Alpine Club in December of that year. Four of the original 12 members of the club (Mathews, Kennedy, Hardy and Ellis) had been on the August Finsteraarhorn ascent. The peak appears to have attained popularity and other eminent British climbers like Tydall, Moore and the Pilkington brothers all subsequently ascended it. And from this initial ascent the development of the Alpine Club and the activities of its members led to the virtual British conquest of the Alps in the following decades, a process exhaustively described and analysed in Trevor Braham's work, *When the Alps Cast Their Spell*, (2004). By the time of Kellas' initial Alpine visits in the later 1890s, the tradition of British climbers spending successive seasons in the, especially, Western Alps, was well established. But there is an interesting footnote to Kellas' own Finsteraarhorn ascent.

The usually reticent Kellas makes his only extended entry in the *Remarks* section of the AC application form, regarding this particular outing. He observes;

The ascent of the Finsteraarhorn was made from Reckingen, the Oberaarhut being reached on the first day, and the ascent made early on the following morning by the Hugi Sattel. This was the first ascent and return made from Reckingen, I was told by the guides (Muller and Alex Blatter).[16]

Reckingen lies to the south-east of the peak, in a valley running north-east from Brig. At that time the mountain was apparently approached from the east by summit devotees. Though it was a fairly minor 'first' in the Alpine scale of things, it was a first ascent of sorts, and Alec was determined to have it recognised and recorded.

The next summer, that of 1901, Kellas decided to forgo the Alps, and went instead on a long cycling tour to Norway, (though this trip actually predated that country's full independence from Sweden in 1905). He started from Hamburg (presumably getting there by boat) and then visited Copenhagen, Gothenburg, Christiana (as Oslo was still called before Norwegian independence) and then headed north to Romesdal and the Fjord country. On this trip he ascended Galdhoppigen from Rodesheim, recording that he hired a guide, K Vole Jr.. Galdhoppigen is a peak of over 8,000ft in the Jotunheimen mountains of Norway and the scenery would have reminded Kellas very much of his native Cairngorms, though on a larger scale. Like its neighbour, the almost identically high Glitter-tind, Galdhoppigen is an easy ascent, although there are summit glaciers on both peaks. There is also now a café at the Galdoppigen summit, which is open in summer.

Kellas returned to the Alps in 1902 and had an unsuccessful season, recording his failure on Monte Rosa due to stormy weather. At PD+, it would have been the hardest climb he had so far achieved had he managed an ascent. Then in 1905 he ascended his loftiest summit to date when he climbed Mont Blanc with his brother Henry who had come out on holiday from Aberdeen to join Alec. Their father had died in January of 1905, and this trip to what was then regarded as Europe's highest mountain can possibly be seen as a sibling bonding after their father's death. The brothers hired a guide, Gaspard Simon, and went by the easiest route, graded as F, via an overnight at the Grand Mulets where a hut had been established as early as the 1850s. Easiest it may be, but as a long glacier plod, the Grand Mulets route is not the shortest or the least fatiguing route on the mountain. Once more it would appear that stamina

THE JOTUNHEIM MOUNTAINS.
Kellas would have considered the Jotunheim as larger versions of his own
Cairngorm Mountains – but with Glaciers. He climbed Galdhoppigen, whose summit
is attained by a long slog over its summit ice-cap (see colour image section).
(IR Mitchell)

as opposed to technical skill was Alexander Kellas' mountaineering forte at this time. It also seems likely that Alec, on this trip especially, must already have been assessing his own bodily reaction to the problems associated with the diminution of the oxygen intake at altitude, though on a mountain barely half the height of Mount Everest.

Kellas was a late developer as an Alpine (and even more so as a Himalayan) mountaineer. But then so too to a very similar extent was Norman Collie. And in the end Kellas, though he never came near to matching Collie's Alpine achievements, was to have markedly more success in the Greater Ranges than Collie himself. After Mont Blanc his next major expedition was to take Kellas from the snows of Switzerland to those of Sikkim in 1907, with much heightened ambitions, including that of 'intending to attack Kangchenjunga from the west...'[17] as he himself put it four years later in his application for membership to the Alpine Club. And by the time Kellas applied for AC membership in 1911, his application was based less on his actually fairly limited Alpine outings than on his much more impressive experience gained in a quite short period in the Himalaya.

NOTES

1   *A Life of Sir William Ramsay*, Morris W Travers (1956) gives a full account of the great scientist's life. Travers states the he himself started work at UCL in October 1894, after the argon discovery, and that Kellas had arrived 'some months' beforehand, (p.147), though it seems clear Alec actually started work at UCL in 1892. *The World of UCL 1829–1990*, Negley Harte and John North, (1991) is an interesting and lavishly illustrated account of the history of the institution where Kellas initially worked in London.

2   *The Discovery of the Rare Gases*, Morris W Travers (1928) p.63. Though Travers might minimise Kellas' role in the inert gases research, the ever-generous Ramsay rated the latter's contribution highly enough to mention it, and Kellas specifically, in his Nobel acceptance speech of 1904. 'Kellas, working in my laboratory, and Schloesing, in Paris, had independently determined the amount of argon in the air: they found almost identical numbers.' We are indebted to Dr Andrea Sella, of the Department of Chemistry, at UCL, for directing us to this quotation.

3   *A Life of Sir William Ramsey*, p.148. Travers is however, expansive in his praise of Kellas' later mountaineering in the same book, stating he 'became very well known as an explorer and mountaineer, spending his long vacations in the Himalayas. He died while a member of the Mount Everest expedition of 1921.' (p.147)... immediately before outlining in contrast his own successful *scientific* collaboration with Ramsay. Travers' own unpublished autobiography shows that he himself in later life had no regard for and hardly any interest in, his early mountaineering experiences, which are dismissed in a few lines.

4   *A Life of Sir William Ramsay*, p.150.

5   *A Life of Sir William Ramsay*, p.146, pp.147–8, p.148.

6   Christine Mill, *Norman Collie, a life in two worlds*, p.101. The most recent resurrection of this claim regarding Collie and the discovery of neon is in the otherwise quite magnificent work, *Ben Nevis; Britain's Highest Mountain*, Ken Crocket and Simon Richardson (2009), p.41. But the claim is without foundation.

7   *The Middlesex Hospital Journal* Vol. XXI, No. 7 (No.135), p.68.

8   *Norman Collie...* p.101.

9   *A Life of Sir William Ramsay*, p.146.

10   *The Discovery of the Rare Gases*, p.68.

[11] *Norman Collie...*p.45 Collie clearly liked and admired Kellas. Indeed, there is hardly anyone who ever said a word against the man. He may have lacked charisma, but no-one appears to have disliked Alec.

[12] *The Middlesex Hospital Journal* Op.cit p.66.

[13] Loc.cit., pp.68–9.

[14] Something on the St Niklaus guides can be had in *When the Alps Cast Their Spell*, Trevor Braham, (2004), pp.234–5, and under the individual guides' indexed names.

[15] *The Alpine 4000m. Peaks*, Richard Goedeke, (2006 edn.) p.59.

[16] *Alpine Club; Application for Membership*, Alexander Kellas (1911), p.1. Under the years 1883–1899 Kellas notes that he 'Made numerous ascents in Britain, climbing the chief summits of the Grampians, Lake District and Wales:' (p.1). It has not proved possible to gain any accounts of his Welsh and Lakes experiences, which were probably undertaken during his time in London. His SMC application notes no ascents in either location before 1897, so we could be looking at the years 1898–99. However, as we have seen, Kellas was quite sloppy with dates, in his SMC application and elsewhere.

[17] Loc.cit., p.2.

CHAPTER FOUR

The Himalaya 1907–1911

Kangchenjunga on his mind

WHEN ALEC KELLAS headed for India in 1907 it was his first trip to the Himalaya. He was then 39 years old. This was a much greater age at the time of such an initiation than was the case with most people before or after him who were to succeed in becoming mountaineers or explorers in the Greater Ranges. He had also, compared with the generality of such individuals, achieved relatively little in terms of mountaineering previous to this first Himalayan venture, as regards climbing on rock or ascents on snow and ice, either in the British Isles or the Alps. Despite these facts, it is arguable that by the time of his death in 1921 Kellas was one of the most experienced of Himalayan mountaineers, with a climbing record and a reputation that few if any alive could equal. That much is evident, what is less clear is – what propelled this retiring and modest man in such a life-changing direction?

As we saw earlier, Kellas worked with Norman Collie in the chemical laboratories at UCL at the time of the latter's tragic journey with Mummery to Nanga Parbat in 1895, and it appears certain that the two chemists must have discussed this trip on numerous occasions. A decade later more resourced expeditions than that of Collie and Mummery to the Himalaya had been mounted. In particular the 1902 expedition to K2 and the 1905 expedition to Kangchenjunga, both of which included Aleister Crowley, had achieved widespread publicity – though not always for laudable reasons. It is not certain that Crowley and Kellas ever met, but Crowley knew Collie, and it is possible that Alec's mind was turned, like that of many others, to the Himalaya by Crowley's expeditions. The Kangchenjunga expedition in particular, where Crowley achieved a height of almost 21,500ft and insisted that the mountain was climbable, may possibly have inspired Alec, despite the deaths of four people on the descent and Crowley's unsavoury refusal to go to their aid.

But the increasing profile of Himalayan mountaineering in those years appears insufficient in itself to have sent Kellas off on his quest. The context of his own life must have had an influence on his decision. In 1907 he was approaching the age of 40, often a difficult time in the lives of men. His father had recently died which might also have focussed his mind somewhat. He had an interesting job lecturing at the Middlesex College Hospital which gave him a comfortable living, but he was clearly not going to shine brightly in the firmament of scientific research, or indeed to advance much further in career terms. He was unmarried, a bachelor living alone in lodgings consisting of one room, with professional associates but apparently no real friends. With few persons, if any, to whom he could unburden himself in conversation or in correspondence, Alec left no record of any discussions, or any letters explaining his decision to go to India. And unlike many isolated persons, he appears to have kept no diary, where he might have engaged in some kind of revealing self-dialogue. We do not know why Kellas took the decision to head for the Himalaya in 1907. But just before he did he made his will. The question of his own death had, it would appear, crossed his mind.

Much of the Himalayan range at this time was problematic of access or out of bounds politically. For example Nepal was (in theory) completely closed to outsiders, as was Bhutan – and entry to Tibet was granted infrequently and on very restricted terms. The easiest parts of the range for access – both politically and in geographical terms – were those within the borders, or within the orbit, of British India – namely the Karakoram, Kashmir and the Garhwal in the west, and Sikkim to the east. And within these areas much of the early exploration, mapping and mountaineering of the Himalaya had taken place.

Kellas' application to join the Alpine Club in 1911 contained in its

KELLAS' PASSPORT PHOTO.
Not quite our normal image of Alec, spruced up in fine clothes and with a waxed moustache. Maybe this was just a special effort for his passport photo, or maybe it reflected increasing self-confidence as an academic and a mountaineer.
(RGS Collections)

supporting evidence an outline of his initial visit to Sikkim in 1907, but the outline failed to note that this trip had been preceeded by a fortnight spent at the north-west rather than the north-east corner of British India, in the Pir Panjal mountains near Srinagar in Kashmir. The boat from Europe docked at Bombay on India's west coast, and possibly Kellas wanted to try himself out in these lesser ranges which were, in a sense, on the way to Sikkim, and which in altitude terms were closer to what he had already experienced in Europe, rather than to those to which he was headed.

In 1918 at the request of Percy Farrar, the President of the Alpine Club, Kellas wrote a letter outlining in more detail his travels in 1907, including those in Kashmir, but insisting that, 'I... sincerely trust that you will not waste a line of the *Alpine Journal* with it at any time.'[1], and adding, modest to a fault as ever, of the whole 1907 trip that, 'I do not consider it as one of my mountaineering expeditions at all, because the climbing done was negligible in quantity.' What is perhaps most striking about this letter is that it was written on 11 November 1918 – the day of the Armistice and the end of hostilities in the First World War. Yet Kellas makes no mention, even in passing, of the significance of the day. His compulsive attention to the details of a trip more than a decade previously appears to have blotted out the wider world for Kellas. A psychologist could have a fruitful field day speculating on what this tells us about Alec's state of mind at this time.

Kellas left Srinagar on 3 August 1907 to cross the Pir Panjal mountains, a range parallel to the main Himalaya, though lower, and lying to the south of Srinagar. He took three men and two ponies with him. Five days later he crossed the main pass at 11,400ft, descending south to Rajaori and reaching Kharian on 15 August, from where he took a train to Darjeeling. The main problem Kellas' party encountered was river crossings, though possibly thinking back to his Cairngorm experiences of crossing rivers in spate he remarked that, 'there was nothing even during the height of the monsoon to stop a well-grown schoolboy, except a few fords between Poshiana and Baramgella.' He does make a note however, under the heading for 11 August that at Rajaori, '3 villagers drowned on preceeding day below ford.' Despite coping well with the physical effort, Kellas was disappointed in this part of his trip as he had had ambitions, spoiled by the poor weather, of camping on the summit of the Pir Panjal Pass, and of climbing a peak of 15,000ft nearby and taking photographs of the Nun

Kun range to the north-east and possibly of Nanga Parbat to the north. He put these disappointments behind him and headed eastwards to Darjeeling where he arrived on 22 August, reaching Gangtok in Sikkim four days later.

When he travelled to Sikkim, Kellas was following in the footsteps of many others, as this was one of the most accessible and travelled parts of the entire Himalayan range. Sikkim was certainly a good place for a Himalayan novice to start. It is a small state, which lies to the west of Bhutan and to the east of Nepal, and where the third highest mountain in the world, Kangchenjunga – with its outlying ridges – forms much of the Nepal-Sikkim common border. To the north of Sikkim lies Tibet. With an area of only 2,750 square miles (Sikkim is – roughly – a 50 mile wide square) it is tiny, less than one tenth of the area of Kellas's own small native Scotland. Theoretically independent, it came early on under the control of the British from Darjeeling, which itself was annexed from Sikkim in 1853. The country was officially made a Protectorate of the Empire in 1890. This state of semi-suzerainty from Dehli continued after Indian independence in 1947, until 1975 when the country formally became a state of India – though retaining some residual local autonomy.

Sikkim's historical importance came from its location on one of the main trade routes from India to Tibet and China, through the Jelep La and the Tang La passes. Its location on the trade route meant that gradually its indigenous people – the Lepchas – became intermingled with incoming Bhotias and finally Nepalese, which latter today constitute the biggest ethnic grouping. Buddism is strong in Sikkim but the main religion is Hinduism. The strategic importance of Sikkim had the effect that after Indian independence this hitherto most open area of the Himalaya became for a while one of the most closed, due to India's multiple border disputes with China. This resulted, for example, in the successful British Kangchenjunga expedition of 1955 having to approach the mountain through Nepal.

The first foray of any significance into Sikkim by a westerner was in 1774. George Bogle was a Scot in the employ of the East India Company, which organisation sent him on a mission to Tibet in order to explore the possibilities for trade. He traversed Sikkim and crossed the Tang La into Tibet, leaving a fascinating account of his sojourn which was, however, of limited economic consequence. A more lasting impact was made by the explorations of Sikkim by the Glasgow-born botanist Joseph Dalton Hooker in the 1840s. His main aim was to investigate its rhododendron population and from his journey dates the craze for the plant in Britain, and its subsequent spread from gardens to the wild, where it has a nefarious weed-like influence, suffocating the indigenous flora. The publication of Hooker's *Himalayan Journals* in 1854 brought 'Kinchinjunga' to the attention of the wider world, through illustrations of its profile, though Andrew Waugh of the Indian Survey had already estimated its height at 28,176ft in 1847.

Mountaineering in Sikkim, as opposed to exploration, begins with the visit of William W Graham in 1883 an English barrister with an impressive Alpine record. With the Swiss guide Joseph Imboden he explored around Dzongri (Jongri) in February and attempted to circumnavigate Kangchenjunga, but failed. He then headed for the Garhwal, and made the claim to have climbed Changabang. A charitable analysis might be that he was mistaken, and that he climbed a lesser neighbouring peak in error. Others were to construct a less charitable explanation when he published the claim, which was rather short on vital detail. Graham returned to Sikkim in September 1883, this time with guide Ulrich Kaufmann, and further claimed an ascent of Kabru (24,258ft) one of the giant Kangchenjunga's neighbouring peaks. Lack of detail, the stated speed of the climb (a mere three days) and the statement that he felt no ill effects of altitude, all tended to undermine Graham's credibility, and the ascent was never officially recorded to him. Victorian gentlemen did not stoop to accusing each other of falsehoods, but the overwhelming rejection of Graham's application to join the Alpine Club speaks volumes. Though Graham failed to circumnavigate Kangchenjunga in 1883, in the following year a Pundit, a trained native surveyor in the employ of the Great Trigonometrical Survey of India, one Rimzing Namgyal, did accomplish exactly that feat in an astonishing display of courage and hardship.

Alec Kellas was a mere stripling when the controversy over Kabru was raging, but he was a mature mountaineer when in 1903 there appeared Douglas Freshfield's *Round Kangchenjunga: A Narrative of Mountain Travel and Exploration*. Freshfield was in many ways an old fashioned Victorian explorer rather than a mountaineer in the then-emerging mould. His book is an account of the circumnavigation of Kangchenjunga which he made from Sikkim in 1899, and his narrative descriptions, the accompanying cartographic work – and additionally the photographic images of Vittorio Sella who accompanied Freshfield on the exploration – all greatly increased the knowledge of this region. Freshfield's credit for this achievement might be seen as being diminished somewhat when it is noted that he was accompanied on the trip – one could actually say guided – by Rimzing Namgyal who had already made the journey in 1884.[2]

Kellas may not have known of Namgyal's original circumnavigation of the Kangchenjunga massif, but certainly he knew the book by Freshfield, and was very impressed with it, apparently to the extent that it turned him from thoughts of Polar exploration, to those of the Himalaya. And by 1911 Kellas also knew Freshfield himself well enough for the latter to be Alec's main proposer for membership of the Alpine Club, largely on the basis of Kellas' Himalayan explorations since 1907. To Kellas' Alpine Club application Freshfield added a personal handwritten note of approval,

KANGCHENJUNGA.
In his trips to Sikkim before the First World War, Kellas was mainly interested in exploring the region around Kangchenjuga, his work being highly regarded by members of the German attempts on the mountain after the war.
(AM Kellas, RGS Collections)

I may add that Kellas has taken a series of [illegible] panoramic views in the Himalaya at altitudes of 15–21,000ft which are of great topographical value & include probably a new view of Mt. Everest.[3]

Freshfield remained a great admirer of Kellas and was to propose him as the leader of the first Everest Reconnaissance in 1921.

Freshfield's 1899 Kangchenchunga exploration had been encouraged by George Curzon, the then Viceroy of India, and indicates the context in which much of the exploration and mountaineering of later Victorian times took place. In fact, from the outset the mapping activities of the Indian Trigonometrical Survey had been largely motivated by the desire to establish the frontiers of first the East India Company's possessions, and subsequently those of British India. Curzon was a firm believer in the civilising mission of the British Empire and sought to extend its territory and influence in what was then called a 'forward' policy. Exploration and mountaineering were seen by Curzon and others as adjuncts of these imperialist drives, and in 1905 just before his retirement the Viceroy offered Freshfield the not inconsiderable sum of £3,000 to stage an attempt on Everest itself.

This was despite the disastrous results of the foray into Tibet in the years of 1903–4, by another of Curzon's protégés, Francis Young-husband. Though no mountaineer himself, Younghusband also became a propagandist for an attempt of Everest. He was more in the mould of the maverick, swashbuckling explorer and imperialist adventurer, and had many feats to his credit, including the crossing of the 18,000ft Mustagh Pass just west of K2. A Russophobe, Younghusband in 1885 came across Charles Macgregor's book *The Defense of India*, written two years previously and he became convinced of the validity of its argument for the need to extend British control into central Asia to ward off the (to many observers more imagined than real) menace from the Russian Bear.[4]

The crowning moment for this advocate of the Great Game in Central Asia came when Curzon became concerned that the Russians were arming the Tibetans, and he sent Younghusband on a military incursion to Lhasa to pre-empt Russian influence there, and seize the weapons of mass destruction which turned out to be a product of fantasy and mis-information. Youghusband's troops vandalised and looted their way to Lhasa, inflicting heavy casualties on the pathetically armed Tibetan 'army' at Guru where in return for five British casualties, as many as 5,000 Tibetans were slain, and on occasion the invading forces massacred numbers of civilians as well, including 700 at Chumi Shengo in April 1904. Though Younghusband was mildly reprimanded for his brutalities and the treaty which he imposed on Tibet, making it effectively a British Protectorate, was repudiated in London, his mission nevertheless put Lhasa under informal British control for decades, and ultimately made possible the Everest expeditions of the 1920s. On Younghusband's punitive expedition was one Captain Cecil Rawling, later to work with Alec Kellas immediately prior to the First World War on detailed plans for an ascent of Everest. Rawling did some limited exploratory work in 1904 and concluded that if Everest were to be climbed it would be from the north-east ridge in Tibet. Rawling was later killed in action during the First World War.

The election of a Liberal government in Britain in 1906 temporarily stayed any further plans for an Everest ascent attempt. Rocked by disasters such as the Boer War the mood in Britain turned anti-imperialist and foreign adventures that might cause international tension were discouraged. John Morley, the new man at the head of the India Office vetoed plans by Charles Bruce, who could be seen as a sort of poor man's, muscular Younghusband, for an Everest expedition in 1906 on 'considerations of high Imperial policy.' Attention turned to more unproblematic objectives and in the following year of 1907 the peak of Trisul in the Garhwal was climbed by a party led by Bruce. The group also included Arnold Mumm, who was in 1911 to second Kellas' application for membership of the Alpine Club. However the actual summit was achieved on 12 June by a party led by Tom Longstaff, supported by the Brocherel brothers (two Swiss guides) and Karbir, one of Bruce's Gurkhas. What was remarkable about this attempt was that not only was Trisul the highest mountain yet climbed, at 23,359ft, but that the summit party had ascended (and descended) 6,000ft from the highest camp to the summit in a single day. Though this might be seen as a triumph for 'rush tactics' Longstaff himself saw it more as a one off and conceded that slow acclimatization offered better chances of success in the Himalaya, a policy which Kellas was later to champion.

Kellas arrived in Sikkim aware of Longstaff's astounding achievement, but with more limited aims himself. As he wrote to Farrar,

As regards the tour from Darjeeling to the Zemu Glacier it was certainly of a very mild order. I had expected to ascend Simvu (22,300ft) and perhaps to attain 23,000ft on Kangchenjunga.[5]

The objective reader might, however, find these not inconsiderable ambitions for a Himalayan novice, and not be too surprised at any subsequent failure to achieve them.

Kellas' route to the Zemu Glacier is now a very popular trek in Sikkim, though he took five days to reach Lachen on 31 August, whereas now that is a day's bus ride from Gangtok. Another five days brought the party of Kellas, two unnamed Swiss guides and 55 coolies to the scenic Green Lake, eight miles east of Kangchenjunga. This lake lies across from Siniolchu which Freshfield had declared was 'the most beautiful peak in the world and a superb triumph of mountain architecture.' Kellas' objective was the slightly lower peak of Simvu (Simvo) to the west of Siniolchu which he attempted with the guides on 8 and then again on 10 September. A snowstorm drove them back at 19,000ft on the first attempt and on the second at 20,700ft the dangerous condition of the snow forced another retreat. Bringing his own Alpine experience to bear to provide context, Kellas remarked to Farrar in the letter already quoted that, 'Our attempts on Simvu were less difficult than an attack on Mt. Blanc from the Grands Mulets after a little fresh snow.'

On 12 and then again on 27 September they tried to reach the Nepal Gap on the shoulder of Kangchenjunga but were once more unsuccessful, reaching a height of 19,000ft on the second bid. They also did

CAMP AT GREEN LAKE.
A place which was to become a regular base for Kellas in his trips to Sikkim, and is now a favourite with trekking parties. The image shows the peaks of Siniolchu and Simvu (which Kellas attempted but failed) and the Kangchenjuga massif itself.
(AM Kellas, RGS Collections)

some exploring crossing the Tangchung La and The La passes to the north of Green Lake. Finally on 27 September they made a third attempt at Simvu, reaching 20,000ft before soft snow and bad weather made then abandon the attempt. Subsequently the party headed back for Gangtok, Kellas having decided that his guides had proved unsatisfactory and had not performed well under 'diminished pressure.' That he possibly found them, in addition, over cautious is indicated on his comments on his Alpine Club application form concerning the second ('Guides consider snow dangerous') and third ('Guides think snow dangerous') attempts to climb Simvu. But just as Kellas was walking out, another party was walking in to an area slightly to the south, and what a pity it was that Alec could not have been on that particular expedition.

In mid-September two Norwegians, CW Rubenson and one Monrad-Aas left Darjeeling, and at the end of the month arrived at Dzongri in the Rathong Valley to the south east of Kangchenjunga. Today this is one of the most popular trekking routes in Sikkim, along with the Green Lake/Zemu Glacier trek. The Norwegians had been hereabouts in a reconnoitre the year before in 1906 and had come back now with the intention of climbing Kabru. Rubenson gave an account of the Kabru attempt in a talk to the Alpine Club in London in June 1908. Kabru was an ambitious objective as Rubenson claimed in the talk to have done little more than some scrambling in his native Norway whilst Monrad-Aas 'had never, previous to the Kabru expedition, climbed a mountain of any description.'[6] They hired 100 coolies, and sent 50 back at Yuksam (Yoksum), taking the rest to base camp at the foot of the East Rathong Glacier and 14 with them on the summit bid on 20 October. They failed possibly 100ft from the summit of the mountain, a fine achievement despite the disappointment, since Kabru is not only higher than Trisul, but is a much more difficult mountain, as is clear from reading Rubenson's account. The pair also stayed for 12 or 13 days above 19,500ft, of which Rubenson correctly states, 'this is, so far as I know, something quite unique' and it made him a believer in slow acclimatization, in 'working one's way carefully up from one camp to another.'[7]

Possibly of even more significance to Kellas would have been – in the light of his own disappointment in Sikkim with European guides – the Norwegians' strong advocacy of the use of coolies in the Himalaya, specifically of the Sherpas, for actual climbing and not just for carrying purposes. The Norwegians had no Empire with its racial overtones, and no tradition of that militarism which meant that many British explorer-mountaineers saw the Gurkas with their army discipline as being ideal for Himalayan work. Possibly with these very points in mind, Rubenson announced to his audience at the Alpine Club, that;

> Another thing in which our experiences differed from those of most other mountaineers who have been in this part of the world was in regard to the usefulness of the natives on such expeditions. We found them very keen and interested people. It is only to their courage and many other good qualities that we owe our success so far. Of course it is no good fitting oneself out like a Polar bear if one does not look after the men in the same way. One must always remember that they have no personal interest in the success of the expedition.
>
> The natives whom we found most plucky were Nepalese Tibetans, the so-called Sherpahs [*sic*]. If they are properly taught the use of ice axe and rope I believe they will prove of more use out there than European guides, as they are guides and coolies in one, and don't require any special attention. My opinion is that if they get attached to you they will do anything for you.[8]

Whether he actually heard, or merely read, Rubenson's account of the attempt on Kabru in 1907, Alexander Kellas was to absorb the Norwegian's recommendations into his own subsequent Himalayan mountaineering. In the light of the Kabru attempt, the talk given by Rubenson at the Alpine Club, and subsequent publication of the latter's article in the *Alpine Journal* arguing for of the value of Sherpas as climbers as well as porters, it is difficult to support without qualification the oft-repeated statement that it was Alexander Kellas who 'discovered' the Sherpas, though he would subsequently use them more often than the once-off Norwegians, and publicise on many occasions their utility.

An example of this tendency to overlook the Norwegians' previous experience with the Sherpas is given in, for example, a letter written from Tibet shortly after Kellas' death and dated 19 June 1921, by a man who figured prominently in the early exploration and climbing history of Everest, JBL Noel. He summarized his opinion of Kellas' 'outstanding points' to Arthur R Hinks, secretary of the RGS;

1 An experienced amateur mountaineer going at Himalayan peaks alone, with supporting party of specially selected and trained native porters;

2   First to discover the best natives for mountaineering, namely Sherpa Bhotias, and first to train teams of Sherpas for high climbing above 23,000ft [7,000m];

3   His tactful and successful handling of natives in regard to successful joint mountaineering projects in the Himalaya;[9]

Kellas did not visit the Himalaya in 1908, but instead returned to the Alps in September where he 'Took tent up to the summit of Corvatsch to carry out scientific experiments in snowstorm.'[10] These experiments were designed to measure the variations in the red corpuscle count of the blood at altitude, and are among the earliest scientific attempts made by Kellas to study the effects of altitude on the human body, and possibly an indication that his mountaineering ambitions were rising. He returned to Sikkim in 1909 in what was to be a more focussed and ultimately more successful Himalayan expedition, which he preferred to designate as his first such, 1907 being relegated to the status of a mere 'tour.'

In 1909 Kellas dispensed with European guides and left Darjeeling on 7 August with 62 coolies and Mr Righi, the manager of a local hotel, a person who had been with Crowley on the 1905 Kangchenjunga expedition. Righi had not impressed Crowley, and neither did he impress Kellas with his lack of adaptability to altitude, though he spoke of Rhigi as 'a pleasant companion and a good walker'. (On 2 September Righi returned to Darjeeling.) The party went by Yumthang and crossed the Donkia La to camp at 19,000ft below Pauhunri (Pawhunri) in north-eastern Sikkim, which they hoped to climb. At 21,700ft on 21 August Kellas and two coolies were driven back in their attempt on Pauhunri by a snowstorm.

TANGU DAK BUNGALOW AND NATIVES.
The bungalow at Thanggu (Thangu/Tangu/Tango) was the usual, comfortable stopping off point before expeditions went further into the mountains to the north-east or north-west of Sikkim, and Alec was a regular visitor here.
(AM Kellas, RGS Collections)

Thereafter the group headed northwards to the Tso Lhamo lake and westwards to Thanggu (Thango). On 27 August with 10 yaks and 12 coolies, the reduced party crossed the Lungnak La (17,300ft), and by 30 August were camped at the Lhonak Glacier. On 4 September Kellas records 'Camp on summit of Jonsong La 20,300ft'[11] The Jonsong (Jonsang) Peak stands at the point where Sikkim shares a border with Nepal and Tibet, and the pass itself had been crossed by Freshfield on his 1899 circumnavigation of Kangchenjunga. Before retracing his steps to the Langbu Glacier, Kellas outlines a further foray in his letter to Farrer of 10 April 1919,

7 September	Descend to Kangchenjunga Glacier
8 September	Camp near Pangperma [*sic*]
9 September	Cross Kangchenjunga Glacier to examine W. face of Kangchenjunga
11 September	Back to S. Langbu Glacier[12]

Kellas had in fact, without official permission or sanction, crossed into forbidden Nepal to gain additional knowledge of Kangchenjunga. (Pangpema is a spot on the Nepalese side of the pass.) Undoubtedly his motivation was to further explore the mountain's vast west face, which Freshfield in 1899 had thought provided the best chance of a possible ascent route.

It is worth mentioning here that in all of Kellas' expeditions before 1914 it is Kangchenjunga which is on his mind. Despite his later wartime planning for an Everest attempt and his untimely death on the approach to that mountain in 1921, *Chomo Langmo* as he himself preferred to call it, is seldom mentioned by him – in all probability because of the political situation which made it then currently unapproachable. His explorations in Sikkim had many objectives, but the reconnaissance of Kangchenjunga, with the prospect of an attempt on the mountain, was foremost amongst those. Hence the descent into Nepal in 1909.

This foray was to be followed by Alec's greatest mountaineering achievement to date, the ascent of Langpo (Langbu) Peak. From the camp on the Langbu Glacier he tried on both 13 and 14 of September to ascend the peak, before achieving the actual summit on 15 September. In the 1919 letter to Farrar Kellas comments;

The incident which pleased me best of all was the ascent of the Langbu Peak (22,800ft) which was my first completed Himalayan ascent, and as I managed to finish it after both the coolies with me refused to move at 21,900ft, it gives me a slight satisfaction even now.[13]

Kellas however states in his chronology of the trip (Letter to Farrar, p.413) that the last 900ft of the ascent were done with one unnamed porter. Possibly after initially refusing to proceed, one of the porters was cajoled into completing the climb.

LANGPO PEAK FROM THE SOUTH.
A fine image of Langpo Peak with a Sherpa and the glacier behind. Kellas managed this on his third attempt in as many days, and it was his first virgin summit and his first over 20,000ft. It was the highlight of his 1909 visit to Sikkim.
(AM Kellas, RGS Collections)

Fired with this success the party went back to the Lhonak Glacier by the Johnsong La and re-established camp. Kellas was now intending to climb Jonsong Peak itself, a very ambitious target and one not accomplished till 1930, when it briefly became the highest peak yet climbed. On 21 September he ascended to a col on the mountain at 21,500ft (approx) and on the next day made slow progress up the North Buttress to 22,000ft, when dense mist and stormy weather aborted the attempt. The group then headed eastwards, over the The La and Tangchung La where Kellas had already been in 1907, to camp by the Zemu Glacier at the Green Lake opposite Siniolchu. With unfinished business in mind, Kellas attempted to do what he failed to do in 1907; on 29 September he tried once more to gain the Nepal Gap, being however forced back by a snowstorm which lasted four days and left a deposit over two feet deep. Forced to retreat from the Zemu Glacier as the coolies who had been sent down for extra supplies could not get back to the main camp, Alec was not finished, but retraced his journey by Thanggu, Giagong (Gyaogang) and the Tso Lhamo lake again to return to Pauhunri by 8 of October. By this time he had traversed Northern Sikkim from and to end – and then re-traversed it! On 9 of October he battled up to 23,000ft on Pauhunri before deep snow, high wind and nightfall forced a disappointing retreat. His Alpine Club application makes it clear that there was at least one Sherpa with him on this attempt, when it states, 'the summit was some distance to the right through deep snow, and, as it was getting dark (4.30pm) and as a strong and very cold gale was blowing we [Authors' emphasis] were forced to retreat.'[14] At this point Kellas and his parter were about 1,700ft higher than on their previous attempt on the 8 August, and only about 200 vertical feet below the summit of Pauhunri. For someone in his first real Himalayan season, this was a hugely creditable feat.

The next day Kellas and his porters headed back over the Donkia La towards Darjeeling which they reached on 18 of October.

By any measure Kellas' Sikkim expedition of 1909 was a major achievement, despite his own modesty making light of it – 'many failures but also a few successes' is how he described it to Farrar. Leaving aside the unreliable Mr Righi, Kellas had spent well over two months exploring Northern Sikkim in the company only of his 'Nepalese coolies' and had come through unscathed. He had climbed a virgin peak of over 20,000ft and nearly succeeded in ascending two more with only Sherpas as climbing companions. It is probably true to say that it was almost entirely on the strength of the 1909 trip – since his other mountaineering credentials beforehand were extremely limited – that Kellas was admitted to the Alpine Club in January 1911. Later on in that year his third trip to the Himalaya was to be even more remarkable, and would elevate Alec Kellas to being considered an almost undisputed authority on questions of Himalayan mountaineering. To being considered as a man who could reasonably be seen as a peer of luminaries such as Longstaff, Freshfield and Mumm, and who would be in demand to give lectures to organisations like the Alpine Club and the Royal Geographical Society, and who would be asked to contribute learned papers to their journals. Alec had come a long way in a short time.

That mountaineering was beginning to dominate Alexander Kellas' life almost to the point of an obsession is shown by the fact that his Himalayan trip of 1911 (and by corollary his absence from work at Middlesex Hospital) lasted a little short of six months, from early April till the end of September, including the sea journeys. By contrast the expeditions of 1907 and 1909 had occupied around three and a half months each. Such considerable time absent from his professional duties in 1911 must have caused Kellas some problems. Comparable absences in later years certainly did.[15] However, the time invested was to be justified, as 1911 was probably Kellas' most successful season, his *annus mirabilis*. The account he read of this expedition to the Royal Geographical Society on 1 April 1912 was the longest mountaineering piece Kellas had written since his extended essay on the trip he made with his brother Henry to the Cairngorms in 1885. It is difficult not to believe that some of the comfort and approval he would have felt back in the 1880s reading to an attentive and appreciative family circle, was experienced again by this shy and lonely man amongst the leading mountaineers and explorers of Edwardian Britain, in the rooms of the Royal Geographical Society on that evening in April in 1912.

NOTES

1   'The Late Dr Kellas' Early Expeditions to the Himalaya'. Letter to Colonel Farrar 11.11.1918 in *Alpine Journal*, 34, No. 225, pp.408–12. Farrar

apparently believed that Kellas' death freed him from the request contained in the letter, not to publish it. Pp.412–14 of the same edition of the *AJ* contains a subsequent letter of Kellas to Farrar of 10 April 1919, outlining the expedition to Sikkim in 1909.

2 For a full account of the work of the Pundits, see the momumental *Mapping the Himalayas: Michael Ward and the Pundit legacy* by Richard Sale (2009), and *Spying for Empire: The Great Game in Central and South Asia, 1757–1947*, by R Johnson (2006).

3 *Alpine Club Application*, Alexander Mitchell Kellas, 1911, p.4.

4 The social and historical contextualisation of Himalayan mountaineering has recently been taken to a higher level in *Fallen Giants: A History of Himalayan Mountaineering from the Age of Empire to the Age of Extremes*, Maurice Isserman and Stewart Weaver (2008). For the specific episode of the Tibet invasion, see Charles Allen *Duel in the Snows* (2004) and 'Officers, Gentlemen and Thieves: the Looting of Tibetan Monasteries during the 1903/4 Younghusband Mission to Tibet', Michael Carrington, *Modern Asian Studies* 1, (2003), pp.81–109.

5 *AJ* 34, p.410.

6 *Alpine Journal*, 24 (1908) 'Kabru in 1907', CW Rubenson, p.310. This, on pp.310–321 is a full account of the attempt on Kabru, read to the Alpine Club on 2 June 1908. It is possible that Kellas was in the audience to hear Rubenson's conclusions about acclimatization and the use of Sherpas. If not he would almost certainly have read the article and the shorter previous account by Rubenson, 'An Ascent of Kabru', published in the *AJ* 24 (1908) pp.63–67. Kellas was aware of the Norwegians' heroic attempt as he mentions it in a letter to Norman Collie from Sikkim in 1921, see *infra*.

7 Op.Cit p.320.

8 Op.Cit p.320–1.

9 Noel to AR Hinks, 19 June 1921 (RGS Archives). In addition to these points dealing with the Sherpas, Noel also mentioned another positive aspect of Kellas' mountaineering, '4. His wonderful energy, perseverance, and drive – the fundamental qualities that enable the mountaineer to conquer his surroundings'

10 *Alpine Club Application*, p.2.

11 Kellas to Farrar, April 10, 1919, in *AJ* 34, p.413.

12 Op.Cit p.413.

13 Op.Cit p.412.

14 *Alpine Club Application*, pp.3–4.
15 For example, in a letter of Kellas to Hinks, the Secretary of the Royal
Geographical Society, 29 September 1917, (RSGS Archives; Kellas File),
we read that he intended to ask the Council of the Medical School to
agree to grant him extra leave at the end of the war, and that 'If they do
not, their attitude to my Himalayan aspirations has been so unsympa-
thetic, that I would be forced to look for another post if I wished to do
more work in connection with high altitudes...'

ALEC KELLAS' CAMERA.
The camera which accompanied Kellas in the Himalaya. Apparently an air bellows
helped with achieving focus. We know that Noel dried his images with yak
dung fires; Kellas possibly did likewise.
(RGS Collections)

CHAPTER FIVE

The Himalaya 1911–1914

Going Native

ALEXANDER KELLAS' PAPER, *The Mountains of Northern Sikkim and Garhwal* was read to the Royal Geographical Society on 1 April 1912 and published in the September edition of the *Geographical Journal*.[1] In it Kellas outlined his experiences in 1911 which probably constituted the most successful Himalayan mountaineering expedition undertaken by anyone up to that date. He also, for the first time, and in some detail, argued for the advantages of using Nepalese Sherpas as both porters and climbers, something which had been advocated in a much briefer way by the Norwegian Rubenson is his talk to the Alpine Club in 1908.

In only the second paragraph of his paper, Kellas nails his colours to the mast, stating his preference for the Sherpas and noting that the fairly small core party that were to accompany him to Kangchenjunga, were composed entirely of that group;

> I have made three journeys to Sikkim in the years 1907, 1909 and 1911. In 1907 Swiss guides were taken but they proved unsatisfactory and in 1909 and 1911 only natives were employed. The natives were either Nepalese, Lepchas or Bhutias. The Sherpas, who come from Eastern Nepal were found to be the best, and they can safely be recommended to travellers...
>
> ...we left Lachen with 31 coolies, eight of whom were Sherpa Nepalese who were to remain with us permanently, the remaining 23 being Lachen men, who were to return after four days march to the north west.[2]

Unlike in many accounts of the time when the natives are anonymous, Kellas gives the more prominent of his porters the dignity of the use of their names, and they emerge as real personalities in his account. Two Sherpas called Sona and Tuny are praised in particular for their ice work, especially the latter 'who is by far the best all round coolie I have ever met with.' Sona on the other hand Kellas notes 'was rather a pessimist' despite his skill, and frequently discretion was to be the better part of his valour.

Kellas also learned from the porters, observing that at one point when they feared incipient frost bite, they removed their boots, rubbed their feet and as insulation 'put dried grass, of which they carried a small supply, into their boots.' He also noted something which Rubenson had remarked upon, which was the Sherpas' unwillingness to cross steep snow roped, their argument being that an unroped fall would lead to a single fatality, whilst a roped fall would multiply this. Kellas when on one occasion faced with a 60–70 degree slope acceded to the Sherpas' wishes to forgo the rope, stating 'the rope would have been cut to pieces on the sharp rocks, so I was quite agreeable.' It became not unknown for subsequent Himalayan expeditions to treat the Sherpas, and porters in general, with less regard towards their safety than was observed in regard to Europeans, with the justification that Asians 'put less value on life' than did Westerners. Such racist special pleading had no place in Alec Kellas' mindset – on the contrary he observed in this 1912 paper at the RGS that, 'Coolies have a very keen sense of the value of their lives, and dislike being taken into places even approximately dangerous.'

The Sherpas were also able to make use of the limited additions to diet afforded by the terrain, appreciating the flavour (and ascorbic qualities) of the wild mountain rhubarb. Alec was a bit dubious about this, but relented and gave the rhubarb plants a try;

> I tried them and found them somewhat insipid, and with none of the sourness of the cultivated plant. As, however, fresh vegetables had been very scarce I asked Sona to cook some and serve with tapioca at dinner. In this form it was more palatable, but I am inclined to think contributed somewhat to insomnia and a peculiar intermittent throbbing in the cerebellar region, which occurred every few minutes for some hours.[3]

Possibly Alec's disturbed dreams that night were of former school dinners at Aberdeen Grammar School. Surprisingly, given the abundance of hares and other small game which Kellas noted even in the higher valleys, no attempt appears to have been made to supplement the party's rations by hunting these.

SHERPAS, TWO PORTERS BEFORE SETTING OFF.
An undated image of some of the porters Kellas worked with. He took many images of them, alas, never captioned with their names. Kellas took great care of his porters' needs with regards to food and clothing.
(AM Kellas, RGS Collections)

SHERPA COOLIES.
A fine group of fellows, the one with the ice-axe presumably the leader. Note three of
them have sun goggles, doubtless supplied by Kellas.
(AM Kellas, RGS Collections)

Kellas paid close attention to the porters' food, noting that on the few occasions he had observed mountain sickness with the Sherpas, it had been associated with inadequate food – 'in nearly every case diet was to blame.' Kellas was eating much the same food as his porters and in some ways this was different from the normal practise of taking large amounts of European tinned food on Himalayan explorations. Again, one senses he was learning from the Sherpas who performed well physically with a largely vegetarian diet. No quail in aspic for Alec then, instead;

> After long and careful experiment, we found that the best mainstay of both the morning and the evening meal was a large bowl of soup, thickened with rice and with added butter… One could then add tongue, boneless sardines etc., as wanted; but it was found that the entire elimination of meat by substitution of four or five freshly baked chupatties (unleavened pancakes) with jam and butter was occasionally a good plan.[4]

In an era when one reads of porters often shivering in the open round an inadequate fire at night, those with Kellas were provided with tents and the same down quilts and 'quite as much clothing' as Alec himself. At the other extreme from this the porters on Aleister Crowley's Kang-chenjunga expedition were ill-fed, went bootless and were subject to physical and verbal abuse. There were tussles with even his favourite duo of Sona and Tuny at times on this trip, but overall Kellas was satisfied with his Sherpas, and they with him. At the end of the trip he records;

> Darjeeling was reached on 25 July, and here we bade farewell to the faithful coolies who had accompanied us for about thee months. In order to prevent misunderstanding, I must state that all of these men were in the best of health and spirits. They were thoroughly satisfied with food and pay and the amount of work expected of them, and when asked at Thango whether they would remain for another month if we decided to attempt the Jonsong peak and the Kangchenjhau, every one of them volunteered to stay without hesitation. These Sherpa Nepalese coolies are, in fact, agreeable to work with, and if treated kindly, will do anything reasonable.[5]

Kellas appears to have found social interaction with the Sherpas more easy than he possibly might have done with other groups. Even his mental problems were turned to a certain advantage in his relationships with the native porters. The eminent biologist JBS Haldane referred to Kellas's auditory hallucinations in a 1962 international symposium on problems of high altitude in Darjeeling;

> Some people hear voices at high altitudes. Dr Kellas also heard them at sea level. Indeed, he once told me that he wondered if a very sensitive microphone might not render them audible to others. This did not prevent him being a good physiologist at one atmosphere's pressure, and much more reliable than my late father when decompressed fairly quickly to 320mm pressure. He said that in the mountains, when no other Europeans were there, he answered these voices, and his Sherpas had great confidence in a man who had long conversations with spirits at night.
>
> International Symposium on Problems of High Altitude,
> Darjeeling, 5–8 January 1962, p.14.

The pleasant personalities of the Sherpa porters are commented on and at times Alec has an almost jocular relationship with them, for example on the occasion the group set out for the Simvu Saddle, when Kellas records;

> At the bottom of the glacier, about 1¼ hours from our previous camping place, the coolies wanted to halt for the night, promising to start at 4 a.m. next morning. Referring to their behaviour on the previous day at the Zemu Gap, I jokingly suggested that it was not 4 a.m. they meant, but 10 a.m., [*on the previous occasion the coolies had refused to start till the sun reached their tents at that hour, Authors' Note*] whereupon they laughed good naturedly, and we went on to the summit.[6]

But there were other reasons than the Sherpas' sociability which made Kellas such an advocate of their use in Himalayan mountaineering. These other reasons were their physical strength and their ability to perform well at altitude; the former Alec thought they did better than their various rivals as porters and climbers in the Himalayan regions, the latter he generously conceded they did better than white men, and better in particular than himself. He had already observed that the Sherpas were preferable to the alternatives available in Sikkim and when in 1911 he moved to the Garhwal, he was able to confirm his impressions by his experience with the porters he hired there for a Kamet reconnaissance.

The men selected were quite different in physique from the Sherpa Nepalese coolies, being tall and slim, and their stamina was found to be inferior. They would only carry about two-thirds of the loads taken by the Sherpas... (They) required more encouragement than the Nepalese coolies...[7]

There were also problems with their food, since the Garhwal men were Hindu and their religion required that they prepare it themselves. This almost drove Alec to distraction, since as they only had one griddle pan between them breakfast took three hours to prepare, each man using the pan in rotation to make his chupattis.

Kellas measured the performance of the Sherpa porters statistically, not just impressionistically. Such practical and objective scientific-minded observations certainly set Kellas apart even further from the 'normal' European mountain explorer of the day. On the ascent of Pauhunri (see below), he took Sona and Tuny's unnamed brother with him. Despite the fact that the latter were lightly loaded, Kellas found that above 22,500ft they outperformed him by 30 per cent, that is 300ft in 1,000. Of his overall experiences in 1911 he concluded;

At any height up to 15,000 to 17,000ft one could hold one's own with the unloaded coolie and easily beat the loaded man. Above 17,000ft however, their superiority was marked, an unloaded coolie climbing much quicker than myself, and even a moderately loaded coolie going up as fast as one cared to go, up to 21,000 to 22,000ft. Above that elevation a moderately loaded coolie could run away from me, and with an unloaded coolie one had not the slightest chance.[8]

Kellas speculated that this ability came from 'greater lung capacity' amongst people born and bred at high altitudes. It must be realized that medical science was years away from even beginning to appreciate the genetic advantages afforded by Darwinian natural selection to these high altitude natives. Kellas carried out experiments on himself on this trip and thought that, though not experiencing 'mountain sickness' his diminished energy and lassitude stemmed from the reduced formation of oxyhaemoglobin in his blood at altitude. To combat this problem Kellas recommended slow acclimatization and the practise of breathing more frequently at altitude than at lower levels. We know today that an individual's chemical responsiveness to hypoxia (the 'hypoxic ventilatory response') can greatly, and automatically, increase the frequency of breathing at high altitudes. This is today recognized as the primary, but not the only, adaption our bodies undergo to ensure efficient acclimatization to altitude. One interesting aside is Alec's optimistic comment (probably thinking of himself, at almost 44 years old) that with regard to high altitude mountaineering 'the effect of age is obviously a variable one, and must be greatly discounted in certain cases.'

The main aim of the 1911 Sikkim trip itself was to further explore the passes and glaciers around Kangchenjunga, but it was to achieve much more than this. Leaving Lachen on 24 April, Kellas and his entourage headed for the Zemu Glacier and Green Lake, with which Alec was now very familiar. On 5 May he ascended to within 50ft of the Nepal Gap at c.21,000ft, and spent the next weeks thoroughly exploring the region, crossing the Lhonak La (19,500ft), and reaching the Zemu Gap (19,300ft) and the Simvu Saddle (17,700ft), and camping at both places. These latter outings gave Kellas the opportunity to examine the north-east ridge of Kangchenjunga, which had been considered as a possible summit route. He was – rightly as it transpired – sceptical, observing;

> On the way the view of the crags of Kangchenjunga was very imposing and we noted that the north-east buttress seemed almost inaccessible, and would in fact, require difficult climbing to get properly onto it, as it degenerates into a narrow rock ridge which rises at the end into a small peak.[9]

In the event, after failed attempts in the 1920s and '30s, this route to the summit of Kangchenjunga was only climbed in 1977 by an Indian team.

On 20 May the party reached the Chorten Nima La (18,300ft) on the Tibetan border, and from there on the following day climbed the first virgin peak of the trip, an unnamed eminence, a 'fine peak', to which Kellas gave the name Sentinel Peak.

> About 7.30 a.m. on May 21, we started on the ascent. Our route lay chiefly up toilsome scree slopes for about 1,500ft, when we reached a crevassed snow slope. From the moment we hit the snow we had to cut steps, although it was only neve. Very soon we were stopped by a wide crevasse, but on traversing horizontally for about 200 yards, we found a narrow bridge, and after that there was little difficulty. First

we proceeded south to what looked like the summit, but near this another higher summit appeared on the left. On reaching this, however, we found it to be merely the heavily corniced edge of a precipice... and a third summit appeared as a sharp snow peak right in front. It was now about 1.30 p.m. and the coolies were discouraged. Tuny, who had cut steps all the way, confessed to being exhausted and Sona was pessimistic as usual, but after a rest they agreed to come up to the top. Unfortunately a small portion of the arête was green ice, and necessitated careful step-cutting, so that it was past three before we reached the summit (about 22,000ft), which had probably not been triangulated, but may be the peak named as 22,060ft and misplaced on the map.[10]

A rapid descent took them back to camp by 5.30pm.

Kellas' next target was the Jonsong Peak to the north of Kangchenjunga. At 24,400ft (later upgraded to 24,550) this would have been the highest peak climbed to that date, higher even than nearby Kabru, itself higher than Trisul which was still the highest mountain that had been summitted by 1911.[11] It is not to be discounted that Alec, shy and modest as he was, was purposefully aiming at Jonsong Peak as its ascent would have greatly raised his own profile amongst Himalayan mountaineers of his day. In order to reconnoitre a route, Kellas decided to re-ascend the neighbouring Langpo Peak which he had already climbed in 1909, but this proved to be in a difficult condition and the attempt, on 26 May, failed.

Kellas' account of this failure on Langpo Peak is very interesting, and one imagines his listeners at the RGS being impressed by the way he compares his two attempts on Langpo Peak in 1909 and 1911 with the experiences he had had in the European Alps.

In August, 1909, the ascent of the Langpo Peak was similar as regards difficulty to that of the Zermatt Breithorn from the Leichenbratter Hut, with the exception that the last 600ft was steeper than anything on the Breithorn. From the denuded appearance of the mountain as seen from the Jonsong La – there is more snow below and less snow above 19,000ft in May as compared with August – we were afraid that the final 1,000ft might be icy and difficult. This proved to be the case. The mountain at this season of the year was considerably more difficult that the Finsteraarhorn via the Hugi Sattel, and we failed to reach the top.[12]

SENTINEL PEAK (L) FROM CHORTEN NIMA LA.
Alec Kellas' second 22,000ft peak, which he named as well as made the first ascent of.
Despite Tuny's exhaustion and Sona's pessimism they both accompanied him to the
summit. The view is looking south from just inside Tibet, Sentinel itself on the left.
(AM Kellas, RGS Collections)

However, there is a deal of spin and gloss taking place here, since the two ascents in the Alps he refers to are not culled from an extensive experience, but – barring a snow plod up Mont Blanc – constitute virtually Alexander Kellas' entire Alpine CV! Shy unassuming and modest as Alec might have been, he is here presenting his mountaineering credentials in a way that, whilst not inaccurate, would tend to make the listener assume they were greater than they actually were.

Having failed on a peak he ascended in 1909, what better was there for Kellas to do to recover from the disappointment than by succeeding on a peak he had failed on in that same year? So with some of his followers sent off to acquire further supplies, and with 'four coolies and two yaks with me to carry wood' he headed eastwards across northern Sikim, reaching Gyaogang on 11 June and camped below Pauhunri two days later at 18,500ft. The ascent of what was at that time and for many years subsequently considered to be the second highest summit – at 23,180ft – ascended by man, proved remarkably straightforward. It was to be the highest point Kellas ever reached apart from on Meade's Col on Kamet in 1920, and his one 7,000m summit.

That Pauhunri was 'subsequently considered' to be the second highest peak ascended until Jonsong Peak in 1930 relegated both it and Trisul from their pedestals, is said advisedly here. Kellas thought Pauhunri to be 23,180ft, taking the then accepted measurement, whilst Longstaff gave Trisul's height as 23,406ft. However the currently accepted height for Trisul is 7,120m, or 23,359ft, while that of Pauhunri is 7,125m or 23,375ft. (see the *Index of Himalayan Peaks*, Alpine Club website). Unbeknown to him, and to Longstaff and to – it would appear – everyone writing about Himalayan mountaineering since then, Kellas was not only the most experienced Himalayan mountaineer at his death in 1921, but was also the holder of the summit height record as well. This fact he was ignorant of, and on Jonsong Peak, on Kamet, and on Kabru it was a prize he attempted to attain, unaware that he already had it, and he held it after his death till 1930. This in no way diminishes Longstaff's pioneering achievement on Trisul, but the common wisdom that he held the world summit altitude record from 1907 till 1930, cannot now be sustained. From 1911 till 1930, that record was Alexander Kellas', and justice is served by crediting it to him posthumously. Here is an extract from Kellas' account of the climb.

PAUHUNRI.
A fine portrait of Pauhunri, the highest summit ever gained by Kellas,
and his one 7,000m peak. Until this book, it was not known that it was the
highest peak to be climbed till 1930, higher than Trisul, which was
previously believed to be the highest summit climbed up till then.
(AM Kellas, RGS Collections)

On the following day an ascent to 20,700ft was made, but we were driven back by a high wind which whirled the fine surface snow into dense clouds. The camp was next moved up to 20,000ft, and on the following day we reached the summit, 23,180ft. The view was unfortunately spoiled by clouds beneath us, but was nevertheless interesting. West and south nearly everything was obscured by a rolling sea of mist, above which some of the great peaks, Kangchenjunga, Chumiumo and the Kangchenjhau showed their crests like rocky islands... We took nearly six hours to ascend, but did not hurry. Keeping close to the edge of the western cliffs until about 1,000ft from the top, we then made a bee line for the summit through snow nearly a foot deep.

...

The summit was corniced to the east, and was some distance from, and much higher than, the western cliffs. We remained on the top about 35 minutes. We felt quite comfortable except for the cold wind and I am confident that there would have been no difficulty in carrying out moderately complicated experiments, such as estimating the number of red corpuscles in the blood... Samples of air were taken and estimations of carbon dioxide started.[13]

Kellas' next objective, after giving up the idea of a repeat attempt on Jonsong Peak because of weather conditions in its vicinity, was to scale one of the summits he had seen from the top of Pauhunri, either Kangchen-

SHERPAS ON SUMMIT OF PAUHUNRI, VIEW TO THE SOUTH.
Not only proof of the ascent, but an image of the Sherpas who accompanied him. Though he trained his porters to use the camera, he never had himself snapped in heroic positions, such was Alec's unassuming nature. We must assume these are Tuny and Sona.
(AM Kellas, RGS Collections)

jhau or Chumiumo. These lay to the westwards of Pauhunri and rose above Gyaogang, the former mountain lying to the south-east, and the latter to the west of that settlement. But before he headed there Kellas spent a while at Thanggu where he replenished supplies, and met the first European he had seen for some time, one Mr Bell, the British Resident in Gangtok, 'who was most kind and hospitable' and whose company Alec enjoyed. This was Charles Bell, who was later to play an important role in easing the way for the 1921 Everest Reconaissance. The first target was Kangchenjhau and crossing the Sebu La on 22 June Kellas investigated the mountain. But the weather was very bad and prevented a clear view of the peak, so the attempt was abandoned and they returned to Thanggu and headed west over the Lugnak La 'in heavy rain' to investigate the western side of Chumiumo. After camping at the south west of the mountain (where the camp was at high risk of rock avalanches) they

CAMP ON CHUMIUMO.
This camp, at 19,500ft, hardly appears the height of luxury, with a flimsy-looking tent erected on what appears to be a boulder-field. It is indicative of the primitive conditions in which Kellas carried out his Himalayan mountaineering.
(AM Kellas, RGS Collections)

moved camp round to the north west, where the site and weather proved more favourable. From this location they moved to a high camp at 19,500ft on 10 July in preparation for a summit bid.

On 12 July we started at 6.30 a.m. The morning was doubtful. Ascending to near the head of the glacier, we crossed, and went up to the right of some seracs which nearly touch the north-west rock arête. At a height of a little over 20,000ft, near the base of the final ascent, were a few awkward crevasses, but after passing these the mountain was surprisingly easy. Tuny and Sona wished to try the north-west rock arête, but I insisted on trying the snow, which, although steep, was in excellent order and probably took not more than a third of the time that the rocks would have taken. I mention this because the coolies always baulked from steep snow under the impression that it was dangerous. We arrived on the summit arête in mist and had to wait for some time before the north top loomed up about 200 yards off. Ascending to this top, which is only a couple of yards broad, and appears as a sharp snow peak, we halted until the mist lifted somewhat, and then proceeded along the arête to the south summit, which is about 300 feet higher. It was a beautiful walk without the slightest difficulty, although in places the way was narrow and we were quite close to the edge of the formidable eastern precipices. The snow was never more than a foot deep. The south top is bounded on the south and east by precipices, but is several yards broad and quite safe. We remained for about half an hour on the summit (22,430ft), and then proceeded back by the way we had come. Mist had interfered greatly with our views from the top, but fortunately we managed to get some photographs, and we took others whilst proceeding along the arête. We were back in camp by about four o'clock, after a day which impressed us all by its easiness.[14]

Kellas found the ascent of Chumiumo easy, but I am sure that JS Haldane found the ascent of Pike's Peak on the very same day of 12 July 1911 even easier, since JSH ascended the mountain by means of the latter's cog railway. For, coincidentally, during this same summer of 1911 when Alec was carrying out his rather basic physiological experiments in Sikkim, Haldane and others were undertaking much more systematic ones concerning the effects of altitude on the human body on Pikes Peak in Colorado, USA. These convinced JSH himself that Everest could be climbed. Kellas

LOOKING INTO TIBET FROM THE SUMMIT ARRETE OF CHUMIUMO.
Again proof, if any were needed, of Kellas, Tuny and Sona's successful climb.
Although Kellas found Chumiumo easy, it was a long time before the climb,
which defeated other very competent mountaineers, was repeated.
(AM Kellas, RGS Collections)

was to become familiar with Haldane's work on its publication when both
men returned to Britain, and he was later to work with JSH himself on
oxygen issues after the war.[15]

After the ascent of Chumiumo Kellas made what he admits was 'not
a judicious decision.' Fearing that bad weather in Sikkim had set in for a
month, he took Tuny and Sona with him and went by train to the Garhwal
region to 'make an attempt on Kamet (25,400ft)' – an extremely ambitious, indeed, over ambitious, objective. A trek of nine days in 'continual
rain' got them to Badrinath. All sorts of frustrations and problems ensued
and Kellas soon realised that, 'It was obvious that we had no time to attack
Kamet seriously.' Nevertheless he did some useful reconnaissance work
and took photographs of the mountain from the summit of Dhonerau
Peak, 'a long easy mountain about 19,000ft high.' This is possibly the
peak 5,815m to the north-east of the village of Danrao, itself north of
Badrinath. Kellas with Sona and Tuny also established camp on the
Khagyam Glacier east of the village of Khagiam, probably climbing the
peak 6,087m to the north of what Kellas calls the Kharian Pass, from
which pictures were also taken of Kamet.

The Kamet coda apart, it would be difficult to select any Himalayan
season by any mountaineer till that time which was on a par with Alec
Kellas' trip of 1911. He had carried out extensive explorations in the
Kangchenjunga region to add to those he and others had already undertaken. He had climbed three virgin peaks of over 20,000ft, one of those
Pauhunri, despite being considered the second highest mountain climbed
to that date and at that time surveyed as marginally lower than Trisul

CHIEF PRIEST OF BADRINATH AND ATTENDANTS.
Although Kellas was hugely interested in his Sherpas, there is little in his writings or
photographic images about the cultural life of the Indian sub-continent, which
fascinated other travellers. This image is very much an exception in his portfolio.
(AM Kellas, RGS Collections)

COOLIES AT MANA.
Kellas took many images of his porters. These were recruited in the Garhwal on his 1911 trip and he commented that in terms of attitude and physical abilities, they were no match for the Sherpas.
(AM Kellas, RGS Collections)

itself, was in fact, as we have seen, the higher of the two, and the highest mountain climbed to that date. But whilst Trisul had been scaled by a very strong team which included Bruce, Mumm, Longstaff and two (unusually) high-performing Swiss guides, the Brocherel brothers, Alexander Kellas himself was the only western mountaineer on his Sikkim expedition four years afterwards. At his death a decade later Kellas had not surpassed the success of his 1911 Himalayan season; and neither had anyone else.

It is a measure of Kellas' increasing stature as a Himalayan mountaineer and explorer, and of his own rising expectations, that his next visit to Sikkim in 1912 should be seen as a relative failure, despite its success in ascending another virgin 20,000ft summit. And whilst the 1912 expedition did not match the achievement of that of 1911, it was nevertheless a more action-packed trip, and one full of human interest. Kellas read an account of the 1912 visit to the Alpine Club on 4 February 1913, and it was published later that year in the *Alpine Journal*, as *A Fourth Visit to the Sikkim Himalaya, with Ascent of the Kangchenjhau.*[16]

Kellas starts with a quotation from fellow Old Grammarian Byron

He who first met the Highland's swelling blue
Will love each peak that shows a kindred hue.

Before commenting that 'Mountaineering, in its widest adaptation, is the most philosophical sport in the world', without however giving us his own cast on this viewpoint, directing us instead to the writings of 'certain veterans of the Club'. Kellas makes clear that his main objective in 1912 was to further explore Kangchenjunga, especially on its northern and western approaches and his failures are attributed to 'the weather being in a hopeless condition for such explorations.' From Darjeeling, which was reached on 22 July, to Lachen attained on 31 July, and then further northwards, the weather was so bad that the initial plans for Kangchenjunga were abandoned and Kellas decided to attempt an ascent of Kangchenjhau (22,700ft, 6,919m – current estimates mostly give the peak as 30m or about 100ft lower than Kellas' figure). He headed there with a small party whilst the main group of porters were sent ahead to the Zemu Glacier and Green Lake to wait for better weather. Kellas was disappointed that his inquiries in Darjeeling had discovered that Sona and Tuny were away in Tibet and unavailable, though a couple of porters from the 1911 trip were recruited, including one who was to be the 'star' of 1912, the marvellously named Anderkyow.

Kellas went by Thanggu, of which he said 'the route is beautiful, many of the hillsides being clothed in dense forest', and then northwards from the town where 'the valley is bare and rocky, but beautiful Alpine plants are present in such profusion that one is kept interested and delighted.' Passing between Chumiumo and Kangchenjhau they turned eastwards and established camp at about 19,000ft on the north side of the mountain. Alec did a reconnoitre of the lower part of the proposed route of ascent on his own and was satisfied that it was possible. Bad weather in the form of a snowstorm delayed the summit attempt for a day before the actual bid was made. (Kellas does not give a date for the ascent, but it would have been around 10 August.) This was possibly Kellas' hardest and most problematic ascent of a Sikkim summit, and it is worth quoting fully his account of the climb.

THE SOUTH FACE OF KANGCHENJHAU.
Taken from Kellas' camp at 15,000ft on the reconnaissance of the mountain.
He was however, to ascend the mountain from its northern, Tibetan side,
which gave easier access to the summit than the southern approach.
(AM Kellas, Alpine Club Collection)

Next morning we started at 7 o'clock, and, keeping close to the rocks, reached the col a few minutes after nine, a speed of over 1,000ft per hour, excluding the single halt. The previous day's snow had frozen firmly to the ice during the night, and the going was easy. At the col we turned to the W. and up the final ascent, which consisted of steep snow at an angle of 45 to 60 degrees, with a belt of rocks (angle 60 to 80 degrees) showing through about 1,000ft above the col. The summit ridge was in mist, but as there seemed to be a chance of it rising, we proceeded. For the first 150ft the snow was so soft that we could kick steps in it, but above that was compacted neve with icy surfaces in places, the S. wind having blown all the fresh snow off this exposed face. There was no difficulty in making steps and we reached the base of the rocks about 11 o'clock, 1¼ hours after leaving the col. The coolies wished to proceed straight up the rocks, which were glazed with ice, but I had already decided that it would probably be better to keep round to the N. of the rocks, and zigzag up a steep snow slope. For about 200 to 300 yards the route looked rather dangerous, because if the snow had avalanched away we would certainly have slipped down 3,000ft on to the glacier below, but I do not think there was any real danger. The ice-axes could always be driven in up to the hilt. Nema, an extraordinarily cautious coolie, was a trifle nervous over this position, and protested several times to Anderkyow, who merely responded with a laconic 'Sahib mahlum' (ie, Sahib understands.) One could hardly be certain that one did understand thoroughly, for Himalayan snow conditions are more variable than Swiss, but we were as cautious as seemed reasonable. Once round the rocks there was no difficulty, and we proceeded slowly to the top, up a steep slope of deep snow, this side of the mountain being protected from the prevailing S. wind. No zigzags were required. The Sherpas indicated clearly that they were more rapid climbers than myself above 21,500ft Above 22,000ft they were certainly 20 per cent. better. At 1.10 p.m. we stepped on to the summit plateau.

A cold wind blew continuously, and dense mist enveloped us for over half an hour. After that, however, the mist broke now and again, and we had magnificent views to the W., N., and N.E. Chumiumo was conspicuous to the N.W...

After remaining on the summit plateau for 1½ hours, during the greater part of which we wandered about in order to keep warm, we started to descend at 2.40 p.m. We proceeded leisurely down to the col, which was reached at 4.30 p.m...

When we started our descent from the col, we found that the condition of the ice-slope had entirely altered since morning. Except when on the summit, the sun had been very powerful, and the snow on the slope had almost vanished. This caused us great trouble, and our progress was very slow. We were slightly tired, and felt lazy, and the ice was extremely hard. Anderkyow led, with Nema next him, I being last. Anderkyow's steps were rather unsatisfactory, but I thought – and as it proved, quite wrongly – that these two men were fairly safe not to slip, and I therefore contented myself with improving the steps for my own use. Only one man was allowed to move at a time. About 300ft from the top we halted on an extremely steep part of the face to discuss how to proceed. The Sherpas, acting in their usual way, wished to take to the rocks on our right, but as they seemed glazed with ice, and as all the ledges dipped downwards, I demurred...

I was re-examining the ice slope to the left, when suddenly, with a startled exclamation, Anderkyow slipped from his steps. Neema seemed to move practically simultaneously, and I certainly did not hold them even for one second. Within a few moments of Anderkyow's slip we were whizzing down that ice-slope with the speed of an express train...

The impact threw me on my side with my length almost at right angles to our direction of motion, and for a critical second my feet were slightly higher than my head. By an extraordinary effort I managed to turn back into the normal glissading position, and almost immediately after, a second jerk threw me onto my back... A few seconds thereafter we slowed down, and the coolies and I half rolled, half scrambled, out of the accompanying avalanche before it packed, and anchored ourselves as best we could.

I felt flushed and exhilarated, and on rising up and looking round, was astonished to find that we were at the top of the lowest pitch of the slope, only 400ft above our camp. This meant a descent of about 1,000ft if my estimate of the height of the col be correct...

Except for a few trivial bruises we were fortunately quite unhurt...[17]

Kellas took full responsibility for the accident as group leader, noting that he should have insisted that Anderkyow, as lead man, had made better steps, and also remarking that the party should not have stopped for consultation at such a steep part of the descent. He further concluded that having three men on a rope was a mistake, as with only two, one of them might have held a fall by the other. A modern climber might also recommend that on such slopes as were climbed that day, belaying might have been a good idea – but such techniques (which consist of anchoring one or more of the party whilst the others move) were under-developed at this time.

There was a sequel to this incident when Kellas sent Anderkyow the next morning to locate an ice-axe that had been lost in the fall. Despite the fact that Anderkyow was the possessor of a fine pair of nailed boots, the Sherpa took soft camp boots on his search and he slipped. As Kellas was getting himself organised in the morning, he found Anderkyow

KANGCHENJHAU FROM NORTH.
The long summit ridge of the mountain, seen across the barren Tibetan plain.
Kellas thought this plateau might be suitable for carrying out high altitude
physiological research and aerial reconnaissance.
(AM Kellas, RGS Collections)

outside covered in blood after a fall, his hands and face badly cut. In a
touching, almost Biblical scene, Alec bathed the porter's wounds in hot
tea and found the injury was not as severe as had at first seemed the case.
Kellas appears to have formed a particular bond with this Sherpa, who
had been on the 1911 expedition and played a bit part, and who had also
been with Alec in 1909. Of him, Kellas comments,

> Anderkyow's character had altered in the last few years. In 1909 he
> might have been described as timid, as he refused to do anything above
> the snow-line, but since then he has developed into the rashest coolie I
> have ever met with…[18]

A real crisis occurred for Kellas when Anderkyow and his men, sent to
obtain supplies, failed to return to the appointed location. A couple of
porters then came into camp and announced that Anderkyow and his
group had absconded into Tibet with the box containing the expedition's
money, scientific equipment and photographic materials. The fact that the
loss of trust weighed greater with Kellas than the loss of the materials is
shown by his statement that 'I was glad to remember afterwards that I
never thought harshly of Anderkyow.' *There must be some explanation*
was Alec's position, insisting to those RGS members listening to his talk
back in London that 'these Sherpa Nepalese coolies are not robbers', and
adding the fall-back position that if indeed Anderkyow had absconded
with the money, it was his, Kellas', fault for putting temptation in the
path of such a poor man. But the issue had been a navigational/logistical
error and eventually Anderkyow turned up. Here is Kellas' reaction, which
says much about both men, and the bond they had established.

He had been as far as the Lhonak glacier looking for us. Anderkyow was greatly distressed because his rapid movements precluded his obtaining fuel, and they had therefore been forced to use some of my private stock of provisions. That, of course, was a trifle. I was so glad to find them all quite well that the comparative failure of the expedition, now practically certain, was felt to be of negligible importance.[19]

Kellas tried manfully again, heading for Jonsong Peak in one of the many forays he made looking for decent weather on this trip, but like the others, this effort was unsuccessful, so he headed for Darjeeling (once more, Kellas is economical with dates for most of this trip). He almost missed his steamer at Bombay because a bridge was down on the road back to Lachen, and the river uncrossable. But a little ingenuity solved the problem.

> Fortunately I remembered having seen a huge block about half a mile back lying athwart the stream. This boulder in form and size somewhat resembled the famous 'Clach Dian' or 'Shelter Stone' at the head of Loch Avon in the Cairngorm Mountains. It was easy to climb to the top from our side, and, by means of ropes, men and baggage could be lowered on a rope near the other side. The last man came down on a doubled rope. Had it not been for this rock, we would have had to go back and cross the Lugnak La (17,300ft) – an extra two days' march.[20]

There is a saying in Aberdeen (doubtless used in variants elsewhere) that *Ye can takk the loon oot o Aiberdeen bit ye cannae takk Aiberdeen oot o the loon.* (You can take the boy out of Aberdeen, but not Aberdeen out of the boy.) An account of a trip which had started with a reference to Byron, the famous poet from Aberdeen Grammar School ended with a reference to the Shelter Stone under which Aberdeen's Cairngorm Club was founded. 1912 was admittedly a mainly frustrating trip, largely due to the weather. But it was a trip which included the ascent of Kangchenjhau as a major compensation, and further it demonstrated the close relationship Alec established with the Sherpas, these very possibly being some of the closest relationships of his life.

Alexander Kellas made two further trips to the Himalaya in 1913 and in 1914, but information on these is almost non-existent. On the 1913 trip he certainly visited Nanga Parbat, viewing it from a neighbouring height, and pronouncing it possibly climbable.

> Nanga Parbat (26,62ft) is one of the most fascinating summits of the main range. Mummery in 1894 carried out the only difficult climb yet affected in the Himalaya, ascending rock ridges of the north face to about 21,000ft. After examination from a spur of the adjacent Ganals peak in 1913, the writer came to the conclusion that the north arête is practicable.[21]

A *Note* in the *Cairngorm Club Journal* of 1920, referring to a slide show Parker gave in Aberdeen of Kellas' mountain images mentions K2 as being one of the Himalayan peaks shown amongst the slides.[22] Possibly that mountain was visited in 1913 also. As to 1914, we only know that he was already out in the Himalaya when the war broke out in August 1914, and that he came immediately home.[23] As with many other aspects of Alexander Kellas' life, with regard to these two visits we simply have to confess our ignorance. He was a shy, modest and private man, who published a limited amount of material, who appears to have kept no private papers and who entered into only restricted contacts with others through letters or social interactions.

Nevertheless, even with what we do know about Kellas, it is possible to argue a case for him being at the very least a peer of the foremost Himalayan mountaineers of his day by the time of the outbreak of the First World War, and even of being their *primus inter pares*.[24] The peaks he climbed waited long for their first re-ascents. Two attempts were made to re-ascend Chumiumo – in 1932 and in 1933 – and one made on Pauhunri in 1934 before they were both climbed again by Tilly and Noyce in 1945. Though the easier Sentinel Peak was scaled by Tilman and Wigram in 1935, Kangchenjhau had still only been ascended by Kellas when in 1948 TH Braham attempted to make a second ascent, and failed.[25] And none of these men, who failed where Alexander Kellas had succeeded, were second-rate mountaineers. That is a sure measure of his achievement.

Comparing Alec Kellas with his contemporaries is revealing. But more astonishing is to compare the Kellas of 1907 to that of 1912, a mere half decade of time having passed. In 1907 he was a man who had done a considerable amount of hard hillwalking in Scotland, and a couple of easy guided Alpine peaks; he even took a guide on his ascent of Galdhoppigen in Norway. Yet this cautious, moderate mountaineer of 1907 had by 1912 ascended five virgin Himalayan summits of over 20,000ft, without guides – and without other European companions, including, unbeknown to even himself, the highest mountain yet ascended in the world. That is an unparalleled progress in mountaineering.

NOTES

[1] *Geographical Journal*, (1912), Vol. XL, No. 3 pp.241–60. This article was also read to the Alpine Club and published in the *Alpine Journal* of 1912.

[2] Op.Cit. p. 241, 242.

[3] Op.Cit. p.254.

[4] Op.Cit. p.259.

[5] Op.Cit. p.256–7.

[6] Op.Cit p.246.

[7] Op.Cit. p.257.

[8] Op.Cit. p.252.

[9] Op.Cit. p.246.

[10] Op.Cit. p.248.

[11] Jonsong Peak briefly achieved this celebrity 'highest summit ascended' status after being climbed by an international expedition including Frank Smythe in 1930. The original intention had been to climb Kangchenjunga itself. See Smythe's *Kangchenjunga Adventure* (1930).

[12] *GJ* (1912) XL. No.3, p.249. There is a late 19th century Aberdeen street-song which Alec might have known, and which has a certain resonance here. (*Sandy* is another form of Alexander common in the North-East.)
I'm nae as daft as I may seen
And I nae as saft as candy
Ye can try yer tricks wi some ither silly Micks
Bit ye'll nivver pit it on wi Sandy.

[13] Op.Cit. p.251.

[14] Op.Cit. p.257–8.

[15] There exists an accessible account of JS Haldane's life and work, *Suffer and Survive* (2007), by Martin Goodman, which includes on pp.331–6 a sketch of Haldane's work in 1919 with Kellas. His work on Pike's Peak is covered on pp.245–6, and his views on the possibility of ascending Everest without oxygen are given on pp.336–7.

[16] *Alpine Journal*. (1913), Vol. 27 No. 200, pp.125–52.

17 Op.Cit. p. 131, 132,133.

18 Op.Cit. p.146.

19 Op.Cit. p.147.

20 Op.Cit. p.151.

21 'A Consideration of the Possibility of Ascending the Loftier Himalaya', *Geographical Journal* (1917), 49, No. 1, pp.26–46. The quote is on p.45. Kellas' slipshod way with dates is again evident; Mummery (and Collie) went to Nanga Parbat in 1895, not 1894.

22 *CCJ* Vol. 10, No. 58, p.81.

23 'Heard of war about Aug. 20th, came home at once. Kept work going at Middlesex Hospital, joined Hampstead Volunteers.' Letter of Rev. John Kellas to Mrs Townend. (21.9.1939) which was based on information given to Rev. Kellas by Nellie Kellas, Alec's sister, then living at 48 Carden Place.

24 The only possible contemporary rival would appear to be Tom Longstaff who climbed Trisul in 1907, and who ascended above 20,000ft several times. But though breasting that height on Nanda Kott, Nanda Devi East and Gurla Mandhata in Tibet, Longstaff failed to summit on all three occasions. In his book *This, My Voyage*, (1950), Longstaff himself generously concedes pre-eminence as a Himalayan mountaineer to Kellas.

25 Braham's account of his attempt on Kangchenjhau – full of praise for Kellas – is in the *Himalayan Journal* 16, (1951), pp.73-85. Tilly and Noyce's re-ascents of Chumiumo and Pawhunri are outlined in *HJ*, 13 (1946), pp.62–72.The other details are taken from 'Exploration and Climbing in the Sikkim Himalaya', K Mason *HJ* 9 (1937), pp.167–171.

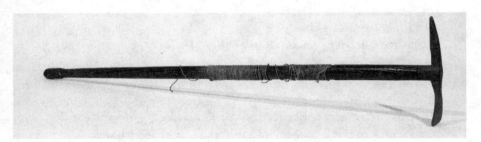

KELLAS' ICE-AXE.

An example of the long, wooden-shafted ice-axe favoured by early Himalayan mountaineers. In Kellas' day, ice-axe and rope techniques were light years away from later practise, and this contributed to the fall on Kangchenjhau.
(RGS Collections)

CHAPTER SIX

The War Years and After

Preparing for Everest

ON HIS RETURN from India in 1914, Kellas showed his support for the war effort by joining the Hampstead Volunteers, a militia unit raised against a possible German invasion that was more a morale-boosting propaganda device than a viable military force.[1] However the reality of the First World War hit home with the Kellas family within the first year of the conflict, when Alec's younger brother Arthur was killed by a sniper's bullet on 6 August 1915, during the Dardenelles campaign. Although Alec's contribution to the war effort was not that of active military service (he was 46 years old at the time war was declared), his responsibilities at the medical school of Middlesex Hospital increased as many individuals on the hospital faculty and staff were mobilized for war-related work elsewhere. To what extent the added stress of a greater workload during the war contributed to the psychiatric issues which became so problematic a few years later is an interesting question. It is not inconceivable that whatever latent or mildly expressed mental disorder he had as a young man may have simply become worse with ageing, whatever the environmental circumstances.

The First World War effectively called a halt to all Himalayan plans for its duration, as life largely became dictated by the country's wartime needs. The war also resigned to obscurity an expedition proposal for exploring and climbing Everest that was intended to be carried out in the years 1915 and 1916. Little was remembered about this scheme in later years, and unpublished material written by Alec concerning this proposed expedition to Mount Everest in 1915–16 had resided in the files of Henry R Kellas (nephew of Alec) for many decades until John B West unearthed it in the 1980s. While the proposed 1915–16 Everest expedition was to be a non-event because of the war, it was to profoundly influence thinking about Everest and the attempts made to climb it after hostilities ended.

Prior to the first successful penetration of the inner sanctum of Mount Everest in 1921, British explorers and mountaineers had for more than two decades shown a serious interest in planning a reconnaissance expedition to the mountain. Several months before the initiation of hostilities that marked the start of the First World War, Colonel CG Rawling[2] the surveyor who had identified Everest for the first time from the north during the 1903–04 Younghusband mission to Lhasa, proposed a reconnaissance of Mount Everest from the north to commence in the year 1915. This was to be followed by an attempt on the summit in 1916. Although this scheme necessarily had to be shelved because of the outbreak of war, it had gained the approval of the Alpine Club and RGS, and Kellas was drafted in to outline a proposal of expedition activities and personnel. A portion of Kellas' proposal for a 1915–16 expedition follows (quoted verbatim):

MOUNTAINEERING

The expedition proposes to examine Mount Everest with a view to ascertaining the possibility of climbing it and to reach the highest point attainable. The experience of the Duke of Abruzzi, Colonel Bruce and others of recent years in the Himalaya has upset many of the old views as to the limits of attainable altitude. It may well be that Mount Everest is unclimbable on the north side by any mountaineer however skilled, or that, even if the mountaineering difficulties are not insuperable, the altitude makes human advance impossible. These questions however have not yet been settled, and it is the aim of the expedition to do something towards their solution.

PLAN OF THE EXPEDITION

Line of approach: The intended route is a direct one: from Darjeeling to Gangtok, the capital of Sikkim, and thence due north to Khamba Dzong (in 1903 the temporary headquarters of the Tibet Mission). From Khamba Dzong a westerly route will be taken until the slopes of Mount Everest are reached.

Area of investigation: The work will be limited to the block of country bounded on the north by the Brahmaputra, on the south by the border line of Nepal and Tibet, and on the west and east by the 86th and 88th meridians of E. Longitude.

Date of operations: The routes out of Sikkim will be practicable about the middle of May 1915, which will allow of the expedition being in the neighbourhood of Mount Everest not later than the middle of June.

Anticipated progress of the work: During the first four months – that is from 1 July to 31 October 1915 – the following work should have been accomplished: the formation of the zoological, botanical and geological collections; the investigation of the deflection of the plumb line, and most of the magnetic and meteorological observations; the triangulation of all visible peaks, and a complete topographical survey of the immediate neighbourhood; a large scale plan of Mount Everest, which, together with the photographs, will show which of the routes hold out the best prospects to the climber. Possibly an altitude of 20,000ft will have been reached, but it is unlikely that any greater height will be attained during the first year. In November 1915 the expedition will return to India to work out the results of the past season and prepare for a return to the same district in 1916, when the scientific work will be completed and the whole efforts of the expedition will be concentrated upon an effort to ascend Mount Everest.

PERSONNEL

The leader of the expedition will be Major C.G. Rawling C.I.E. [Companion of the Indian Empire], Somerset Light Infantry. In addition to important journeys in other parts of the world, Major Rawling has travelled in Tibet on five separate occasions, and in northern Tibet has explored and surveyed 40,000 square miles of unknown country. He was employed throughout the Tibet Mission under Sir F.E. Younghusband, and was in command of the Gartok expedition from eastern Tibet to the sources of the Brahmaputra, Sutlej, and Indus. He is familiar with the Tibetan language.

As medical officer, botanist and entomologist, Mr. A.F.R. Wollaston, if his services are then available. Mr Wollaston has travelled extensively in the Sudan, central Africa, the Pacific and New Guinea, and had fulfilled the same duties with notable distinction on three separate expeditions.

As chief Surveyor and officer in charge of the survey, plumb-line and magnetic operations, Captain H.T. Morshead R.E., Survey of India, whose services have been lent by the Surveyor General of India. Capt. Morshead accompanied Capt. F.M. Bailey in the successful exploration of the lower Brahmaputra and reached to within three days march of Lhasa. He will be assisted by a native surveyor.

As transport officer and photographer, Lieutenant J.B.L. (John)

Noel, East Yorkshire Regiment. This officer has had considerable experience on the frontier roads of Sikkim and is familiar with mountain transport.

A Meteorologist (with approval of the Director General of Observatories).

An officer or assistant of the Geological Survey of India (with the approval of the Director General).

A Tibetan interpreter from the Magistrates Court at Darjeeling (with the approval of the Government of Bengal).

Three Alpine climbers, one of whom will be Mr A.M. Kellas. In the Himalaya, Mr Kellas has made the first ascents of Chumiumo (22,450ft), Kangchenjau (22,700ft), Powhunri (23,180ft), and Langpo (22,800ft). Two other members of the Alpine Club, and it is hoped that Dr Longstaff may also join this expedition. A Swiss guide will be added who has had experience in Himalayan climbing. The members of the expedition destined for the attempted ascent of Mount Everest will only join during the second season.

A staff of Gurkhas, Bhutias, and Tibetans.

COST OF THE EXPEDITION

It is anticipated that the total expenditures on the expedition, including wages, travelling expenses, transport, food, equipment, and instruments will reach 4,500 pounds sterling for the first year, and 2,500 pounds sterling for the second year – a total of 7,000 pounds sterling.[3]

Even though war put a reconnaissance of Everest on hold, whenever the opportunity presented itself during the years of the First World War, John Noel would visit Kellas in his chemical laboratory at Middlesex Hospital to talk about Everest. John Baptist Lucius Noel was educated in Switzerland and at the Royal Military Academy, Sandhurst, after which he joined the Army and was posted to India. In 1913, during leave from the Army, he travelled in disguise (without permission from his military superiors) into Tibet in order to reconnoiter the northern approach to Mount Everest. After serving in Europe during the First World War, he lectured about his travels near Everest to the Royal Geographical Society in 1919. Noel subsequently joined the 1922 Everest expedition as the official photographer and filmmaker, and produced a short film, *Climbing Mount Everest* (1922).

Alexander Kellas' birthplace at Regent's Quay. A fine merchant's house from the 1780s, note the Venetian windows. Family living quarters were above the offices of the Aberdeen Marine and Mercantile Board, where his father worked.
(IRM)

The substantial house in the bourgeois West End where the Kellas family moved in 1878 as Alec's father's career blossomed. A far cry from the crowded alleys of the Aberdeen dockside.
(IRM)

Sluivannichie, the farmhouse in Ballater of Alec's mother's people, the Mitchells, who were prosperous tenant farmers and horse-coach operators. Alec spent many boyhood holidays here within sight of the Cairngorm Mountains.
(IRM)

The new buildings of the Aberdeen Grammar School, which Kellas and his brothers attended in the 1880s. The statue, erected later, is of Lord Byron, its most famous former pupil. (IRM)

Alec's favourite howff, the Shelter Stone near Loch Avon below the Shelter Stone Crag, a refuge in use for 500 years. Seen here with a member of the Scottish-American Kellas expedition of 2010. (IRM)

Ballater Station, opened in 1865, closed in 1966. Alec would arrive here from Aberdeen to engage in his mountain tours from *Sluivannichie*. Another regular to use the station (in her own private train) was Queen Victoria.
(IRM)

The Angel's Peak of Cairn Toul and Lochan Uaine from Braeriach. Alec and Henry would have a little local difficulty when attempting to climb this after Ben MacDhui in 1885.
(IRM)

Lochnagar. Kellas climbed this Deeside mountain from *Sluivannichie* in Ballater.
Here it is stunning in its winter raiment, presenting a different image from
Byron's characterisation of it as Dark Lochnagar.
(IRM)

University College, London (UCL).
In this building's basement and
ground floor was housed the
Chemistry Department when
Kellas worked under William
Ramsay and alongside Norman
Collie, at the time of the discovery
of the inert gases.
(IRM)

Middlesex Hospital. Where Kellas worked after UCL, during the time of his greatest mountaineering exploits. He instructed medical students in chemistry. The building has since been demolished.
(GR)

St Mark's Square. Kellas rented a room in this building whilst he was working in London.
He could walk through Regent's Park to UCL. This remained his main residence till his death in 1921.
(IRM)

The Breithorn. Alec Kellas' first 4,000m Alpine peak, climbed from Zermatt.
It is reckoned to be the easiest of all the 4,000m peaks.
(IRM)

The Finsteraarhorn from the north. Alec's second 4,000m peak was climbed from the
far, southern side, from Reckingen. It was a tougher proposition than the Breithorn.
(Dick Sale)

A long line of penitents trudge their way over the ice cap to the summit of Norway's Galdhoppigen. Unlike in Alec Kellas' day, they now have the incentive of a summit café in the summer months.
(Pete Drummond)

Kangchenjunga (on left) from Gantok. A view Kellas (and thousands of tourists) would have been familiar with. The dense jungle between Gantok and Kangchenjunga, through which expeditions had to travel, is shown.
(AIAS)

Kangchenjunga at dusk from Mugutang (4,533m). Alec Kellas' explorations of the Kangchenjunga region are possibly even more unrecognised than his contributions regarding the explorations of the Everest region.
(AIAS)

Kangchenjunga massif from Sandakphu (3,636m), West Bengal, India. Sandakphu is situated at the edge of the Singalila National Park in Darjeeling district on the West Bengal-Sikkim border, and is the highest point of the Singalila Ridge. This view of Kangchenjunga and its satellites from Sandakphu is known as the *Sleeping Buddha* or the *Sleeping Shiva*.
(GWR)

The Lhonak Valley seen from near the head of the col between Kellas and Jonsong Peaks. The Lhonak Valley is the approach route (from the Sikkim side) to Jonsong, Kellas and Lhonak Peaks, and the 2009 party was following in Kellas' footsteps.
(AIAS)

The image gives an idea of the tough conditions Alec would have faced in Sikkim's mountains after the frequent heavy snowfalls. The party is crossing the Lungnak La, a route Kellas took on several occasions.
(AIAS)

Icefall below Kellas Peak. An example of the difficult conditions found by the expedition of 2009. These were compounded by dangerous ice conditions and rotten rock higher up and by a compressed schedule due to transport delays in Sikkim.

(AIAS)

North face of Jonsong Peak. This was a mountain Kellas attempted to climb in 1909, reaching over 22,000ft. It was finally ascended by Frank Smythe and other members of the International Kangchenjunga Expedition in 1930, and at 24,482ft (7,462m) became the highest summit climbed to that date.

(AIAS)

Camp below Kellas Peak. Jonsong Peak is to the left and Lhonak Peak to the right. Kellas Peak (21,916ft [6,680m]) was named in his honour by the International Kangchenjunga Expedition of 1930. It remains unclimbed.

(AIAS)

Peak at 6,252m on ridge between Kellas and Jonsong Peaks. This is the route Alec took on his 1909 attempt, and he gained a point higher than the peak shown here, before steep rock turned him back.

(AIAS)

Kellas Peak from the ridge of Jonsong Peak. Compare this image with that taken by Frank Smythe in *Kangchenjunga Adventure*, reproduced on p.203. This point is roughly where Kellas reached in 1909, looking across to the peak that would later bear his name.

(AIAS)

Kellas' grave at Kampa Dzong photographed on the 1922 Everest Expedition and looking across the arid Tibetan plain to the mountains he first climbed in northern Sikkim.

(RGS)

Kamet (on the left) was the target of Kellas and Morshead's expedition of 1920 when they reached their highest point at Meade's Col. The long walk in, now a popular trek, goes over the Kuari Pass.

(Priyardeshi Gupta)

Much of Kellas' exploration before 1914 centred on the region around Kangchenjunga, and his work was highly regarded by the German expeditions attempting the summit between the wars.
(Priyardeshi Gupta)

Alec Kellas visited the Nanga Parbat region in the years before 1914, following in the footsteps of Norman Collie who tried to climb the mountain in 1895. We know little of Kellas' explorations in this region.
(Shutterstock)

The north face of Everest – the view Kellas never saw. Though he had taken telephoto images of Everest from the south-east, Alec died on the day before the 1921 reconnaissance came within sight of the mountain.
(Shutterstock)

This outer space image, courtesy of NASA, shows the northern and eastern approaches to Everest.
(Courtesy of Earth Sciences and Image Analysis Laboratory, NASA Johnson Space Center http://eol.jsc.nasa.gov)

In 1924, Noel formed a private company that paid for the photographic rights for the Everest expedition. Noel reached the North Col and used a specially adapted camera to film the attempted ascent of the peak. A note from George Mallory to Noel was the last contact with the lost explorer before his body was discovered in 1999. The disappearance of George Mallory and Andrew Irvine added drama to the film, *The Epic of Everest* (1924). Noel lectured widely in North America and published a book about his adventures, *Through Tibet to Everest* (1927).

During these discussions, Kellas told Noel 'many things that have never been made known about his plans and work concerning the mountain'. In *Through Tibet to Everest*, in a chapter titled 'Dr Kellas' Plan' Noel described Kellas as;

> ... a pioneer in every sense. He established new records in Himalayan travel and climbing and in feats of physical endurance. Furthermore, he pioneered in ideas and methods. He devised the plan of using the natural resources of the country – yaks and mountain ponies – for transport on the lower heights, as the Tibetans do themselves, and he employed the Sherpas, one of the hardiest mountain tribes of the world, dwellers in the highest mountain valleys of the Himalaya, as porters. What General Bruce was to the Gurka, so Kellas was to the Sherpa. Kellas discovered the use of the Sherpas on high ascents. They are simple Shepard people, as hard as steel. They can run up mountains with immense loads on their backs, and then yodel their songs in pure delight, when the plainsman following them, panting and blue of lips, will fall exhausted to the ground. Kellas found them cheerful under all conditions, willing to undertake risks, and faithful. He made friends with these rough mountaineers, and with their help he conquered virgin peaks one after another with an ease and rapidity that astonished the world... Kellas did not advertise; few people knew about him. He would emerge each year from his chemical research work at the hospital. He did not tell the newspapers when he set out to climb a mountain higher than any climber had ever tackled before. He just went unobserved... He told me how he got his wonderful photographs of Everest's glacier from the Tibetan side. He had shown them to geographers, but would tell no one how he obtained the pictures. He had been among the mountains of Nepal west of Kangchenjunga, but not so far west as I had reached at Tashirak. He trained a native to photograph, and sent him to Kharta

and the Arun Gorge to get the pictures of the valleys and the eastern glaciers of Everest.[4]

Noel also relates how Kellas had;

> ... worked out a plan to lay depots of food in uninhabited high valleys west of Kangchenjunga by means of his own trained Sherpas, and of his hopes of reaching Kharta, crossing the river and going up to the eastern glaciers of Everest by the Kama Valley, escaping the watching Tibetans.

Apparently, so detailed was the plan, and so confident was Kellas that he could reach Everest (Noel had seen Kellas' reconnaissance photos of the aforementioned area), that Noel had agreed to accompany him on this adventure 'as soon as the War was finished and we could both get away'. However, this proposed 'furtive private raid', as Noel termed it, never came to fruition after the end of hostilities. To leap ahead in time just a little, what we know about Kellas' thoughts regarding the details of an approach to Everest is laid-out in the post-lecture discussion section of the paper Noel read to the RGS (just a few months after the armistice) on 10 March 1919 and subsequently published as *A journey to Tashirak in Southern Tibet, and the eastern approaches to Mount Everest.*[5] The primary purpose of the paper was to render the account of Noel's secretive journey – in native disguise – to Tashirak, undertaken in 1913 in order to reconnoiter the approaches to Everest beyond the Sikkim frontier in Southern Tibet. Noel's 1913 reconnaissance was meant to inform the proposed (above-mentioned) expedition to be led by General Rawling.

After Noel's RGS lecture, Kellas was joined in the immediate discussion by Douglas Freshfield, JP Farrar and Francis Younghusband. But it was Kellas who had had taken the time and made the effort to carefully study the approaches.

> The problem of the approaches to Mount Everest attracted me when I first visited the Himalayas about 12 years ago, and since then I have studied the matter rather closely, and come to the conclusion that the route described by Major Noel is one of the best from many points of view.[6]

Not surprisingly, he was able to provide by far the most distinctly detailed recommendations regarding an approach route to Everest. These were later summed up in his posthumous article 'A Consideration of the Possibility

MOUNT EVEREST.
Kellas took many images, including some of the earliest, if not the earliest,
of Everest before and after the First World War. However he did not label or date them,
but this in all probability dates from 1920–21, from around Kabru. The prominent peak
just to the right of centre is Makalu. The upper east face and summit of Everest
is just visible to the right of Makalu's summit (rising over the long ridge between
Makalu and Kanchungtse (AKA Makalu II).
(AM Kellas, RGS Collections)

of Ascending Mount Everest' (actually written in 1919/20), and finally
published in 2001.

As regards access, the mountain has so far never been visited by
white men, and it is unlikely that any mortal has reached an altitude
of even 20,000ft (6,096m) upon it... The nearest route would be
through Nepal, but as it is likely that access will be more readily
granted through Tibet, only routes through the latter country need
be considered. The base from which a start should be made would
be either Darjeeling or Siliguri, and the length of the route would be
approximately 300 miles. A good pony track leads northwards through
Sikhim up the valley off the Teesta River for about 140 miles, passing
Gangtok and Lachen. Proceeding due North from Gyamtshona, where
the Teesta Valley bends to the East, one would cross the Tibetan
frontier by two easy passes, the Koru La (16,900ft, 5,121m.) and the
Sepu La (17,200ft). Twelve miles (approx.) would bring one to Kampa
Dzong, an important village of S. Tibet, whence the route would lie

N.W. to Kanjoonglabran, where the Phungtu Chu, the westerly branch of the Arun River, may be crossed by a hiderope bridge. The Arun River is the only serious obstacle to reaching Mt. Everest by this route.[7]

As it turned out, the Kampa Dzong, thence Kanjoolglabran route was chosen as the most practical and expedient route by the time of the 1922 assault on Everest – after the fine points of this approach had been worked out during the 1921 reconnaissance.

As the protracted and devastating First World War reached its mid-point, Alec's thoughts started to seriously turn once more to the Himalaya. In 1916 a letter was written by Kellas to AFR Wollaston. Wollaston served as medical officer and naturalist to the 1921 Mount Everest Reconnaissance Expedition, and corresponded with Kellas regarding the practical difficulties involved in climbing at great altitudes in the years leading up to the Reconnaissance. In the letter, Kellas states;

> I am of the opinion that Mt. E. can be climbed without aids, but that an average of 300ft [91m] to 350ft [107m] per hour would be all one could expect between 25,000 [7,620m] and 29,000ft [8,839m]. This would mean a camp at 24,000ft [7,315m] as a minimum. A preliminary expedition to Kamet, on which a camp could be formed at 22,000ft [6,705m] or over would be of great value in order to gain experience regarding effects of prolonged camping at 22,000ft [6,705m], suitable diet, etc.[8]

He then discusses the question of supplementary oxygen;

> The oxygen necessary for the work of ascent is the difficulty and I have been considering whether a climbing suit like that of a diver, with a thin copper or aluminium head piece and a small pump to raise the internal pressure to about half an atmosphere, would not be a great advantage on the first ascent of Mt Everest.

A couple of months later, AR Hinks wrote to Kellas inviting him to a meeting of the RGS to give a paper,

> with some general title like 'The possibilities of Climbing above 25,000ft [7,620m]' as it would be a subject of first-rate interest... especially since no one perhaps in the world combines your enterprise as a mountaineer and your knowledge of physiology.[9]

Kellas replied to Hinks accepting the invitation but stating that he was not entirely comfortable speaking as an authority on the subject as his visits to the Himalaya 'have generally been hurried holiday visits' which prevented him from 'carrying out much scientific work'. Kellas closed his letter with the following sentence:

> Had one been able to attack Kamet (25,440ft [7,756m]), and study physiological conditions from a camp at 23,000ft [7,000m], one would feel more competent to write a paper on the subject, but kindly inform the President and Council that it will give me pleasure to do what I can in the circumstances.[10]

Incidentally, this paper in question was read before an afternoon meeting of the RGS on 18 May 1916, and was titled 'A Consideration of the Possibility of Ascending the Loftier Himalaya'. It was published in the *Geographical Journal* in 1917, and was the basis for the somewhat expanded and more detailed 'A Consideration of the Possibility of Ascending Mount Everest' previously referred to. This latter work lay out of sight in the archives of the RGS and Alpine Club for nearly 70 years.

Regardless of the fact that Great Britain was still deeply mired in the First World War, the RGS was sufficiently impressed by Kellas' exploratory mountaineering record as well as his scientific background and ideas that Hinks wrote to his old Cambridge acquaintance, Edwin S Montagu, the Secretary of State for India, on 21 September 1917 regarding matters concerning Kellas that can be classified as official in nature.

> I take it that the question of the effects of high altitude, important as it has been in the past, is likely to have much more importance in the future of India, since the change in the character of our relations with Russia it is certain that we shall have much more intercourse with the north, and people are already talking of air-plane posts between India and Central Asia. Although this possibility may be somewhat distant there is, I suppose, no doubt that the Survey of India will be pressing forward across the high peaks of the ranges, and that we may hope for a considerable extension of detailed exploration and survey at extreme altitudes. Finally, it is to be hoped that the Government of India will not look with disfavour upon the attempts which they will be asked to authorize after the war is over for a systematic attack upon the highest peaks.[11]

Hinks goes on to introduce Kellas' altitude-related interests and accomplishments to Montagu. He then proceeds to suggest that not only would it be in the best interest of the Government of India to favorably consider sponsorship of a systematic examination of high-altitude physiology, but it would be highly desirable to appoint Dr Kellas to such special duty 'for a term of years to conduct systematically what he has only been able to do in hasty trips from England.'

> It would seem to be a great pity if the remarkable enthusiasm and skill of such a man cannot be applied systematically to the service of the Government of India, since the combination of great scientific ability with remarkable powers of organization and endurance are not frequently found.

Unsurprisingly, Montagu replied to Hinks saying he did not want to consider funding any Himalayan exploration until after the end of the military conflict. Hinks counter-replied,[12] indicating that the possible need for military air travel at 23,000 [7,000m] to 25,000ft [7,620m] over the Himalayas prior to the cessation of hostilities was a good excuse to allow Kellas to carry out government-funded high altitude investigations immediately. The Secretary of State for India, however, remained unconvinced.

Regardless of this tepid 'official' response, the wheels were turning in Kellas' mind, and by early October of 1917 he posted a detailed seven page letter to Hinks containing his thoughts on possible future physiological research above 20,000ft [6,100m]. Considering that many of the predictions in 'A Consideration of the Possibility of Ascending the Loftier Himalaya' were of a speculative nature (not data-based), Kellas indicated:

> Further research would mean either a scientific study of the effects of living at about 23,000ft [7,000m] for some time – say a month – or the possibilities of climbing to the top of Chomo Langmo [Mt. Everest], and making approximate observations on the physiological effects of altitudes at different elevations above 20,000ft [6,100m].[13]

Kellas was well aware of several locations in northern Sikkim where semi-permanent camps could be made above 6,800m that might serve as a platform for a series of experiments similar to those performed by Haldane and co-workers during the Anglo-American Pikes Peak Expedition in 1911. Kellas suggested that a prime position for such investigations 'would be the summit plateau of Kangchenjau (22,700ft [6,919m]).

The area at this elevation is considerable, being several hundred square yards... It might even be possible to drag up in small parts the frame-work of a small wooden hut.' He suggested, however, if the more pressing problem 'set for solution' was to try to ascend the highest Himalayan peaks,

> ... and incidentally study the effects of altitude, which would in my opinion be the better plan, as thorough scientific investigation might come later, then I would suggest at least a couple of the following mountains as suitable for experiments:

1	Kamet	25,443ft	[7,756m]
2	Nanga Parbat		
	A north summit	25,586ft	[7,799m]
	B main summit	26,620ft	[8,114m]
3	West peak of Kangchenjunga	25,900ft	[7,894m]
4	Chomo Langmo	29,141ft	[8,882m]

Attempts would be made to solve two important problems:

> 1 The best method of preparing and using oxygen at high altitudes. This would mean studying types of helmets, etc., and part of such work could be carried out in this country in an airchamber, if one were available.
>
> 2 Practical investigation of the more suitable types of diet for high altitudes.[14]

MAZENO PEAKS ON LEFT AND DIAMIRIA PEAKS IN CENTRE, LOOKING SW ACROSS DIAMIRAI GLACIER.
Kellas visited the area of Nanga Parbat before the outbreak of the First World War, but we have almost no information on his visit, where he was following in Collie's 1895 footsteps. This image shows outliers of Nanga Parbat, explored by Mummery and Collie.
(AM Kellas, RGS Collections)

Kellas' curiosity in the Himalaya and its exploration did not end with matters terrestrial. On 18 March 1918, he read a paper at an afternoon meeting of the RGS which he entitled 'The Possibility of Aerial Reconn-aissance in the Himalaya'. Before the presentation, looking forward to man's future efforts to gain the poles via air in the following decade, the chairman of the session stated:

> At the present time we are looking forward to the close of the war for a great increase in the scientific use of aviation, and there is no department where it could do more than in the inaccessible portions of the Earth's surface, whether in the polar regions or high mountains.

Kellas presented a plan for airmen to fly over the Himalayan mountains and through the gorges, and carry out survey work from the north side of range in the summer months. He indicated:

> That there is no physiological difficulty in flying for some time at 25,000ft if there is a plentiful supply of oxygen and a suitable apparatus for utilizing it to the best advantage... a base camp might be chosen to the north of the main chain between the Great Himalaya and the Ladakh range at an altitude from 15,000 to 17,000ft Such a position would offer advantages... There are many comparatively flat areas which would make landing-places after preparation. The advantages of acclimatization at such an altitude would be considerable. Airmen in thorough training should require very little oxygen below 22,000ft, if properly acclimatized at 15,000 to 17,000ft [and in fact German scientists in the 1930s went to great lengths to investigate the potential of this idea during mountaineering expeditions to Nanga Parbat].[15]

This proposal (somewhat surprisingly) met with much scepticism from the aviators in the audience. The mountaineers, interestingly enough, were more enthusiastic. During the post-presentation discussion, Douglas Freshfield reminded listeners that the interest in aviation for mountain exploration purposes had a long history. He maintained that:

> A very similar [proposal] was entertained by no less a person than the founder of scientific mountain exploration, H.B. de Saussure, as long ago as the year 1785

> ...

When last year I discussed possible attempts on Mount Everest after the war with General Rawling, whose loss we so deeply regret, one of the ideas we entertained was that from a base camp established on the Tingri Maidan aircraft might be employed for reconnaissance of the environs of Mount Everest and the unknown ranges of Nepal lying south and west of it

Unfortunately aerial reconnaissance was not employed for the benefit of the British attempts on Everest in the 1920s. However, the Houston expedition of 1933 did eventually accomplish flights over Everest and around the high 8,000m peaks east of Everest (Makalu and Kanchenjunga). The photographs these aviators brought back from their flights were of great benefit to climbers who subsequently attempted these peaks in later years. Once again, on the issue of aerial reconnaissance, as with so many others, Alexander Kellas was a (largely unrecognized) Himalayan pioneer.

Another example of his broad interests was Kellas' study of Himalayan mountain nomenclature. In a letter written to the editor of the *Geographical Journal* in 1918 entitled 'The Nomenclature of Himalaya Peaks', Kellas demonstrated his support for the native peoples of the Himalaya by suggesting that he 'did not agree that the time has come for regarding the name 'Everest' as a suitable designation for the loftiest mountain of the whole system.' He reminded the reader that General CG Bruce and himself had independently found the native name 'Chomo Langmo' given to the mountain by the highland people that lived in its shadow. Kellas concluded that;

> ... until this name has been tested it would be advisable to refrain from a decision. In any case, one would prefer to see a Tibetan or Nepalese name applied to the mountain.[16]

In December 1918, a few short weeks after the armistice, RGS President Sir Thomas H Holdich resumed official RGS contact with the Secretary of State for India, stressing the need for support for scientific-oriented high altitude exploration. Perhaps because the war was now history, the RGS did not at this time stress the potential military benefits of high altitude exploration. Holdich made the theme of his letter plain in the second sentence, 'The ascent of Mt. Everest is the outstanding task which remains for geographers to accomplish'[17]. He requested that the government of India consider lending its technical and logistical support to Kellas's proposed high altitude physiological investigations. Citing

Kellas's proposals for a renewed attempt at the ascent of Kamet, with the planned investigation of problems related to the need for supplementary oxygen and adequate diet at high altitude, Holdich explained that the expedition to Kamet was to be organized as the first step in operations aimed at the eventual conquest of Mount Everest.

Two months later in February 1919, the Oxygen Research Committee of the British Admiralty responded to a RGS resolution concerning the recommendation of Kellas to the Committee in connection with the proposed Kamet expedition. The Oxygen Research Committee communicated in turn to the RGS that they had decided to assist Kellas's expedition 'by advising as to the methods of oxygen supply and the kind of equipment to be used.' They also agreed to recommend that the Department of Scientific & Industrial Research authorize the provision of the oxygen equipment needed for the Kamet expedition. But Alec was not meanwhile sitting around waiting to go to Kamet to study the effects of diminished pressure on the human frame.

In the immediate post-war situation Kellas had an opportunity to utilize a hypobaric (low pressure) chamber for research purposes during a set of experiments he performed at the Lister Institute in London with JS Haldane and EL Kennaway during 22–26 April, 1919. This research focused on the acclimatization obtained by relatively short, discontinuous exposures to progressively lower atmospheric pressures as well as the benefit derived from using a small supply of supplementary oxygen to facilitate climbing work. Kellas and Haldane spent several hours a day for four consecutive days in a hypobaric chamber at altitudes equivalent to 11,600ft [3,536m] (day one), 16,000ft [4,877m] (day two), 21,000ft [6,400m] (day three), and 25,000ft [7,620m] (day four). On day four, with the barometric pressure at 312 Torr, Haldane's alveolar PCO_2 was 19.8 and PO_2 30.1 Torr. The results of these studies were published in the *Journal of Physiology*.

This is a rather long, but at times quite entertaining article. Some of the results reported in this paper certainly applied directly to the projected experimental plans for the Kamet expedition. On the fourth and last day of their acclimatization experiments at the Lister Institute, within one and a half hours of lowering the chamber pressure to an estimated altitude equivalent of 25,000ft [7,620m], JS Haldane did 3,300 foot-pounds of work on an ergometer for four minutes before being forced to stop due to exhaustion and blurred vision, being described at this point as 'quite blue'!

Oxygen was then added to his inspired air through the latest form of Haldane mask as supplied to the Army for oxygen administration. One litre a minute (measured at normal pressure) was turned on shortly after the work was stopped. The effect was very striking. The light seemed to increase and there was a short apnea. At the same time the lips and face became bright red. It now became quite easy to do the work, which was accordingly increased to 5,000 foot-pounds. After 1½ minutes of this, however, the panting was so great as to be exhausting, though vision remained clear and there seemed to be no evident lack of oxygen.[18]

Haldane concluded that at a pressure corresponding to 7,620m, there were clear indications that with the use of proper apparatus 'as little as one litre of oxygen a minute was an enormous help in doing work'. Not only did these results support the assertion that even short periods of acclimatization increased altitude tolerance, but it showed how important the use of low-flow supplementary oxygen could be in improving performance during exposure to extreme hypobaric hypoxia. Perhaps it goes without saying, but 'extreme' human experimentation such as this would be difficult to reproduce today because of institutional human subjects' protection policies (aka. Health and Safety regulations)!

As clear and convincing as these results were, the issues surrounding the use of supplementary oxygen for high altitude mountaineering were anything but straightforward. As we shall see, in the following year Kellas provided the first scientific evidence in the field that supplementary oxygen was very effective as long as it was provided in containers that were relatively light in weight. Although further (and very convincing) low pressure chamber experimentation with supplementary oxygen was undertaken by Oxford pathology Professor George Dreyer prior to the 1922 and 1924 British Everest expeditions, the use of bottled gas as an aid to climbing the highest mountain on earth remained a very contentious matter. This was partly due to ethical concerns (ie. could such an aided ascent really be counted as a true ascent?) and partly due to practical concerns (weight and reliability of the oxygen apparatus). George Ingle Finch and Geoffrey Bruce proved the efficacy of supplementary oxygen during their summit attempt on Everest in 1922 when they bested the altitude of the non-oxygen party that year, but doubts still lingered. There was not to be a full-on commitment to an oxygen-aided ascent of Everest until the 1950s, during the 'Golden Age' of 8,000m peak ascents

– when the object was to obtain the summits of these peaks by virtually any means necessary.

However by the mid 1970s, advocates of ascents 'by fair means', such as Reinhold Messner, once again questioned the ethics of climbing the world's highest peaks aided by supplementary oxygen. The debate still rages. Whether climbers really think they are meeting the mountain 'by fair means' *without* supplementary oxygen but *with* the latest and greatest science and technology can provide in the way of clothing, tents, climbing gear, pharmaceuticals, nutrition, radios, etc. is an open question. The observations and logic of George Finch in his 1925 book *Der Kampf um den Everest* is possibly as relevant today as it was in the 1920s;

> No one takes offence at the fact that we wear special garments to combat the cold; no one denies the importance of thermos bottles, which, especially on this mountain, have almost life-saving status; no one opposes the fact that we use stimulants or specifically designed foodstuff, providing both strength and energy; no one takes exception to the use of snow goggles to protect the eyes from the sun's ultraviolet radiation and the extreme cold of the piercing winds; and no one criticized the use of caffeine to invigorate an exhausted climber. In short, if scientific research were to produce oxygen in easily ingestible tablet form, one can be sure that not a soul would oppose its use so violently during the climbing of Mount Everest, and no-one would label the use of supplementary oxygen 'artificial, dishonest, unsportsmanlike and un-British.'[19]

But to return to Kellas. The government of India officially agreed to assist him with the preparations for an attempt on Kamet by May 1919, but encouraged all concerned to postpone the expedition until 1920. The reason given for this suggested postponement by the India Office was that the Survey of India was 'very short of surveyors.' Given that Kellas had not requested any surveyors from the Indian government to accompany the expedition, it would appear that perhaps this was the government's way of politely refusing to sanction the Kamet undertaking for the year 1919. (Incidentally, the Survey of India did in fact detail a deputy superintendent of the Survey, Major HT Morshead, to accompany Kellas on the Kamet expedition the following year.)

A more potent reason for delaying the Kamet expedition till 1920 was the political situation in the Indian sub-continent. Nationalist agitation

KAMET GROUP WITH SHERPAS IN FOREGROUND FROM THE
KAURI LA (19,300FT).
Kellas visited the Kamet area twice before the expedition of 1920, more in an
exploratory fashion than with a view to attempting an ascent of the mountain.
This image dates from 1911, when he established camp on the Khagyam Glacier,
west of Kamet.
(AM Kellas, RGS Collections)

led by the Indian National Congress had led to the massacre of over 400 persons in Amritsar by Gurkha troops under British command. The failure to prosecute General Dyer, the instigator of the massacre, led to greater unrest. In addition Afghanistan had revolted from its position of semi-suzerainty under the British, and its army was threatening to invade the North-West provinces, which led to another doomed (though unfortunately not the last) British military intervention in the country in 1919. That Kellas did not live entirely in an ivory tower and was aware of at least some of the political issues of the day is shown in his letter to Adrian Lumley, of the Oxygen Research Committee of the Medical Research Council of 15 May 1919, where he notes;

> I should have written before to thank you for sending the haemoglobinometers...
>
> I am awaiting a letter from the Royal Geographical Society regarding the Kamet expedition. The Afghan trouble seems quite remote from Kumaon and Garhwal, but of course one must abide by the decision of the Indian Govt. If permission is not granted for the Kamet expedition perhaps Prof. Haldane might continue his experiments at the Lister Institute, and I would be glad to assist.[20]

As we previously saw, early as February 1919 the ORC had adopted a resolution to support the proposed Kamet expedition, possibly influenced by a paper Kellas presented to them in that month entitled 'Comparisons of Airman and Climber as Regards Oxygen Equipment'. There might have

SUNRISE ON KAMET FROM THE KHARIAN (KUARI LA).
The 1911 expedition to Kamet also left us this fine image of sunrise over the mountain from the Kuari La, the pass Kellas attained to take the image. He also climbed a nearby 20,000ft unnamed peak as well.
(AM Kellas, RGS Collections)

been limited general interest in problems faced by climbers at altitude, but with the prospect of a massive growth in air travel for both military and civilian purposes, it was quite the opposite with problems faced by pilots at this juncture. Alec held out a carrot to the ORC in this regard, by stating;

> scientific results obtained by climbers could be of value in considering problems connected with airmen... By varying and noting the volume of Oxygen used per minute [*by climbers, Authors' Note*] results should be found comparable with those which might be expected to obtain with airmen at definite heights.[21]

If the Indian Government was not keen on a 1919 Kamet expedition, the ORC gave Kellas all the help it could, sending him equipment, as well as books and pamphlets he requested on diet and nutrition, and they further wrote to several people, including Professor Leonard Hill, an eminent physiologist at UCL, asking them if they could be of help to Kellas. In the event, the expedition was postponed until 1920.

As well as the lack of enthusiasm on the part the government of India for undertaking the Kamet expedition in 1919, Kellas was at the time also struggling with a serious personal issue that may have contributed to the delay. In October 1919, Kellas mentioned the problem in a letter to RGS Secretary AR Hinks.

> I am suffering from a slight disability at present, but my fixed intention is to make an attempt upon Kamet (25,447ft [7,756m]) next year, even if the peculiar and continuous annoyance described when I saw you continues until June next. In fact, I am looking forward to the journey as a means of finally getting rid of a disturbance which medical men tell me is due to overwork, and which takes the form of malevolent aural communications, including threats of murder.[22]

Modern psychiatry might consider such a complaint as due to something other than merely the stress of overwork. In 1920, however, this diagnosis was in keeping with accepted state-of-the-art psychiatric practice. As such, we should not be surprised to learn that the disturbance persisted, even after Kellas took a leave of absence from his teaching position at Middlesex Hospital Medical School in London in the autumn of 1919, for an extended rest in his hometown of Aberdeen. However, though he may have rested physically when back home at Carden Place, there was no let up in Kellas' Everest preparations, and specifically in planning for the now agreed-upon preparatory expedition to Kamet.

NOTES

1   Letter of Rev. James Kellas to Mrs Townend, 21.9.1939. (This letter has been mis-typed out by a subsequent hand and its author is given as John. But John, the father was dead by 1939, and James the son was the author). The relationship of Rev. James Kellas to the Kellas family of Alec is unclear. Nor do we know who Mrs Townend was, or the nature of her interest in Alec Kellas. James Kellas was born at Rathen, Aberdeenshire in 1898 and attended Aberdeen University from 1920, and would thus not have known Kellas himself. His father, John Kellas (1866–1925) however was born in Mortlach near the lands of Alec's ancestors in 1868 and attended Aberdeen Grammar School whilst Kellas himself was there in the 1880s, and it is possible the pair knew each other. John Kellas became a Church of Scotland minister at Rathen, which lies in the Old Deer parish, but alas only in 1895, a decade or so after Alec had gone there, apparently to recuperate from some unspecified ailment, so Alec did not go to stay with his eponymous family. Rev James Kellas became the minister of Mannofield Church of Scotland in Aberdeen's West End, and knew the Kellas family, so we can assume there was some, if quite distant, blood relationship. He died in 1977. See *Fasti Ecclesiae Scoticaniae* Vol. 6, p.239 for the John father and Vol. 8, p.527 for James the son. For the Holy Ghost, keep looking.

2   Brigadier-General Cecil Godfrey Rawling, CMG, CIE, DSO, FRGS (1870–1917) published two books detailing his experiences as soldier and explorer. In 1904, then Captain Rawling was attached to the Younghusband mission to Tibet, charged with exploring and surveying the mountainous terrain. During this diplomatic expedition and the campaign which followed it, Rawling surveyed over 40,000 square miles (100,000 km²) of Tibet in addition to his military duties. His team even explored the foothills of Everest and included parts of the mountain in his survey, confirming it as the highest mountain in the Himalayas. He wrote a book about his experiences in Tibet titled *The Great Plateau* which was published in 1905. He served in the British Army on the North-West Frontier of India and in France during WWI. He was killed in the latter conflict at age 47 during the Battle of Passchendaele.

3   Rawling CG. *Unpublished 1915–1916 Mount Everest Proposal*. Henry R Kellas collection, 1914.

4   *Through Tibet to Everest*, JB Noel (1927), Ch. 5, pp.60–62

5   Noel 'A journey to Tashirak in Southern Tibet, and the eastern approaches to Mount Everest', *Geographical Journal*, 1919. No. 53, pp.289–308.

6   Kellas, quoted in Noel, *Geographical Journal*, 1919. No. 53, pp.289–308).

7   Kellas AM. 'A consideration of the possibility of ascending Mount Everest'. *High Altitude Medicine & Biology* 2001, No. 2, pp.431–461.

8   Kellas AM to AFR Wollaston. (Alpine Club Archives,) 27.2.1916.

9   Hinks AR to AM Kellas. (Archives of the RGS), 14.4. 1916.

10 Kellas AM to AR Hinks. (Archives of the RGS), 24.4. 1916.

11 Hinks AR to ES Montagu. (Archives of the RGS), 21.9.1917.

12 Hinks AR to ES Montagu (Archives of the RGS), 28.9.1917.
    Hinks was not exaggerating when he mentioned the possibility of flying over the Himalayas at altitudes of over 7,000m in 1917. Robinson mentions that in 1914 a German pilot flew to 25,780ft [7,858m] in a DFW biplane with a 100hp Mercedes engine. There is mention that in 1918 the Germans possessed a reconnaissance plane with a *service* ceiling of 24,000ft [7,315m] (Robinson DH *The Dangerous Sky: A history of aviation medicine*, (1973), p.69).

13 Kellas AM to AR Hinks. (Archives of the RGS), 9.10.1917

14 Kellas AM to AR Hinks 9.10.1917. A project of this sort, specifically designed to study the long-term effects of extreme altitude on human physiology, was not actually undertaken until 1960–61 during the Himalayan Scientific and Mountaineering Expedition (popularly known as the Silver Hut Expedition). Several physiologists spent an entire winter season in a specially designed, prefabricated wooden hut erected at 5,800m on the névé at the head of the Mingbo Glacier in the Everest region of Nepal.

15 Kellas AM. 'The possibility of aerial reconnaissance in the Himalaya'. *Geogaphical Journal*. 1918, No. 51, pp.374–389. Freshfield's comments on Kellas paper are given in the discussion section following the published article.

16 GJ 1918, No. 52, pp.272–74.

17 Holdich TH to ES Montagu (Archives of the RGS), 19.12.1918.

18 Haldane JS, Kellas AM, Kennaway EL. 'Experiments on acclimatization to reduced atmospheric pressure'. *J.Physiol. Lond.* 1919/20, No. 53, pp.181–206.

19 Finch GI. *Der Kampf um den Everest*. (Leipzig) 1925. English edition, *The Struggle for Everest*, (2008), pp.121–3.

20 Kellas to Lumley (ORC) 15.5.1919 (National Archives, MRC papers.)

21 'Comparison of Airman and Climber as Regards Oxygen Equipment' p.1, 2 (National Archives MRC papers).

22 Kellas AM to AR Hinks (Archives of the Royal Geographical Society), 21.10.1919.

CHAPTER SEVEN

Prelude to Everest

The Kamet Expedition of 1920

SO FAR WE HAVE covered Alec Kellas' pioneering role in Himalayan exploration and his record of high altitude climbs before 1914. We have also seen how during the First World War he engaged in detailed planning and research concerning both the physical and physiological issues relating to plans for an assault on Everest. Kellas' contribution in these areas lies largely under a cloud of unknowing. But the neglect of his contribution to Himalayan mountainering does not end there. No one has revisited and examined in any detail what was the most ambitious high altitude physiological field study undertaken until the third decade of the 20th century, Kellas and HT Morshead's 1920 Kamet Expedition. This undertaking by Kellas and Morshead was unique because it specifically emphasized investigation of the practical difficulties inherent in climbing at very high altitudes. During this endeavor, with Morshead's assistance, Kellas carried out the first rigorous tests of the value of supplementary oxygen for climbing at high altitude.

Henry T Morshead was commissioned in the Royal Engineers in 1901 and joined the Survey of India five years later. He took part in the 1921 and 1922 Everest Expeditions and on the latter reached an altitude just shy of 8,225m as a member of the climbing team. Incidentally, this foray in 1922 to 8,225m, accomplished with Edward Norton, Howard Somervell, and George Mallory, was the first recorded climb above an altitude of 8,000m. Morshead was appointed Director of the Survey of India in Burma in the late 1920s. There his life came to an unfortunate end on Sunday 17 May 1931, when he was murdered while out horseback riding.

Kamet (7,756m) lies in the Garhwal Himalaya on the Indian–Chinese (Tibetan) border approximately 300km northeast of the Indian city of New Delhi and roughly 75km northwest of the more famous peak Nanda Devi (7,816m). The exploration and mountaineering history of the Kamet, leading up to and including its first ascent, is thoroughly documented in Meade's *Approach to the Hills* (1940) and Smythe's *Kamet Conquered* (1932). Kamet was surveyed in the 1840s but mountaineers did not make an attempt upon the mountain until 1907. Although an actual attempt to climb Kamet was not undertaken until that date, the brothers Adolphe and Robert Schlagintweit from Munich made what they thought was an early probe of Kamet's slopes. The two brothers, along with a third brother Hermann, travelled to India in 1854 at the invitation of the East India Company. In spring and summer of 1855 they began a series of Himalayan journeys, eventually crossing into Tibet. Pioneers far in advance of their time, the brothers Schlagintweit approached the Garhwal region from Tibet in early August of 1855 and reached a height of over 6,700m on a lower neighboring peak of Kamet, Abi Gamin, on 19 August.

The brothers had actually intended to attempt Kamet, and it was not realized for several decades that they in fact attempted Abi Gamin, which lay between their approach route and Kamet. Nonetheless, this attempt was quite significant in the annals of early high altitude Himalayan endeavours. Their description of the effects of the harsh environment on their bodies may well have been the very first of many such laments to be uttered by Himalayan mountaineers in the subsequent decades;

> We had got much accustomed to the influence of height, especially during our Thibetan [*sic*] journey, but here not one escaped unhurt; we all felt head-ache and more or less severe pains in the eyes, the latter being especially caused by the furious wind which constantly blew the fine snow dust into our eyes. The night [after reaching their high point] was a very bad one, we had scarcely any fuel left for cooking, the wind threatened every moment to tear to pieces our light tent, the cold was intense, and our people, with the exception of one, had entirely lost courage and the faculty of thinking.[1]

Between 1907 and 1914, seven small climbing parties visited the mountain. In 1907, TG Longstaff, CG Bruce, and AL Mumm reached over 6,100m. on the eastern side of Kamet before being driven off by avalanche worries. Their prodigious efforts on this expedition did result subsequently in the ascent of Trisul (7,120m) in the Garhwal, which established a new mountaineering summit altitude record. The classic account of Himalayan mountain exploration, Mumm's *Five Months in The Himalaya: A Record of Mountain Travel in Garhwal and Kashmir* (1909), gives a delightful and detailed account of the travel and climbing exploits of this important 1907 undertaking. Incidentally, the first recorded use of supplementary oxygen also occurred on this expedition. Small oxygen generators were taken along, but no serious attempt was made to evaluate the value of oxygen supplementation at high altitudes.

Other notable attempts on Kamet occurred in 1912 and 1913 when AM Slingsby and CF Meade reached 7,000m, and Meade also managed to gain the col (Meade's Col, 7,140m) between Kamet and Abi Gamin from the eastern side. The first ascent of Kamet in 1931 by Frank Smythe, Eric Shipton, and RL Holdsworth, with Sherpas Lewa and Nima Dorje, is a notable mark in mountaineering history if only because it was at that time the highest summit to have been attained by humans, though, of course, it was significantly lower than altitudes already achieved on Mount Everest in the previous decade. We have examined in detail in the previous chapter how Kellas, who had already visited the Kamet region twice before the outbreak of the war, was preparing from 1916 for an attempt on the mountain's summit as a prelude to that which was to follow on Everest. We take up the story again after his return to Aberdeen in the autumn of 1919, following the breakdown of his health and his taking extended leave of absence from his post at Middlesex College Hospital Medical School.

KAMET AND EAST ABI GAMIN.
An image showing the Kamet Glacier, with East Abi Gamin attempted by the Schlagentweit brothers in 1854, and Meade's Col between it and the summit of Kamet on the left. This was to be the high point reached in 1920 by Kellas and Morshead.
(AM Kellas, RGS Collections)

The Aberdeen Alexander Kellas returned to in the autumn of 1919 whilst on indefinite leave from his post at the Middlesex College Hospital Medical School, was a very different place from the town he had left in the 1890s to go and study in London, or even from the place it had been before the First World War. The latter world-shattering event had changed everything, even life in the provincial backwater that Aberdeen had previously been. The war and its impact had led to the emergence of political agitation in the city, to strikes, demonstrations and to agitation against continuation of the war, which was followed by a political radicalisation which broke the hold of a century of moderate Liberalism in the town. In 1918 a Labour MP, one of the first in Scotland, was elected to Parliament for Aberdeen North and the party also made gains in the local town council. Indeed for a while Aberdeen was the main conduit through which exiled revolutionaries returned to Russia after the Revolution of 1917.

None of this appears to have made any impact on Kellas, and he never comments on events such as these, if indeed he noticed them at all. We have already observed that Alec could write a letter on Armistice Day in 1918 without even mentioning the end of the greatest conflict and slaughter in human history. It appears that Kellas was living increasingly in a parallel universe of his own obsessions which clouded out all else. If Kellas had any political, or indeed religious beliefs, then we have absolutely no knowledge of what they were, unlike, for example with George Mallory. Kellas returned to live at the family house in Carden Place, which was still occupied by his widowed mother and an unmarried sister, and seems to have lived quietly there over the next few months, physically resting on medical advice and hoping for a recovery of his health. Over the winter of 1919–20 Alexander Kellas would have much time on his hands to think about the point his life had reached – and where it might go from there.

Kellas was now over 50 and, though yet strong and fit, must have realised that a limited period was left to him to make his further mark on international, specifically Himalayan, mountaineering. He was unmarried and – barring some near-miracle – certain to remain without a personal family till his death. He had taken indefinite leave from his post at Middlesex Hospital, a post he was becoming increasingly disenchanted with, as he felt it restricted his mountaineering. Whilst in Aberdeen he was to transform this leave of absence into a definite resignation of his teaching post at the hospital. In addition he was ill, and despite the Aesopian language of family and associates, it was clear to them, and possibly might have been to Kellas himself, that he was mentally ill. In every respect, Alec's life would have appeared to have reached an impasse, or a set of cul de sacs. But for just one thing – his mountaineering.

Far from taking a complete rest whilst in Aberdeen, Kellas was engaged in continuing correspondence with Hinks about preparations for the proposed expedition to Kamet in 1920, as well as with Lumley of the Oxygen Research Committee, to whom he wrote on 21 October 1919 regarding his Kamet scientific aims. That these were wider than those simply relating to oxygen *per se* is shown by the list of dietary questions he hoped to investigate;

> The different types of Carbohydrates, fats and proteins should be tried. The calorific value of the different foodstuffs used should also be known... Vitamines [sic] would also have to be kept in view.
>
> Special foodstuffs, such as plasmon, glycerophosphates, Lacto-phosphorus, Benger's food, etc., would be tested and dilute phosphoric acid would also be tried to promote acidosis of the blood.[2]

It appears to be no exaggeration to suggest that Alexander Kellas' scientific approach to a whole range of issues concerning the possible ascent of Mount Everest, from the use of aerial reconnaissance, to the development and testing of oxygen equipment and to the investigation of questions of diet and physical performance, was light years away from the gentlemanly, amateurish atmosphere which dominated British attempts to climb Everest before the 1950s. But his supreme contribution was yet to come, though like much of Kellas' work, it was to remain unsung and become largely forgotten.

On 21 November 1919 Kellas received a communication from Capt. TEC Eaton, secretary of the British Section of the Alpine Congress, inviting him to give a paper at the forthcoming Alpine Congress scheduled to take place in Monaco in May 1920, and stating:

> Mr Henry F. Montagnier has suggested that I should write to you and ascertain whether you would feel disposed to prepare a paper on the possibility of attaining an altitude of 8,800m? He adds that you are one of the best authorities on the subject and he is sure that a paper by you would be very much appreciated.[3]

Kellas replied on 2 December agreeing to the invitation 'to write a paper on the possibility of ascending Mt Everest (Chomo Langmo)...' only expressing the reservation that as he expected to be in India for the Kamet attempt by May 1920, he was concerned that he would be expected, but unable, to deliver the paper personally in Monaco. Once he had been re-assured that the paper need not be delivered in person, Kellas formally accepted the proposal on Christmas Day 1919, and began work on the manuscript that was to become his 'A Consideration of the Possibility of Ascending Mount Everest.'

Kellas appears to have been under pressure to complete the text to schedule. In mid-January he wrote to Eaton:

> I will do my best to comply with the wish of the Directors of the Alpine Congress to have the paper on the possibility of ascending Mt. Everest ready by the middle of next month, or failing that, at latest by the end of the month... I am supposing that 40 to 50 pages would be the maximum length allowed.[4]

Further pleas from Eaton for the paper led to Alec replying on 11 March that he had had problems getting the manuscript (now finished) type-written in Aberdeen, and in getting his lantern slides to accompany the lecture made up. But on a trip to London at the end of the month Kellas was able to deliver both the paper and the slides to Eaton personally at the Alpine Club. It is worthwhile to present here a short summary of Kellas' 'A Consideration of the Possibility of Ascending Mount Everest', which was undoubtedly the most interesting and extensive paper he ever produced.

Kellas began this work by stating his primary question: 'Is it possible for man to reach the summit of Mount Everest without adventitious aids, and if not, does an ascent with oxygen appear to be feasible?' He then divided the difficulties into two groups – physical and physiological. The physical difficulty concerned access to the mountain. As seen elsewhere in this book, Kellas knew of three possible routes from Darjeeling – the feasibility of any given route ultimately depending in whether it was the government of Nepal or Tibet which eventually granted permission.

When considering the physiological difficulties of Everest's extreme altitude, he reviewed the experiences of early balloonists, particularly the French and English, who ascended to altitudes of 8,000m and beyond on several occasions (often with disastrous results due to the severe acute

3̲14747

CONGRÈS DE MONACO

POUR FAVORISER LE DÉVELOPPEMENT

des Stations Hydro-Minérales
Maritimes, Climatiques & Alpines

DES NATIONS ALLIÉES

MONACO — 1er au 10 MAI 1920

CONGRÈS DE L'ALPINISME

COMPTES RENDUS

TOME Ier

Préliminaires et Commissions scientifiques

PUBLIÉ PAR M. MAURICE PAILLON, SECRÉTAIRE GÉNÉRAL

EXPANSION SCIENTIFIQUE FRANÇAISE
23. Rue du Cherche-Midi, 23
PARIS
—
1921

MONACO ALPINE CONGRESS.
The frontispiece of the published proceedings of the 1920 Alpine Congress in Monaco, which included a French translation of Kellas' paper on the possibility of ascending Mount Everest. It was to be 80 years before this received its first publication in English.

hypoxia). Kellas also considered studies performed in low-pressure chambers that simulated a high altitude environment, including one such experiment he carried out with John Scott Haldane and EL Kennaway at London's Lister Institute. More than a dozen pages of the paper were then devoted to mountain sickness, and Kellas rightly attributed the condition to hypoxia. He knew that to tolerate the extreme hypoxia high on Everest one would require adequate acclimatization in order to be able to function with any degree of effectiveness. This realization led him to ask whether sufficient physiological adaptation could occur to allow a climber to ascend from a camp at 25,000ft (7,772m) to the summit of Everest, and return, in one day. In the process of addressing this matter, Kellas focused on estimating the value of oxygen in the alveoli (tiny air sacs) of the lungs on the summit of Everest. The values he suggested were for many years thought to be much too low, but samples of arterial blood taken for blood gas analysis in four subjects almost 500m below the summit of Everest in 2007 support the assertion that Kellas' calculations were actually reasonably accurate – especially given the fact that he had so few data with which to make estimates of this nature in 1920!

It is quite interesting as well to note that Kellas was able to conclude, based on assumed arterial oxygen saturation, that the maximum climbing rate near the summit of Everest (*sans* supplemental oxygen) would be in the range of 300–350ft/hour. This estimate was given confirmation by the first ascent of Everest without supplemental oxygen by Reinhold Messner and Peter Habeler in 1978. Messner wrote of the 1978 climb in *Everest: Expedition to the Ultimate* (1979) that 'The last 100m took us more than an hour to climb'.

In the last paragraph of 'A Consideration of the Possibility of Ascending Mount Everest', Kellas summed up his views in an amazingly prescient fashion;

> Mt Everest could be ascended by a man of excellent physical and mental constitution in first rate training, without adventitious aids [i.e. supplemental oxygen] if the physical difficulties of the mountain are not too great, and with the use of [supplemental] oxygen even if the mountain can be classified as difficult from the climbing point of view.[5]

At the same time as Alec was engaged in writing his Everest paper he was continuing with the plans and preparations for the Kamet expedition. However, all was not well back at Royal Geographical Society head-quarters, where Secretary Hinks was seriously concerned about Kellas's health and his ability to undertake an assault on Kamet. On 20 March 1920 Hinks wrote a letter headed **Private**, to Henry Kellas, Alec's brother in Aberdeen, expressing his concerns on behalf of the RGS,

Dear Sir,

I have to ask you if you will kindly help me by giving me some information on the state of health of your brother... as we have been involved in his plans for the ascent of Kamet as a preliminary to the Mount Everest expedition.

When your brother called upon me last, in September, I was sorry to see that he was evidently suffering from a serious breakdown in health, and I hoped that rest would restore him. As he now writes that he has resigned his post at the Middlesex Hospital I fear that his progress has not been what we should all desire.

Nevertheless he talks of starting next month for India in order to carry out the work he has planned on Mount Kamet. The Survey of India had nominated an officer to assist him in this work and provide the necessary transport. I shall have to write to India very shortly on this matter, and I must therefore know whether it is really possible that your brother is in a fit state of health to undertake this expedition. His letters to me are perfectly clear but he continues to speak of the 'aural trouble which has continued for some time' I cannot help feeling anxious about him, and should very much value your opinion as to the possibility and desirability of his proposed journey this year.[6]

Henry Kellas, acting in some respects as his brother's keeper, replied in a combination of wishful thinking and well-meaning intentions, to the effect that he thought his brother's health was 'improving', and adding 'he is extremely anxious to visit his beloved mountains,' and further commenting that;

Professor Ashley MacIntosh [sic] of this Town has been consulted, and it has been decided that it is inadvisable to place any difficulty in the way of his going to India and endeavouring to carry out his plans.

We are hopeful that a sea voyage and sojourn among the Hills may expedite a recovery, and so far as I can judge there is a fair prospect of my brother successfully carrying out his intentions.[7]

As Professor of Medicine at Aberdeen University and manager of the Aberdeen Asylum, Mackintosh was one of the top medical professionals in Aberdeen. He had experience of treating mental illness and had published papers on neurology. He favoured the humane Weir-Mitchell method of tackling mental illness, which pleasantly consisted of rest, massage and good food. Alec appears to have consulted him privately as there is no record of his attending the asylum; it is likely that Mackintosh may well have been a family friend, as he would have been the immediate superior of Alec's brother Arthur Kellas, who was deputy superintendent at the asylum until he volunteered in 1914 and was killed a year later. Consulting Mackintosh is an indication, that whilst Alec himself may have been in denial in saying that medical science could find nothing wrong with him, the family were privately agreeing that he was mentally ill.

Despite being apparently re-assured somewhat by Henry Kellas' comments, Hinks was not entirely convinced that Kellas was fit, or at least fit enough even after the Kamet attempt, to be a part of the actual Everest Reconaissance in 1921. As late as December 1920 he was writing to Norman Collie regarding the Dalai Lama's granting his consent to the proposed Everest expedition. But the bulk of the letter to Collie is taken up with his concerns about Kellas, and whether he should be of the reconnaissance party. Reading between the final lines, one suspects that Hinks was trying, almost Pontius Pilate like, to transfer the decision about Kellas onto Collie's shoulders.

I hope that this Christmas time you will be thinking over the right and available people for a climbing reconnaissance, I understood from Kellas' letter that he is remaining in India hoping to climb again next year, and evidently one of the first things to be decided will be whether Kellas should be of the party. I imagine that he has every claim, except possibly that of good health. I suppose that if he has got to 25,000ft [sic] this year, it will be difficult to plough him on that score. I do not know whether you have heard anything from Morshead about his state of mind.

I am often writing to Kellas, and I should find it difficult to write again without mentioning the Mt. Everest prospects of which I had promised to keep him informed. I shall be glad if you will let me know whether in your opinion Kellas should form one of the reconnaissance party this next summer. If you think so there would be no harm in talking about the general plans, and allowing him the opportunity of asking him to take part.[8]

Hinks' reservations about Kellas' health were well-founded, but once Collie pronounced himself in favour of Kellas for inclusion in the Everest Reconnaissance, Hinks went along with the recommendation. Hinks appears rather unforceful in all this, being swayed probably against his better judgement by Henry Kellas and then by Norman Collie, and endorsing the choice of a man who was clearly ill, to go on an expedition which was to result in his death. And though there is no connection directly between Kellas' mental illness and the physical cause of death, it appears likely – as we shall see – that Alec's increasing obsession with Everest led him to neglect his personal welfare in the last months of his life, and that the resulting decline in his physical condition undermined his general health and in all possibility hastened his demise.

In any event, right up to the moment of his departure for India, Kellas was informing Hinks that he was still being troubled by aural hallucinations. For example, in early February 1920, Kellas wrote to Hinks while on leave in Aberdeen (Kellas, 5 February 1920): 'What I complained of before has gone on day and night since then, and I have therefore consulted several specialists both in London and here who can find nothing wrong whatever, physically or mentally.' A month later, Kellas again wrote to Hinks from Aberdeen 'As the aural trouble has continued for some time, I have resigned from my post at the Middlesex Hospital, and am to take a good holiday before starting systematic work again.'[9] Prevailing medical theory gave him hope that open-air activity in the mountains would be a legitimate means of ridding himself of the unsettling disturbance. Hence, with the support of the government of India, the Admiralty, and the RGS, Kellas readied himself for the Kamet expedition in the spring of 1920.

Much of the scientific equipment the Kamet trip would need was requested from the Oxygen Research Committee of the Admiralty. On 22 April 1920, approximately one week before he was to sail for Bombay, Kellas drafted a rather extensive letter to the Oxygen Research Committee outlining his expedition plans and equipment needs (Kellas, 22 April 1920).

It is obvious, when looking through this list of scientific apparatus requested by Kellas, that examination of the efficacy of two forms of supplementary oxygen – chemically produced via Oxylithe vs. bottled oxygen in steel cylinders – for improving climbing performance at high altitude, was a primary scientific aim of the expedition. The oxygen apparatus requested from the Oxygen Research Committee reads (in part) as follows;

> 72 oxygen cylinders
> 2 Leonard Hill bags, capacity 60 liters each
> Oxylithe for Hill's bag_45 lbs.?
> Caustic soda for Hill's bag_20 lbs.?
> 3 Airmen's lined helmets
> 3 sets of valves and connections to oxygen
> cylinders with volume recorders, etc.[10]

This oxygen apparatus, as well as numerous other pieces of scientific equipment, was to be sent to Kellas at Niti, Upper Garhwal, such that it would reach there by 31 July 1920. Why Kellas waited so near to his sailing date to make the equipment request is a bit of a mystery. One could surmise that the question of whether Kellas was capable of such an undertaking in his present state of health was of concern to a number of people including the expedition sponsors and Kellas himself, up until very shortly before his projected departure date for India. Perhaps this question lingered for some months in early 1920 prior to all parties committing to the venture.

It is certainly not an overstatement to suggest that Kellas had given much preparatory thought to the research he was planning to undertake on Kamet. In the manuscript titled 'Report upon Expedition to Ascend Kamet (25,447ft), and Investigate the Physiological Effects of High Altitude' sent from India by Kellas to the RGS in the month (December 1920) after completion of the Kamet expedition, and published only in part in the *Geographical Journal* as 'Dr Kellas' Expedition to Kamet' and in the *Alpine Journal* as 'Dr Kellas' Expedition to Kamet in 1920', Kellas outlined the expedition's intended experiments and observations;

I
Experiments as to the possibility of using cylinders of compressed oxygen in ascents of the loftier Himalaya.

II

Investigation of utility of Prof. Leonard Hill's rubber bag and Oxy-lithe in a similar connection.

III

Observations regarding incidence of 'Mountain Sickness.'

IV

Observations as to the possibility of acclimatization to high altitudes.

V

Observations regarding suitable diet for high altitudes.

VI

Experiments with Major Flack's mercury manometer to test any variation of strength and energy with increase of altitude.

VII

Estimation of haemoglobin values at different heights.

VIII

Determination of the variation of the number of red and white corpuscles at different altitudes.

IX

Determination of the variation of alveolar oxygen and carbon dioxide with altitude, by means of Prof. Haldane's apparatus.

X

Observations regarding the cooling power of the atmosphere at high altitudes, using Prof. Hill's wet and dry bulb thermometers – Kata-thermometry.

XI

Observations of meteorological conditions with maximum and minimum thermometers, wet and dry bulb hygrometers, etc.[11]

It had been arranged for part of the scientific apparatus to be delivered by the Indian Stores Department to the railway terminus of Kathgodam, approximately 400km from Kamet, by early July 1920. Most of the remainder of the scientific equipment was to be delivered to the village of Niti, about 64km from Kamet, by the end of July. Kellas started from Darjeeling (a very familiar base for him), the legendary British hill station perched in the foothills of the Himalayas in the northern extreme of the Indian state of West Bengal, on 25 June. He arrived at Kathgodam three days later, expecting to find his supplies waiting. However, Kellas found that no apparatus had arrived from England, and it was only after a delay of many weeks that all requisite material for the planned experimental program arrived at Kathgodam. This very serious delay was due to shipping problems associated with the oxygen cylinders and to the discovery that the very light oxygen cylinders, which passed their tests when newly made, lost strength rapidly and were not safe.

Apparently an unexpected decision was made by the shipping authorities in England to classify the cylinders as 'high explosives' after the initial delay when the Oxygen Research Committee decided it necessary to send heavier cylinders. Finally, on 4 August 1920, Morshead, who was to join the expedition in about two weeks' time, wrote to the RGS informing them that 'the apparatus has all duly arrived' and that the expedition was now underway for Niti. This unfortunate delay in Kellas's start meant he had to abandon his plans for 'comparative observations on acclimatization en route'. The primary mission became pushing forward with all possible speed in the endeavor to reach high altitude before the onset of winter conditions, with the hope that the comparative observations could be accomplished on the return journey.

The key to the eventual ascent of Kamet was found by CF Meade. After a short east-side reconnaissance in 1912, in 1913 he navigated a way through the east Kamet Glacier and ascended to over 23,000ft. Here he set up camp at the wide col (subsequently designated Meade's Col) between Kamet itself and East Abi Gamin, the mountain's subsidiary peak. Subsequent attempts on the mountain, including the successful ascent involving Shipton and Smythe in 1931, followed this route.

Meade had suffered from altitude sickness on his attempt and encountered a stiff bit of work above camp at 21,000ft in the form of a steep rock and ice slope that persisted for approximately a thousand feet:

> We found the ascent of the precipice trying owing to the quantities of fresh snow lying all over the rocks. Bhotias are in their element wherever there are crags to be climbed, but snow-covered rock is not what they are accustomed to, and consequently we had some anxious moments when the men launched themselves on to this snow-bound face, heavily laden as they were. A slip would have been fatal... however, all the men climbed admirably, and at last we found ourselves on the supreme promontory of the precipice, where it abutted on the snow- or ice-slope that formed a sort of forehead just under-

neath the spacious plateau leading to the saddle, as we had noticed from the camp. It was disconcerting when we came to the 'forehead' to find that it was a slope of steep, tough ice... [necessitating] prolonged step-cutting. At the top of the 'forehead' began the lofty glacier-plateau sloping at an easy angle up to the saddle between Kamet and Eastern Ibi Gamin.[12]

Meade's attempt stalled at just over 23,000ft – a short distance above the saddle, or Col, that bears his name – his party finding that the deep snow and the team's exhaustion conspired to halt the progress of that year's effort.

Both Kellas and Morshead wrote up accounts of the 1920 attempt on Kamet, Kellas for the Oxygen Reasearch Committee and Morshead for the Surveyor-General of India. The bulk of both of these accounts was published in the *Geographical Journal* for 1921.[13] Morshead's account is the more detailed on the actual mountaineering, and differs from that of Kellas on slight points of details such as dates, heights and camps. Given Alec's repeated sloppiness over such things, we are probably safe in taking Morshead's version concerning such details.

The pair left Niti on 29 August with 21 yaks and 40 porters. It is worth recording that on this occasion the personnel was much greater than Kellas had been accustomed to using in Sikkim. Part of the reason for this was undoubtedly the need for extra porterage caused by the transport of the scientific equipment Kellas required for his oxygen experiments. Partly however, the greater numbers were due to the addition, not so much of Morshead himself to the expedition, but also of his transport officer and 11 attendants, who were to carry out survey work during the expedition. These personnel included Laltan Khan who subsequently produced the first accurate map of Kamet. The provisioning of such a large group – which did not work perfectly – was undoubtedly a reason for its slow progress late in the season, compounding problems caused by the delays already incurred. These factors stand as probable contributions to the failure of the attempt on Kamet in 1920. This expedition was not 'Classic Kellas'.

On August 31 the party reached base camp at the end of the Raikana Glacier. Morshead records that;

From the Raikane base camp our route was identical with that of C.F. Meade in 1913, and led over the moraines and crevasses of the

east Kamet glacier for a distance of ten miles... We were fortunate
in having with us some of Meade's old coolies, whose knowledge of
previous camping grounds proved invaluable...[14]

Delays in obtaining provisions to allow the large party to proceed held
then back till 3 September when they moved along the glacier to establish
another camp at 16,800ft. Further delays in obtaining sufficient wood to
proceed meant they next moved on 10 September (Kellas gives 8 September
for this move forward) and established a further camp at 18,500ft Kellas
calls this Camp Three, whereas Meade designates it merely as Camp Two,
a usage we will follow.

Kellas describes the route ahead from Camp Two (Kellas Camp Three):

The increase of height between this third camp and the saddle – namely,
5,000ft – consisted firstly of 2,500ft of sharp ascent, chiefly steep
scree, but partly debris–covered glacier, then came 1,000ft of precipitous rock, and finally about 1,700ft of snow and ice.[15]

On 11 September the party moved over the steep screes and established
Camp Three (Kellas 4) at 21,000ft. There appear to have been no technical difficulties in gaining this height at Camp Three, though progress
was undeniably slow. Partly this was because Kellas, with Morshead
acceding to his views on the matter, believed that slow acclimatisation
would help them avoid the altitude associated debilities experienced by
Meade. But it is clear that they were making a virtue of necessity.
Problems with porter indiscipline, and illness, as well as insufficient
supplies of wood and food slowed the party down. Indeed Meade stated
bluntly that 'the daily convoy of provisions and firewood ceased to
function...', and he left Camp Three on 15 September and went back
down valley to deal with some of these issues, not returning till 17
September, thus leading to further delay.

Finally on 19 September the party moved from Camp Three (Kellas 4)
to Camp Four (Kellas 5) at a height of approximately 22,000ft, Kellas
simply states that 'On September 19 we climbed the rocks, and formed
a camp on snow at approximately 22,000ft.' A certain understatement is
evident here, which is corrected in Morshead's account. The attempt to
prepare to climb this section had actually started two days after Camp
Three (Kellas 4) was reached on 11 September.

The majority of the coolies showed signs of distress and complained
of violent headaches on arrival at this altitude; we accordingly sent

them back to the last camp, keeping only two as guides for the 600ft of rock climbing which lay ahead. After a day's halt for acclimatization we successfully reconnoitred the rock face on the 13th, finally emerging at the top on to a smooth dome of glassy ice, up which we had time to cut 45 large steps before returning to camp – a delightful day of real mountaineering.[16]

In Morshead's absence down valley from 15 to 17 September Kellas had ascended to the previously gained high point with the remaining two porters/guides and cut another 35 ice steps to successfully complete this section of the route, and thus when they climbed to Camp Four (Kellas 5) on 19 September it was over a well reconnoitred and prepared route.

When Smythe and his party climbed this section of Kamet in 1931, they found the route from Camp Three to Camp Four hard going. A full account of this section of the ascent of Kamet is given in Chapter XII of *Kamet Conquered* (1931), where it is clear to the reader that this is serious high altitude mountaineering of technical difficulty, and that Smythe was not certain of success. Smythe comments that,

Above Camp Three is a steep rock and ice face nearly 1,000ft high. As this was plastered with new snow and promised difficulties, we decided to make Camp Three our advanced base...

The Meade and Kellas expeditions experienced no great difficulty beyond a bout of step-cutting in ice while climbing the face above Camp Three, but now, owing to the snow and ice covered rocks, it took us three days to work out a safe and practicable route for porters. We first of all prospected a wide couloirs running up between the icefall to the right of the face and the cliffs of the Eastern Ibi Gamin, but this proved much too dangerous. Finally, two separate parties worked out a route slanting diagonally in its lower portion from left to right across the face and then directly upwards. Six hundred feet of rope fastened to pitons had to be fixed before it was safe for porters unaccompanied by Europeans. Fortunately we were spared the bout of step-cutting found necessary by Meade and Kellas in the upper portion, owing to a foot or more of firm snow covering the ice.[17]

Or, as Smythe was to put it subsequently after mature reflection in his book of the expedition, *Kamet Conquered*, 'It was the first time in my Himalayan experience that anything Himalayan had proved possible when it looked impossible, and I felt it to be a happy omen.'[18] It is

KAMET, CAMPS THREE TO FOUR.
This shows the difficult ground between Camps Three and Four which caused Smythe and his party so much trouble on the first ascent. Alec Kellas climbed it (with porters) and prepared the route for himself and Morshead to move to Camp Four.
(Frank Smythe, courtesy of the Smythe Estate)

testimony to Alec Kellas' skill as a mountaineer by 1920, that he, alone with his porters, prepared a route to Camp Four on Kamet which later caused Smythe and his party such difficulty. Kellas and Morshead stayed at Camp Four on 20 September, according to Kellas to allow acclimatization to take place though Morshead attributes this more to having to send the porters back down on the evening of 19 September, to bring up cooked food for the party on 20 September as cooking was almost impossible at that height with the stoves the party had, and firewood could not be portered up the rock-face. On 21 September they headed for Meade's Col, hoping to make Camp Five (Kellas 6). That day is best described in Morshead's words,

> The thermometer next morning registered a minimum night temperature of 15 degrees below zero on the surface of the snow, and our blankets were as stiff as boards where one's breath had congealed on them. Rising from our beds on the snow was therefore more than the work of a moment. However, after heating ourselves a tin of soup on the spirit stove and thawing sufficient snow to fill the thermos flask with Bovril, we started at 9 a.m. – our two selves and three coolies on the rope. Taking the lead in turns, and steering a winding course to avoid the giant crevasses, we gradually emerged onto the wide flat valley which separates Kamet from E. Ibi Gamin. On our left the summit of Kamet showed clearly 2,000ft above us, connected to the valley by two well-defined arêtes of easy slope. Either of which must have been easily climbable, had time permitted. It was now 3 p.m. however and our coolies were dead beat, so after a brief halt for food and a round of photographs, we had to turn regretfully homewards from Meade's col to avoid being benighted. The view from this col is magnificent, comprising the whole Tibetan portion of the Sutlej valley to the north, while 100 miles to the east- south-east the stupendous massif of Gurla Mandhata towered head and shoulders above the intervening army of lesser ranges.
>
> Had we been able to induce the coolies to carry our camp one march further forward to the flat, open neve near Meade's Col, it is hard to believe that anything could have prevented our reaching the summit.[19]

Kellas is briefer, merely stating that the porters,

> ... refused to entertain the idea of moving a camp up to the saddle,

alleging that the winter storm was due, and that we would be snowed up. The threatened incidence of this winter storm had been their continual complaint since reaching Camp No. Three, but otherwise the men from Mana village (10,000ft [3,048m]), some of whom were coolies who had been with me previously in 1911 and 1914, behaved very well, and indeed were the mainstay of all the hard work carried out.[20]

Morshead says nothing of the descent but Kellas adds the comment that 'A considerable amount of step cutting was required, which was shared' – showing possibly that he had learned his lesson the hard way from his descent of Kangchenjau in 1911 when he and the porters fell due to insufficient attention given to protection on descent. Morshead himself ends his account of the expedition by expressing his highest praise for Kellas' skill as a mountaineer.

Could they have summitted?

One cannot simply take Morshead's belief that they could have done so at its face value. For example, the view from Meade's Col of the Kamet summit considerably foreshortens the angle of the final slope, which is much steeper than it appears. Smythe's account of this section in *Kamet Conquered* and his *Alpine Journal* article also show that it is – whilst technically not complicated – more than a simple snow plod. The route from the col to the summit consisted at times of unremitting 50 degree ice slopes, and took the party eight and a half hard hours from Meade's Col.

The snow, although soft, was at least consistent for the first few hundred feet, and we mounted at quite 500ft an hour. But then it became progressively worse. From straightforward stamping we were reduced to floundering frequently over the knees in the vilest stuff we had ever encountered. The whole weight would be put on the foot and then the crust would break and the leg would go in to the knee. Rhythm, so important in high altitude climbing, could not be maintained. Taking it in turns to lead, we toiled upwards. Here and there were choked crevasses, the upper lips of which sometimes necessitated some toilful kicking or cutting, but these crevasses were securely bridged. Our pace dropped from about 500ft an hour to about 200ft...

The ascent of [the final] 300ft... to the summit ridge will remain in the memory of all of us as the most exacting and exhausting piece of climbing any of us have ever endured. The slope was very steep, consisting of loose snow and skavala overlying hard, icy snow. Steps had to be made, since the penalty of a slip was the great eastern precipice. I remember that towards the top I drove my ice-axe in before me, with both hands hauling myself up on it while kicking steps with feeble viciousness. We were in a cold shadow, but a few yards above the declining sun illuminated a small flake of ice on the summit ridge with a clear gleam. We were drawing on our reserves of energy. Faculties were numbed, action automatic.[21]

However, when one considers that Kellas, initially without and later in the company of, Morshead managed the ascent between Camps Three and Four with equal – if not greater – facility than Smythe's party over a decade later, it must be at the very least a reasonable assertion to say that, had Kellas and Morshead been able to induce the porters to establish camp on Meade's Col, they would have had a realistic chance of attaining the summit of Kamet in 1920. It should also be pointed out that neither did Smythe's party find the ascent from Camp Four to Meade's Col as straightforward as Kellas and Morshead had done.

With his leave from the Survey of India coming to an end and the season now too far advanced for further efforts at the highest altitudes, Morshead bade farewell to Kellas on 22 September and turned his steps toward home. In his report on the Kamet expedition in the *Geographical Journal* Morshead later discussed what he believed to be the primary reasons underlying the failure to reach the summit: (1) Lateness in the year due to unforeseen delay in the arrival of oxygen cylinders from England, (2) failure of porters recruited from the middle Himalayas to stand the climate and altitude of the higher ranges, and (3) inadequacy of arrangements for cooking at high altitudes. The expedition's primus stoves were very inefficient above 6,100m, and they discovered that their one small methylated spirit stove was far superior at the higher altitudes (though too small for all the cooking chores). 'Lack of properly cooked food, combined with the intense cold, had however undermined the stamina of the coolies, who absolutely refused to carry forward any further loads.' as Morshead stated. Regardless of the disappointments encountered during the expedition, Morshead had nothing but praise for the few Bhotia porters of the higher Himalaya that had joined the expedition. His following assessment suggests a very perceptive grasp of the shape of things to come,

ROUTE TO KAMET SUMMIT FROM CAMP FIVE.
With the tracks of Smythe and his party showing, this may look an easy route to the summit from Camp Five. But as Smythe says in *Kamet Conquered*, the slope is much steeper than it appears. But the possibility of a Kellas/Morshead summit was there.
(Frank Smythe, courtesy of the Smythe Estate)

On rock they can climb like goats, while on ice they readily learn step-cutting.

It appears very doubtful if the present-day expense of importing Alpine guides can ever justify their employment in future Himalayan exploration.[22]

After several frustrating and unsuccessful days of attempting to induce his remaining porters to help him to pitch a camp on a pass between the Raikana Glacier and the Ganeshganga valley to the north for purposes of facilitating the completion of several physiological experiments, Kellas decided retreat was in order. A double march was made to Niti on 1 October with the ambitious intention of visiting the area of the Bagini Glacier to the southeast (closer to Nanda Devi) for the purpose of setting a high camp on Dunagiri (7,066m) in order to continue physiological experimentation. Reaching Dunagiri village (3,399m) on 5 October, approximately three day's march from the mountain of the same name, Kellas quickly began to realize that his present group of porters were no more mentally or physically prepared for the rigors of cold and high altitude than were most of the men he had employed on Kamet earlier in the season. Thus, it became clear that the idea of placing a high camp at 6,248m on Dunagiri was untenable. Kellas eventually settled for a camp at approximately 5,486m on a considerably smaller peak to the northwest of the Bagini Glacier. After a week's worth of experimental work at this camp, Dunagiri village was regained on 16 October, with Kellas eventually returning to Darjeeling on 9 November after an absence of four and a half months.

In a letter written to Hinks in mid-November 1920, shortly after his return to Darjeeling, Kellas expressed his intent to organize a small expedition for a return to Kamet in 1921 in order to complete the ascent. Aside from simply wanting to make the first ascent of Kamet, Kellas wished to undertake a systematic investigation of the completeness of human adaptation to altitudes in excess of 7,000m, as this would have been invaluable information for the projected ascent of Everest. However, Kellas's receipt and acceptance of the Everest Committee's invitation to join the 1921 Everest Reconnaissance Expedition while wintering in Darjeeling, and his subsequent demise on that trip, meant that there would be no return to Kamet in 1921.

The Kamet expedition of 1920 did yield useful results with regard to the value of supplementary oxygen for high altitude mountaineering. The 72 oxygen tanks sent from England were approximately three times heavier than Kellas had planned for, but the lighter tanks he was expecting turned out to be unsafe and heavier models were shipped out to India instead. Upon receipt of the heavier tanks at Kathgodam, Kellas was almost certain they would prove to be too heavy for high altitude work. The weight of each tank with regulator, nearly 9kg [and capacity of 300 litres], was as much as Kellas believed most porters were able to manage as a load even at 6,100m. Preliminary experiments on Kamet at 6,400m confirmed that they were unsuitable, but not until Kellas reached the 5,486m camp on a smaller peak to the northwest of the Bagini Glacier (after Kamet was abandoned) was there an opportunity for systematic experiments designed to determine the usefulness of the oxygen tanks for practical climbing work. During the week of work in the vicinity of the 5,486m camp, climbing trials with the oxygen tanks were carried out over three different courses: (1) a long course involving an easy snow ascent of approximately 1,000m and return, (2) a medium course involving an ascent of 200m over rough snow and return by a rock scree, and (3) a short ascent along a stony arête of about 70m. Regardless of the course undertaken, the porters Kellas enlisted for these experiments consistently had greater elapsed times *with* supplementary oxygen from the cylinders than without. He concluded, no doubt rightly, that 'the cylinders are too heavy for use above 18,000ft, and below that altitude they are not required. They would be quite useless during an attempt on Mount Everest'. A possible resolution to this problem that Kellas proposed in the same report, but ultimately never had the opportunity to test, involved experiments

> with cylinders of double the capacity filled to half the pressure, so that a light cylinder similar to that shown to me in 1919 by Colonel Stewart could be safely employed. A volume of 140 litres of oxygen might be helpful, if the weight of the cylinder were not above, say, 7 lbs.[23]

Interestingly, Kellas does not discuss oxygen flow rates utilized (or suggested) with this open-circuit system in the published report. However, examination of correspondence in the RGS archives shows that he had suggested 1.5 to 2 litres/minute when climbing at altitudes over 6,000m (Secretary, 6 February 1919). Given the weight of the oxygen delivery system that Kellas used on this expedition, it is hardly surprising that there was no improvement in ascent rate with its use. The oxygen flow rate of 3.5 to 5 litres/minute then recommended for airmen operating at altitudes near 6,000m would have been appropriate for high altitude mountaineering as well in 1920.

As well as experimenting with oxygen cylinders, Kellas also tried out a further method of obtaining supplementary oxygen at altitude. Professor Leonard Hill of University College, London, suggested that Kellas carry out practical climbing trials using rubber bags containing oxylithe (sodium peroxide), which produces oxygen when water is added. When sodium peroxide combines with the water of expired gas, oxygen is liberated with the formation of sodium hydroxide (NaOH). The NaOH then absorbs expired CO_2 to give sodium bicarbonate. Therefore, oxylithe has the dual property of both generating oxygen and absorbing CO_2.

In the event, Kellas performed two sets of experiments with the Hill bags. In the first set the subjects breathed oxygen from a bag freshly filled with Oxylithe and caustic soda for about five minutes, shaking the bag from time to time to promote absorption of CO_2. The subjects were then timed negotiating the short course described previously without breathing any additional supplementary oxygen. After the subjects had rested for approximately 15 minutes, a repeat experiment was carried out without breathing from the Hill bag prior to climbing. 'As a rule the times were practically identical, so that it seemed that no benefit accrued from breathing oxygen while resting, and that the excess amount in the lungs at starting was of negligible value in promoting ascent.'[24] Kellas indicated that this result was predictable based on what was known about the very limited stores of oxygen in the body. Subsequent high altitude mountaineers have not always been aware of this. In the spring of 1952 a Swiss team, attempting the then unclimbed South Col route on Mount Everest, barely missed making the first ascent, and might well have been successful were it not for misguided reliance on an oxygen system that was only useful when the climbers were at rest. (It can also be argued that the Swiss were seriously handicapped as well by lack of adequate hydration during their time at extreme altitude.)

The second set of experiments performed with the Hill apparatus required *continuous* breathing from the freshly filled bag during ascent. No special provisions had been made for attaching this equipment to the user, so it had to be rather inconveniently carried under the arm. Regardless, Kellas indicated that during these trials 'the gain while using oxygen was quite decisive, the advantage being up to 25 per cent. This again was to be expected, and clearly indicates that the light oxygen cylinders suggested above might be of considerable value as regards increase of rate of ascent at high altitudes'.[25]

As well as these experiments on oxygen, Kellas was interested in estimating times of ascent by mountaineers in oxygen depleted atmospheres. He had a great interest in trying to determine if a relationship existed between oxygen pressure in the lungs (known as alveolar oxygen pressure in medical circles), breath-holding time, and possible rate of ascent at high altitudes. In his paper on the possibility of ascending Everest, he takes into account alveolar oxygen pressures when he calculates the expected rate of ascent at 29,000ft [8,839m] (Table 8 in Kellas, 2001).

TABLE 8
Calculation of rate of ascent at 29,000ft. From the amount of oxygen required while walking at 4 and 5 miles per hour respectively at Sea Level

Energy	Altitude feet	Alveolar oxygen pressure	Oxygen absorbed per minute calculated at 0°c and 760mm.	Oxygen available for climbing after subtraction of 400 cc. as a constant factor for vital processes	Rate of climbing in ft. per hour
Energy used corresponds to 5 miles per hour at sea level	16,000	49.5	2000 c.c.	1600 c.c.	1,000
	23,000	33.0	1333	933	584
	29,000	24.0	970	570	356
Energy used corresponds to 4 miles per hour at sea level	16,000	49.5	1600 c.c.	1200 c.c.	1,000
	23,000	33.0	1068	668	557
	29,000	24.0	776	376	313

It is evident to the reader of the Kamet report that Kellas was rather disappointed with the relatively small scientific return of the expedition. As an example of the problems the expedition encountered in attempting to complete the intended research program, the late arrival of the scientific apparatus rendered impossible a thorough study of acclimatization rates as evidenced by the alteration of haemoglobin value. Late arrival of the scientific apparatus also affected Kellas's ability to determine the variation of the number of red and white corpuscles at different altitudes. However, factors other than slow equipment transport and consequent late season conditions contributed to the expedition's investigative difficulties. Certainly one of the more interesting and important aims of the scientific program was to be the determination of variation of alveolar oxygen and carbon dioxide at different altitudes using Haldane apparatus. After some preliminary work with the apparatus early on in the expedition, studies with this equipment soon ground to a halt when a tap started to leak, followed closely by a broken water jacket and then a broken case.

As stated above, Kellas intended to rectify the deficiencies and problems of the 1920 expedition in an attempt on Kamet the following year. Plans were taking shape in the autumn of 1920 and early months of 1921 for a return, but were put on hold when Kellas received (and accepted) an invitation from the Mount Everest Committee to accompany the 1921 Everest Reconnaissance Expedition. Regardless, the 1920 Kamet Expedition provided strong support for the use of supplementary oxygen at high altitude, provided it could be supplied in a relatively lightweight form. After Kellas died on the approach march to Everest in June of 1921, insufficient interest and technical expertise in the oxygen systems guaranteed neglect of the apparatus by other expedition members.

Thanks to the efforts of George Ingle Finch, the 1922 Everest Expedition made reasonably extensive use of supplementary oxygen for high altitude climbing. However, the pioneering experiments of Kellas were virtually ignored, even though the scientific results of the Kamet expedition were published in February 1921. The British mountaineering establishment did not again have a proponent such as Alexander Mitchell Kellas, willing and able to systematically evaluate the value of supplementary oxygen for climbing at high altitude, until physiologist Griffith Pugh once again took up the challenge in the early 1950s in preparation for the successful 1953 ascent of Everest.

NOTES

[1]   Schlagintweit A, Schlagintweit R, 'A Short Account of the Journey from Milum in Johar, to Gartok in the upper Indus Valley, and of the ascent to the Ibi Gamin Peak'. *Journal of the Asiatic Society of Bengal* (1856) No. 25, pp.125–133.

[2]   Kellas to Lumley 21.10.19 (RGS Archives)

3   Eaton to Kellas 21.11.1919 (Alpine Club Archives)
4   Kellas to Eaton 17.1.1920 (Alpine Club Archives)
5   Kellas AM 'A Consideration of the Possibility of Ascending Mount Everest', *High Altitude Medicine and Biology*, 2001.
     A detailed analysis of Kellas' 1920 manuscript was undertaken by John B West in 1987 for the *Journal of Applied Physiology*. This article titled 'Alexander M. Kellas and the Physiological Challenge of Mt Everest' was actually the first detailed treatment of Kellas' life and work to appear in English – only some 50 plus years after several German authors paid tribute! West's article was a great improvement on previous studies of Kellas, largely because it dealt with Kellas' altitude-related scientific interests, not just his Himalayan exploration and climbing. Permission from Professor West and the American Physiological Society has allowed us to reproduce the section of the 1987 article dealing with the 1920 manuscript in Appendix 1 of this book.
6   Hinks AR to Henry Kellas. (Archives of the RGS), 20.3.1920.
7   Henry Kellas to Hinks 23.3.1920 (RGS Archives). We are indebted to Fiona Watson of Grampian NHS archives for the information on Professor Mackintosh.
8   Hinks to Norman Collie 22.12.1920 (RGS Archives).
9   Kellas AM to AR Hinks. (Archives of the RGS), 7.3.1920.
10   Kellas AM to the Oxygen Research Committee Secretary. (Archives of the Royal Geographical Society), 22.4.1920.
11   Kellas AM to the Oxygen Research Committee Secretary. (Archives of RGS), 22.4. 1920.
12   Meade, CF, *Approach to the Hills* (1940), pp.249–250.
13   *Geographical Journal* (1921) No. 57, pp.124–30 (for Kellas) and pp.213–219 (for Morshead). Laltan Khan's map of Kamet from 1920 is reproduced in Morshead's article on p.216.
14   Morshead, *GJ* Op.Cit., p.215.
15   Kellas, *GJ* Op.Cit., p.125.
16   Morshead, *GJ* Op.Cit., p.217
17   Smythe, FS (1931). 'The Kamet expedition, 1931', *Alpine Journal*, 43, (1930), p.297.
18   *Kamet Conquered*, Frank Smythe (1932) p.160.
19   Morshead, *GJ* Op.Cit., pp.217–218.
20   Kellas AM *GJ* Op.Cit., p.126
21   Smythe, FS (1931). 'The Kamet expedition', 1931. *Alpine Journal*, 43, (1930), pp.299–300.

22 Morshead HT. *GJ* Op.Cit., p.219

23 Kellas AM. *GJ* Op.Cit., p.127

24 Kellas AM. *GJ* Op.Cit., p.127. It is thus something of a mystery why Kellas ordered additional NaOH, or caustic soda, from the Oxygen Research Committee. Given his knowledge of chemistry, one would think that Kellas was not confused about this issue. However, he did list a question mark after 'caustic soda' on the list he sent to the Oxygen Research Committee (as noted above). It is not outside the realm of possibility that he thought additional NaOH added to the Oxylithe was insurance against rising CO_2 levels in the closed system after prolonged periods of use. Conceivably, this additional NaOH might have permitted a longer period of use of the Hill bag before recharging it became a necessity. Recharging the bag with Oxylithe and/or NaOH in a high altitude field setting would undoubtedly be an unsavory task.

25 Kellas AM. *GJ* Op.Cit., p.128

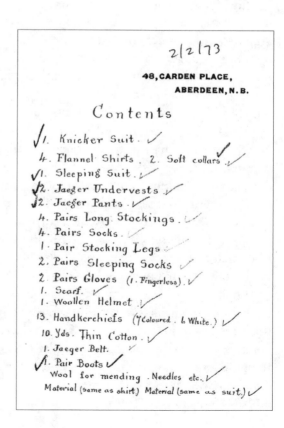

KIT LIST.

Alec's handwritten kit list for his trip to the Himalaya in 1920. Mountaineers would expect something a bit more high-tech today, and would probably take fewer handkerchiefs.

(RGS Collections)

CHAPTER EIGHT

Sikkim and Everest 1920–21

No Country for Middle-Aged Men?

AFTER THE FAILURE of the attempt to climb Kamet, Kellas found himself back in Sikkim and he took up residence at The Pines Hotel at Ghum near Darjeeling at the beginning of November 1920. Having no job – or family ties – which demanded his return to Britain, and in high expectation of being invited to join the Everest Reconnaissance scheduled for 1921, he decided to spend the entire winter in India. There he intended to do what he did best and enjoyed most. That is, to carry out further explorations in the company of his Sherpa guides. And whilst it is true to say that the area around Kangchenjunga was the main focus of his activities before 1914, on his return to Sikkim it was Everest, its approaches and the technical difficulties its ascent posed, which now loomed largest in his mind, carrying forward the obsession with the conquest of the mountain which had dominated his thinking during the war itself.

Kellas' death meant he never wrote up his exploits in Sikkim in 1920–21, as he had done in journal articles detailing much of his pre-war exploration between 1907 and 1911. However, while in Sikkim between the Kamet expedition in 1920 and that to Everest in 1921 he was in regular correspondence with both Arthur Hinks at the Royal Geographical Society and with Norman Collie of the Everest Committee. As these letters have never been published, and as only the briefest reference to them has been made elsewhere, their contents will form the backbone of our narrative of Kellas' final journeys through Sikkim.

On his return from Kamet, Kellas had made a trip to the Kabru region, and after coming back from this, wrote to Collie in January 1921 from the hotel at Ghum, where he appears to have been comfortably ensconsed, commenting, 'This hotel is owned by a Scotswoman, and consists of six bungalows of which I have had one for my sole use, which is quiet and convenient',[1] whilst to another correspondent he wrote that 'The above address will find me for a long time.'[2]

India had changed since Alec had last been there in 1911. The war had given an enormous impetus to the nationalist independence movement led by Ghandi's Congress Party, and much of India was in a state of turmoil. In addition the Amritsar Massacre in 1919 had dealt a body blow to the moral authority of the British in the sub-continent. But in the stations in the Himalayan foothills, always the favourite resort of the colonial ruling class, life went on – apparently – much as before. In his *Through Tibet to Everest* Noel describes life at Darejeeling after the war. Reached by the crazy loops and zig-zags of the miniature Himalayan Railway, where tigers and elephants were obstacles on the track, life in the town centred round clubs like the Gymkhana where a quartet played day and night and consisted of endless parties followed by dawn rickshaw rides to watch the sunrise over Kangchenjunga. Alec was apparently as little aware of, or interested in, the political awakening taking place in the vast sub-continent, as he was of, or in, the social life of the settler set. He had quite other preoccupations in his increasingly parallel universe.

DARJEELING HILL RAILWAY.
The crazy little hill railway that led to the servants of the Raj's paradise in Darjeeling.
The Everest Expedition of 1921 got free passage from the railway company for its men
and goods. Elephants and tigers on the track added to the excitement.

At the end of the previous November Kellas had set off for the Nepal frontier via Dzongri through thick mist, but he rose through this at 10,000ft and spent a month 'in nearly continuous sunshine' and 'reached the Kang La without fresh snow falling.' From here Kellas took various telephotographic shots towards Mount Everest, further stating that 'It is my intention to write a short illustrated account of the phases of Mt. Everest from the East' – and adding that he hoped to measure the heights of certain unsurveyed peaks captured in his images. Kellas was clearly beefing up his credentials with regard to a possible invitation to join the actual Everest expedition.

As we saw earlier Hinks at the Royal Geographical Society had allowed his doubts over Kellas' health to be put on one side, especially after Collie's strong endorsement of Kellas. At the end of December 1920 Hinks had written to Kellas informing him that all political objections to the reconnaissance had been overcome and sounding Kellas out about the possibility of his joining the party. Grabbing the bull by the horns, Kellas not only gave his agreement in principle to join the expedition, but sent a long letter to Hinks containing his opinions on various matters concerning such an undertaking. The forcefulness of this letter rather undermines the accepted image of Alec as shy and unassuming, and shows a strong determination on his part not only to be included in the expedition, but to influence its programme, especially on the question of using European guides.

> My dear Hinks,
>
> Many thanks for your interesting letter of 30th Decr. just received. I had of course seen in the Press that the Royal Geographical Society had overcome the political difficulties against an expedition to Mt. Everest.
>
> The rough draft of the scheme proposed seems to me to be admirable, and I am thoroughly in agreement with the President's opinion that this year's reconnaissance party should not only select a route, but should if possible push up to at least 25,000ft
>
> As regards the joining of the reconnaissance party if asked to do so either by the Royal Geographical Society or the Alpine Club, I would naturally be very glad to have the opportunity, and would consider myself honoured by the request.
>
> ...

So far as my knowledge of the mountain goes, the S.E. arête may probably be the best route, but the N.E. arête seems practicable, although of extraordinary length. If the S.E. arête proves to be the best on close examination, the route to be followed would be up the N.E. Mount Everest glacier to a Col. between Mount Everest and the peak to the S.E. visible in the photographs sent, and in the well known view from Sandakhpu. A base camp could be readily formed near the Col. At a height of about 22,500ft, from which camps could be pushed towards the summit. The west side of the mountain is unknown and might modify the procedure.

From what you say I gather that the advance will be made through Tibet, and that probably Dingri and Kharta will be bases for supply. If it has not already been done it might be advisable to ask the Nepalese government to allow the use of the Kampa Dzong, Saar, Nila La, Tashiraka and Hatiya route...

...

There is one point connected with the ascent on which I might venture to give you my private opinion. The question will probably arise as to whether the expedition should be guided or guideless. I am strongly of the opinion that the whole expedition should be guideless, and that to employ European guides in connection with reconnaissance work would probably be useless.

Mountaineering is a sport, and may be learned either from professional guides, from one's friends – who would rarely take the responsibility, especially for snow and ice work, or from personal experience, the latter being the most dangerous method. Having learned the sport, one should be able to act alone. Golf and cricket are comparable sports from some points of view, and may be learned by similar methods, but one should not be allowed expert advice – which one might not agree with – during a real game of either.

In my opinion the Expedition would be to some extent spoiled if any foreign guides are employed. Their use would be a reproach to all concerned, and would seem to indicate that we had not learned the technique of the game...

We have at hand mountaineers who rapidly learn the use of the ice-axe, and are good on rocks. Three of the men who were with me on Kamet last year are very good climbers and their services could probably be obtained, as they agreed to come back to Kamet this year.

...

I am aware that my opinion may be regarded as somewhat hetero-dox, and that first rate men like Meade will probably be against me, and I can only say that if guides be taken, I will work with them to the best of my power, if asked to be a member of the reconnaissance party. I might add that foreign guides would not be as efficient as they are in Europe because the problems of acclimatisation and mountain lassitude are there practically non-existent.[3]

By the time Hinks received Kellas' communication, the former was able to reply both that Kellas was 'now a fully accredited member of the expedition' and that,

There is a general agreement with you that European guides are a mistake in the Himalaya – Meade quite concurs and we have not the slightest intention of using them.[4]

Meanwhile Alec had been busy studying his photographs and maps and on 9 February sent an almost identical letter to both Hinks and Collie. We will use the letter to Hinks since it also contains Kellas' acceptance of a position on the Everest expedition,

Yesterday morning I received your cablegram from the special committee of the Royal geographical Society and the Alpine Club asking me to join the Mt. Everest Expedition, and I at once cabled acceptance as follows:–

'Geographical' London. Accept Committee's kind invitation join Everest Expedition. Kellas.'

As an aid to the interpretation of the telephotographs sent recently, I have worked out the positions of all the loftier peaks seen, and plotted their positions graphically so as to show their respective mileage from Mt. Everest...

My method of procedure was to calculate exactly the distance of Makalu from Peak N53, which I make to be 3.3 miles, and then work out the rest graphically from Latitudes and Longitudes.

The results are interesting. The great snow dome seen in all the photographs is 7 miles from Everest, and the rock peak of the same range about 12. The table shows the other relationships.

The length of Mt. Everest from N. to S. horizontally appears to be about 3 miles, which would make the N.N.E. arête about 4 miles long from the N.Col seen in Photo IV, without counting irregularities of course. This is the longest arête and is much shorter than the tremendous arêtes of Kangchenjunga. The S.E. arête is short.[5]

Kellas was before long back in the field again, and his next letter to Collie was received when he was camping at Dzongri to the south-east of the Kabru massif in early April 1921. Alec's supply of ink must have run out, as he replied to Collie's letter in pencil. Kellas informed Collie that he had ascended another virgin peak, though it was not one of his more notable achievements,

You may be interested to learn that a few days ago – 5 April – along with 4 Sherpas I was fortunate enough to be able to make an ascent of Narsing (19,130ft) from a camp at about 14,700ft. We were

MAKALU, EVEREST, CHOMOLONZO.
Kellas was making a composite panoramic telephoto image of the Everest range, and it can be seen from the photograph on p.131 that this image adjoins it directly. So far the other images, mentioned to Collie, have not been discovered.
(AM Kellas, RGS Collections)

favoured that day with exceptionally good weather, and the snow was in excellent condition.[6]

This climb may have been in the nature of a training day, as Kellas' main intention on this April trip was to climb Kabru. Part of the reason for climbing Kabru was because Kellas hoped that its summit's vantage point would give the best possible views towards the Everest region and be of great help in the forthcoming Reconnaissance. Kellas had already taken telephoto images back in December 1920 from the Kang La, and on this later trip he pushed further, noting in the above letter 'on the 26th March I crossed that pass to the N. of the Kang La (which is not correctly given on any map) and ascended the highest peak to the W. of the Kang La Nangma, the extreme N.W. point overlooking the Yalung Glacier: the height is nearly 18,000ft.' Cloud however prevented him getting his photographs and he concluded that 'I hope to get a better view from near Kabru in the course of the next fortnight.'

But there was possibly another reason for Kellas' aiming at Kabru. Alec had tried to climb Jonsong Peak before the war, and after the conflict had ended he had attempted Kamet, coming close on both occasions. Had he climbed either he would have officially achieved the summit height record for a mountain ascent. The same was true with Kabru. The fact, unknown to himself, to any of his peers – and to anyone at all till the publication of this book – that Kellas already had this height record with his ascent of Pauhunri, was an aspect of the almost Greek tragedy of his life. Was Kellas pushing himself to the limit, and undermining his constitution, in the pursuit of a Golden Fleece he already unknowingly possessed?

Kellas knew of the failure of the Norwegians, Rubenson and Haas, on Kabru in 1907, but there remained the prior claim of Graham to have conquered Kabru back in the 1880s. But by now Kellas knew the topography of the region around Kabru as well as any man living or dead, and he was adamant that Graham had not climbed the peak. His detailed researches confirmed what he had previously felt. To Collie he wrote,

You may remember that several years ago I pointed out that Graham could not have ascended Kabru, because even a photo. of the real Kabru showed that there was no relationship with Graham's mt., and his statements were entirely at variance with my scientific conclusions. Graham unfortunately mistook Kabru for Kangchanjungi, and the

Rathong Glacier for the Yalung Glacier. I will write to you again more fully with regard to this matter…

I enclose 2 telephotographs which may interest you, one of Kabru showing the summit plateau, and one of Jannu.[7]

Kabru was up for grabs, and Alec was hopeful of grabbing it. Alas, the photograph of Kabru appears lost.

The only information on Kellas' attempt on Kabru comes in letters to Hinks and Collie written on the same day – 18 May 1921, from the Mt Everest Hotel in Darjeeling where Kellas had moved to prepare for the reconnaissance with the rest of the Everest party. To Hinks he wrote,

> After the ascent of Narsing we were somewhat delayed by heavy fresh snow and thunderstorms, but made a sustained attack on Kabru during the last fortnight of April, and had reached the comparatively easy snow below the final peaks (21,000ft approx.) at the end of the month when we were forced to descend for lack of time. My main object in ascending Kabru (besides training coolies for the Mt. Everest expedition) was to obtain for your use a photograph of Mt. Everest and all the peaks to the N.W., which should I think be of great interest. A glance at the diagrammatic plan which I sent you some time ago shows that nearly all these peaks should be visible from Kabru. Foiled on Kabru I spent the 2nd and 3rd May on peaks of the Nepal frontier… The weather was unpropitious however and although I could see the Mt. Everest group for a time, it would have been useless to take photographs.[8]

Kellas mentioned to Hinks that after the Everest reconnaissance he intended to return to Kabru and make another attempt on the mountain. (As he had previously stated his intention to return to Kamet later in 1921, Kellas was clearly not short of ambitious plans for his future mountaineering!). In the letter to Collie written on the same day as that to Hinks, Kellas goes into more detail, indicating that he feels he had 'cracked' the mountain,

> Since I spent so much time working through the Kabru icefall, and have now a fairly good route I think, my intention is to return to Kabru in Octr. or Novr. and try and get a photograph of Mt. Everest from the top.[9]

However the fact that Kellas was still over 3,000ft from the summit means that, unlike Kamet, Kabru cannot be regarded as a near-miss mountain. His ability to succeed on Kabru where Rubenson and Haas had failed, and on a peak whose upper reaches were possibly more technical than was Kamet, was not a forgone conclusion, though it was by no means excluded, either.

But Alec Kellas was not to be given the opportunity for a further attempt to climb either Kamet or Kabru. The day after he wrote these letters to Hinks and to Collie, he set off from Darjeeling on the expedition to Everest, a journey from which he would not return. But before dealing with that fateful expedition, we need to go back and cover the complicated prelude to it.

Ever since Younghusband had suggested an attempt on Everest in 1893 to his fellow buccaneering frontiersman Bruce, many people had dreamed of climbing the mountain. We have examined some of these dreams and schemes already. Everest was increasingly to become seen as the 'Third Pole' after the conquest of the Arctic and Antarctic ones, and in 1920 things took a series of giant leaps forward. Lt.Col. CK Howard-Bury, an independently wealthy traveller with experience of Tibet and contacts in India visited the country in that year and with the support of the Indian Government, met with Sir Charles Bell, the Political Officer in Sikkim. Bell was prevailed upon to visit the Dalai Lama in Tibet in the autumn of 1920 and sound him out about a possible expedition to Everest. He left the Dalai Lama with a map of the proposed expedition route and when he returned a few days later, found to his surprise that permission had been granted. Apparently believing that the sahibs were on some sort of religious pilgrimage, the Tibetan government not only agreed to the venture, but also issued orders to the local governors (Jongpens) and village headmen along the proposed route that they were to offer all assistance possible to the expedition when it arrived. On 15 December 1920 the Viceroy of India, Lord Chelmsford, telegraphed London explaining that Bell had been successful in obtaining permission for an expedition to Everest the following year. Interestingly, in the light of the debate as to whether the Tibetans really had a name for 'Everest', the communication from the Prime Minister of the country to his subordinates mentioned above noted that the sahibs were intent on visiting 'Cha-mo-lung-ma mountain'.

This development galvanised all concerned into the formation of the

Everest Committee in January 1921, under the chairmanship of Young-husband. Its secretary was Hinks from the RGS, with two other RGS members, and it also included Norman Collie, CF Meade and JP Farrar from the Alpine Club. The composite body passed the following resolution,

> The main object this year (1921) is reconnaissance. This does not debar the mountain party from climbing as high as possible on a favourable route but attempts on a particular route must not be prolonged to hinder the completion of the reconnaissance.[10]

The route chosen was that through the Jelep La to Tibet, as it was the main trade route to Tibet, was easier than other possible routes to provision, and along it decent communications could be maintained between the expedition itself and India, and thus with home.

The initial choice for expedition leader was Bruce, but he was unavailable and – as he was prepared to make a substantial personal financial contribution and had done much of the preliminary work, Howard-Bury was chosen instead. Kellas was an almost automatic choice for inclusion, and was duly invited to join the reconnaissance. Douglas Freshfield had actually proposed Kellas as expedition leader, but this was strongly opposed by Farrar, who had previously commented negatively on Kellas' climbing abilities

> Kellas has never climbed a mountain, but has only walked about on steep snow with a lot of coolies, and the only time they got on a very steep place they all tumbled down and ought to have been killed.[11]

Whilst Farrar wanted the expedition to be as strong as possible in climbing terms, Hinks' concern was to strengthen its exploratory, geographical element above all else. Personal animosity as well as differing objectives also hampered relationships between the two men.

Whilst the judgement from Farrar is grossly unfair to Kellas, it under-lines Farrar's belief that the expedition should be as strong as possible in climbing terms, and go for the top if possible. He was a strong advocate of the inclusion of George Finch, probably one of the best climbers of the day, but Finch was rejected on medical grounds. The climbing party finally chosen consisted of Harold Raeburn, who was 56 and not in the best of health, and George Mallory who, though a climber with a good reputation, had no high-altitude experience – with Finch's place being taken by GH Bullock. Mallory was strongly supported by Farrar, but regarded with suspicion by Hinks, who feared (well-foundedly) that Mallory had ambitions to attempt the summit in 1921.

The Survey of India appointed and paid for the survey party which consisted of EO Wheeler and Major Morshead, who had been with Kellas on Kamet the previous year. AM Heron was added by the Geological Survey of India, and AR Wollaston was appointed as the medical officer. There is a photograph of the members of the expedition of 1921, a famous photograph, which shows them all – except Kellas. By the time it was taken he was dead, and this reflects – as well as in itself being a contribution towards – his fall into relative obscurity. He is The Man Not In The Photograph.

To help finance the expedition, the Everest Committee and Bury entered into binding negotiations with newspapers, including *The Times*, and with Edward Arnold book publishers, about the rights to the endeavour's publications. As a result there is an official account of the expedition which was written by Bury, the other members being pledged to silence,

MEMBERS OF THE 1921 EXPEDITION.
The official photograph of the Expedition was apparently taken after Kellas had died, but before Raeburn had been sent back. It shows (standing, left to right) Wollaston, Howard-Bury, Heron, Raeburn, (seated, left to right) Mallory, Wheeler, Bullock, and Morshead.
(RGS Collections)

except in so far as some of them contributed Appendixes to the official story. (In compensation for this self-denying ordinance preventing them writing about the expedition, each member was given £100 for personal equipment; this translates roughly as £7,500 in today's terms, a not ungenerous allowance). As we travel through Sikkim and Tibet on what was to be Kellas' death-march, it is informative to compare and contrast the official and rather dry account given by Bury, with the extensive but private comments made by George Mallory in his correspondence.

The members of the expedition had all arrived in Darjeeling by the middle of May, 1921. Bury comments that 'Owing to the heavy deficit in the Indian Budget... the Government of India were unable to give us financial assistance.'[12], but that the Darjeeling-Himalayan Railway gave the expedition and their equipment free passage and that the customs service had waived duty on their goods and supplies. Bury was a High Tory, an aloof and superior man, who appears to have engaged little on a personal level with the other expedition members, and indeed his account does not go into much detail about them, and is largely written from a personal standpoint. However, his first mention of Kellas is a rather censorious one, noting that due to his recent attempts on Narsing and Kabru, '... when he arrived at Darjeeling a few days before the expedition was due to start, he was not in as fit a condition as he should have been.'[13] Never of a stocky build, Alec had lost a stone in weight over the winter.

Compare this with Mallory's first impression of Kellas in a letter to his wife,

> Kellas I love already. He is beyond description Scotch and uncouth in his speech – altogether uncouth. He arrived at the great dinner party ten minutes after we had sat down, and very dishevelled, having walked in from Grom, a little place four miles away. His appearance would form an admirable model to the stage for a farcial representation of an alchemist. He is very slight in build, short, thin, stooping and narrow-chested; his head... made grotesque by veritable gig-lamps of spectacles and a long pointed moustache. He is an absolutely devoted and disinterested person.[14]

Mallory's admiration of Kellas is interesting as he was critical of certain others on the expedition, seeing Bury as a skinflint and reactionary, and Raeburn as a pig-headed boor.

The reconnaissance members left Darjeeing in two groups, on 18 and 19 May, Kellas being in the latter group. They went by Kalimpong (from where Alec sent apparently his last communication, a letter copied to his brother and mother, stating optimistically of the expedition that 'the outfit was admirable' (cited in Henry Kellas to Hinks 14.6.1921 RGS Archives), then by Peshole, Pedong and Gnatong to the Jelep La, where they left Sikkim. They had not their troubles to seek. The government-issued mules proved unsatisfactory and they were delayed by the need to replace most of them with local animals. It rained almost continually on the Sikkim side of the mountains, and this had a further unpleasant side effect in that as Bury noted, 'The constant rain had already brought out the leeches and on most of the stones or blades of grass beside the path they sat waiting for their meal of blood.'[15] At first things appeared to improve when they crossed the Jelep La and descended towards the Chumbi valley 'and obtained glimpses of a really blue sky such as we had not seen for weeks. We had arrived in Tibet.'[16] Despite being at 9,400ft the Chumbi valley has a pleasant climate and apples, peas, barley and potatoes grow, as well as wild roses. Here too at Yatung lived Mr MacDonald, a British Trade Agent, who put a spare bungalow at the expedition's disposal, and where Bury noted approvingly that 'Mrs MacDonald had with much thoughtfulness sent over her servants who had tea and dinner prepared for us on a generous scale.'[17]

From then on things got increasingly more difficult. The group arrived at Phari their next encampment which Bury described as 'an extremely dirty village.' It stood at 14,300ft and he added that 'the climate there is always cold, as it is never without a strong wind.' The Jongpen presented them 'with a dried sheep which looked mummified and smelt very strongly.'[18] Possibly this sheep made a bad situation worse, and was a contribution to what followed, as described by Bury,

> The change in the climate and the bad cooking had affected the stomachs of all the members of the Expedition, and none of us was feeling very well. Dr Kellas was the worst and as soon as he arrived at Phari he retired to bed.
>
> ...
>
> (The cooks) were very bad cooks, and usually drunk, and the fact that all of us had been ill was solely due to their bad cooking... Dr

Kellas was getting no better; he refused to take any food, and was very depressed about himself.[19]

Earlier in his account Bury had noted that one advantage of the Sherpas as porters was that they had no caste system and would touch or eat any food. But this expedition revealed that there was a rigid caste system on the trip; the caste system of the British Raj. It is inconceivable that subsequent parties would allow drunk and unhygienic cooks to prepare and serve their food; they would have taken charge and done the cooking themselves. But the members of the 1921 Expedition would appear to have preferred to allow themselves to suffer food poisoning rather than take control of the cooking situation. Gentlemen did not do such lowly labour – even if failure to do so made them ill. Or possibly coming from a social strata such as they did, most members of the party might actually have been unable to even boil an egg. These were people brought up in Victoria's reign – or in Mallory's case in the Edwardian period – and they apparently regarded themselves as being exempt from such degrading labour as cooking, as did any Hindu Brahmin. It is difficult to imagine the next generation of Himalayan mountaineers – Shipton, Tilman and Smythe – allowing such a problematic gastronomic situation to go unchallenged.

The next day on leaving Phari (Bury does not give dates for the expedition's progress in the book, but it was 31 May) Kellas was not fit to ride and was carried in what Bury describes as an 'arm-chair', the day afterwards in a 'litter.' The party crossed the Tang La at over 15,000ft to Tuna, and then gained Dochen where they were now on the main road to Lhasa. After that, they passed through Khe and arrived at Tatsang, Kellas making up the rearguard, as Bury noted;

> Dr Kellas had had a very trying day. He had been rather better, and had started riding a yak, but he found this too exhausting and coolies had to be sent back to bring him in a litter so that he did not arrive at Tatsang till late in the evening.[20]

With Raeburn also chronically ill, Mallory was falling into semi-despair about the chance of success of the expedition, 'Can you imagine anything less like a mountaineering party?' he wrote to his wife.

On 5 June the party started towards their next stop, at Kampa Dzong.

For a change it was a beautiful sunny day and quite warm, which appeared to have rallied Kellas, as Bury observed;

> Dr Kellas started off in his litter at 7 a.m. in quite good spirits. I did not start off till an hour later... On the way we passed Dr Kellas in his litter, who then seemed to me to be still quite cheerful.[21]

Bury arrived at the fort of Kampa Dzong first and was engaged in conversation with the Jongpen, when the tragic news arrived of Kellas' death.

> While we were talking a man came running up to us very excitedly to say that Dr Kellas had suddenly died on the way. We could hardly believe this, as he was apparently getting better; but Wollaston at once rode off to see if it was true, and unfortunately found that there was no doubt about it. It was a case of sudden failure of the heart, due to his weak condition, while being carried over the high pass. His death meant a very great loss to the Expedition in every way, as he alone was qualified to carry out the experiments in oxygen and blood pressure which would have been so valuable to the Expedition, and on which subject he was so great an expert. His very keenness had been the cause of his illness, for he had tried his constitution too severely in the early months of that year by expeditions into the heart of the Himalayas to see if he could get fresh photographs from other angles of Mount Everest. The following day we buried him on the slopes of a hill to the south of Khamba [sic] Dzong, in a site unsurpassed for beauty that looks across the broad plains of Tibet to the mighty chain of the Himalayas out of which rise up the three great peaks of Pawhunri, Kanchenjhow and Chomiomo, which he alone had climbed. From the same spot, far away to the West – more than a hundred miles away – could be seen the snowy crest of Mount Everest towering far above all the other mountains. He lies, therefore, within sight of his greatest feats in climbing and within view of the mountain that he had longed for so many years to approach – a fitting resting-place for a great mountaineer.[22]

Four days after Kellas' death, at Tinki Dzong, Bury wrote an account of the Expedition's progress since it had left Phari on 31 May. This account reached Simla 26 June and was telegraphed to *The Times*, where it appeared on the following day – although the actual news of Kellas'

KAMPA DZONG.
The bleak plains of Tibet where Alec died, beside the fort of Kampa Dzong, shown.
Alec was buried here, within sight of some of the Sikkim peaks he had climbed.
The present state of the grave, lying in a restricted military area, is not known.
(RGS Collections)

death had been published in the same newspaper 13 June. Most of the account matches that of the official narrative made by Bury later apart from one, that is an item relating to the actual cause death. In his *Times* contribution this is give again as 'heart failure', but earlier in the article Bury mentions that 'Dr Kellas was unfortunately rather seedy with a bad attack of diarrhoea...' This information is not given in the 'sanitised' official account. It is given however in the letter Bury wrote to Hinks from Kampa Dzong on 7 June, the day after Kellas' death, which he writes of, also mentioning the similar diarrhoetic state of Raeburn, and the decision taken to send him back to Lachen. Bury concludes bluntly, 'It does not pay to send middle-aged men out to this country.' (Bury to Hinks, 7.6.1921, RGS Archives).

Within sight of Everest as he is from his resting place, Alec had died the day before the 1921 Expedition actually sighted the mountain. It is an event which strikes you as – once again – almost worthy of Greek tragedy: the greatest Himalayan mountaineer of his day being denied, by a death brought on by his passion for Everest, a sight of the Mother Goddess of the World. As noted, Mallory had been greatly taken with Kellas and was moved by his death, writing to Geoffrey Winthrop Young;

> It was an extraordinarily affecting little ceremony burying Kellas on a stony hillside – a place on the edge of a great plain and looking across to the three great snowpeaks of his conquest. I shan't easily forget the four boys, his own trained mountainmen, children of nature, seated in wonder on a great stone while Bury read out the passage from Corinthians...[23]

It is clear that Kellas took four of his own trained Sherpas with him on the 1921 expedition. We do not know who they were, their names or whether they had been with him on previous expeditions. Neither Bury nor Mallory give their names; one thinks that, had Kellas himself lived to write about the 1921 Reconnaisance, he would have done so.

Malory added in another communication to his wife,

> ... he died without one of us anywhere near him. And yet it was a difficult position. The old gentleman (such he seemed) was obliged to return a number of times en route and could not bear to be seen in distress, and so insisted that everyone should be in front on him.[24]

Alec died alone, as he had lived much – indeed most – of his life, on the mountains and elsewhere. And despite the cause of death being given as heart failure (a commonplace verdict at that time) it is clear that gastric troubles resulting in acute dysenteric symptoms had led to his death. It was an unpleasant way to die.

Mallory did not forget Kellas, quite the contrary. With Bullock later on in the 1921 Expedition he climbed a summit facing Everest at 22,500ft which he wanted to call Mount Kellas. Hinks wrote to Mallory's wife on this issue of her husband's nomenclatural enthusiasms, 'He must not keep calling mountains by personal names like "Kellas" or "Clare" for they certainly will not be "allowed to stick". The idea is enough to make poor Kellas turn in his grave at Kampa Dzong'.[25] Indeed this did not 'stick' and the mountain is now called Ri-ring. But in as close proximity to the Everest massif another summit was named by the 1921 Expedition as Kellas Rock Peak. At 23,190ft it was first climbed by a party led by Shipton in 1935, and this name *has* stuck. A further commemoration to Kellas was of course the memorial at the foot of the Rongbuk Glacier dating from 1924 which also commemorates Mallory, and which we have already mentioned more than once.

KELLAS ROCK PEAK.
The 1921 Expedition named two eminences in the Everest area after Kellas, but only this one, Kellas Rock peak, has stuck. The other – Mount Kellas – was replaced by Ri-Ring, though the former appellation was later applied to a different summit in Sikkim.
(RGS Collections)

And though he is missing from its 'team' photograph, the expedition of 1921 itself did not forget Alec either. After it had completed its work and was on its way home, the entourage passed by his gravesite once more. As Bury records in his official account;

> On 11 October we arrived at Khamba [*sic*] Dzong... In the course of the afternoon we put up over Dr Kellas' grave the stone which the Jongpen had had engraved for us during our absence. On it were inscribed in English and Tibetan characters his initials and the date of his death, and this marks his last resting place.[26]

– unfortunately Kampa Dzong and Kellas' grave now lie in a restricted military area and the current condition of the memorial is unascertainable.

There is no doubt that Bury's view that Kellas' death was a major blow to the 1921 Expedition was correct, and it was echoed by the analysis, subsequently given by AR Hinks of 'The Scientific Equipment' on the expedition. In Appendix IV of the official Expedition account, where he states;

> The most important scientific work of the first year's expedition should have been the study of the physiological effects of high altitude that Dr Kellas had undertaken, with the support of Professor Haldane, FRS, and of the Oxygen Research Committee of the Department of Scientific and Industrial Research...
>
> He was prepared to make several difficult researches into the physiological process of adaptation to low oxygen pressure; and some delicate research apparatus was prepared and sent out to him by the Oxygen Research Committee. Unhappily these interesting and important enquiries came to naught, for there was no one competent to carry them on after his lamented death at Kampa Dzong; and the Expedition of 1922 was thereby deprived of much information that should have been at its disposal in studying the use of oxygen for the grand assault.[27]

Everest has its one Great Mystery. What happened to Mallory and Irvine? But there is another Great Mystery; why did a man who was so highly regarded by his contemporaries as Alexander Kellas, and whose death as seen by his peers as a serious blow to subsequent plans to climb the mountain, all but disappear from the subsequent narrative of Everest?

NOTES

1   Kellas to Norman Collie, 12.1.1921 (RGS Archives)

2   Kellas to Dr EL Kennaway 14.2 1921 (NLS Acc.9603)

3   Kellas to Hinks, 26.1.1921 (RGS Archives). Kellas was clearly so excited by the prospect that he would be on the Everest reconnaissance that on the same day, 21 January, he wrote and informed Collie. Though Kellas climbed little with Collie, the older man does appear to have acted as a sort of father figure to Alec.

4   Hinks to Kellas 17.2.1921 (RGS Archives)

5   Kellas to Hinks 9.2.1921 (RGS Archives)

6   Kellas to Collie 9.4.1921 (RGS Archives) p.3

7   Kellas to Collie 9.4.1921 pp.3–4.

8   Kellas to Hinks 18.5.1921 (RGS Archives)

9   Kellas to Collie 18.5.1921 (RGS Archives)

10   Quoted in Michael Ward, *Everest; A Thousand years of exploration* (2003), p.48.

11   Farrar to Montagnier 15.5.1919, (Alpine Club Archives).

12   *Mount Everest, the Reconnaissance 1921*, CK Howard-Bury (1922), p.23.

13   Op.Cit., p.26

14   Quoted in *George Mallory*, D Robertson (1969) (1999 edn.) p.151.

15   Howard-Bury, Op.Cit., pp.34–5.

16   Op.Cit., p.36

17   Op.Cit., p.38.

18   Op.Cit., p45.

19   Op.Cit., p.46, 47.

20   Op.Cit., p.53.

21   Op.Cit., p.53

22   Op.Cit., p.54. Kellas' death appears to have focused minds wonderfully, and Bury adds (p.56) that 'Raeburn, who for some time had been suffering from the same complaint as Dr Kellas, was unfortunately getting no better and was getting weaker every day. We were therefore reluctantly compelled to send him back again into Sikkim to Lachen...' Raeburn survived, and it is possible that Kellas would have done so also, had he too been sent back to Sikkim earlier. Raeburn incidentally became clinically insane soon afterwards and spent most of the rest of his life in a mental asylum, one of his delusions being that he was convinced that he himself had actually killed Kellas. During the walk-in on the 1922

Everest Expedition, Henry Morshead wrote to his wife on the 31 March... 'Did you hear that old Raeburn has been off his head since his return to England last autumn? He is apparently under the delusion that he murdered Kellas!' That Morshead heard this out in India indicates that it was a widely disseminated story. The quotation is given in *The Life and Death of Henry Morshead*, Ian Morshead, (1982), p.89. I am grateful to Robin Campbell for drawing my attention to this quotation.

23 Qu. In Walt Unsworth *Everest*, p.91. Bury remarks in his article in *The Times* which covers Kellas' death that, 'His coolies made a rough cross out of the lovely wild flowers that spring up everywhere in this dry soil'. Mallory comments that there were four such Sherpas of Kellas' personal training and retinue. Sadly, as Alec never wrote about this trip, we do not know their names.

24 Qu. In Robertson, Op.Cit., p 154.

25 Hinks to Ruth Mallory, No date given. Qu. In Unsworth *Everest*, p.58.

26 Bury, Op.Cit., p.164. For a full account of the further progress and results of the 1921 Reconnaissance after Kellas' death, see Michael Ward, *Everest*... pp.55–69.

27 *Mount Everest, the Reconnaissance*... Appendix IV, p.341.

KELLAS GRAVE AT KAMPA DZONG.

The stone the Jongpen of Kampa Dzong had engraved between visits of the 1921
Expedition to Kellas' grave, and which was laid above his remains. It shows his intials
and the date of his death in English and Tibetan characters. A poignant memorial.

(RGS Collections)

CHAPTER NINE

Kellas' Place in Mountaineering History

The Man not in the Photograph

WHEN HE DIED IN 1921, and for a considerable number of years subsequently, the status of Alec Kellas in the international – and specifically Himalayan – mountaineering world was unrivalled and unquestioned.[1]

This was reflected in the publication of a wide range of obituaries and tributes to Kellas which appeared subsequent to his death at Kampa Dzong, all of which bear eloquent testimony to the esteem in which he was held. From newspapers to scientific and geographical journals and in all the important mountaineering periodicals, writer after writer spoke of Kellas' outstanding and unique contribution.[2] Possibly the most representative of these, as well as being the most informed both as to Kellas' life and of the broader Himalayan mountaineering context, was that by Norman Collie who had known Kellas since their time together in the chemistry department at UCL in the 1890s. It is politic to speak well of the dead, but Collie's sincere admiration for Kellas is evident in his obituary;

> Although he was keenly interested in chemistry, he was also even more interested in mountains; and during the latter part of his life, his scientific researches all were connected with problems elucidating the effects of high altitudes on the human system; in fact, he was probably the best authority of the subject, for there was no one who had such a practical knowledge, or who had worked scientifically and with more persistence on the subject than he.
>
> ...
>
> He had a unique knowledge of the Sikkim Himalaya, and his death deprived the Mount Everest expedition of one of its most valuable members, for he had studied the country round Mount Everest more deeply than anyone... he has left behind him a mountaineering

record of a very high order, and a scientific one that is founded on the results of painstaking, conscientious, and accurate hard work.[3]

With the repeated attempts which were made on Everest subsequent to the 1921 Reconnaissance, a virtual industry of Everest publications began to emerge, mostly written by participants in the various attempts on the peak, many of whom had known Kellas personally. Again, Alec Kellas' pioneering role is testified to by everyone, for example in Noel's *Through Tibet to Everest* published in 1927. This actually contains a whole chapter entitled 'Dr Kellas's Plan' relating to Alec's schemes for approaching Mount Everest prior to the one adopted in 1921. Noel comments that;

> I, who knew Kellas well, believe that if he had not died, Everest would have been conquered by now, and by nothing other than this – the combination of Kellas' Himalayan knowledge and Mallory's dash.
>
> Mallory's spirit and boldness and pluck and courage needed tempering by Kellas's knowledge and mountain wisdom. Kellas was hardly less powerful physically, except that he was older – and age tells on Everest – but Kellas and Mallory were the perfect pair to forge a way to the top.[4]

This speculation of Noel's, that Kellas could have summitted Everest, is one which is unverifiable. Certainly on Kamet he showed a high level of technical skill that indicated he was possessed of possibly more than simple physical strength and stamina. On the other hand, had Kellas lived and his pioneering work on oxygen been continued into the 1920s, then – given how close to success the Everest efforts subsequent to 1921 actually came – it is not beyond the bounds of possibility that Noel's opinion might have been vindicated, by others than Kellas using supplementary oxygen equipment in the design of which he had been involved, and gaining the summit.

When an official narrative by Younghusband on behalf of the Mount Everest Committee, of the various attempts made to date on the world's highest mountain was published in 1926, Kellas is again singled out for praise, his only flaw being seen as a selflessness which made him neglect his own personal welfare;

> Kellas had made many expeditions in Sikkim and other parts of the Himalaya. He was a lecturer in chemistry who had for years made a study of the use of oxygen for climbing at high altitudes. And he was one of those indefatigable men who cannot be torn away from

their special pursuits. In the previous summer he had made an ascent to 23,000ft and should during the cold weather have taken a rest. But he spent all the time climbing in Sikkim, living on very poor and insufficient food.[5]

G Bruce in his *Himalayan Wanderer* (1934) added his voice to what was a virtual chorus of praise for Alexander Kellas that continued for many years after his death;

> Dr Kellas lived harder than almost any mountaineer that has ever visited the Himalaya. His camp was hardly a camp at all: he lived entirely with his Bhotia porters and his success, not only as a traveller and an observer but actually as a mountaineer, was phenomenal. I put down very largely the success of the Sherpa and Bhotia porters whom we have used so much on Everest and who have been used by other expeditions, to the splendid training which they had under Dr Kellas and the confidence which they thus obtained. But poor Dr Kellas was a little too old for that very hard life, and extreme exposure and rough feeding was his downfall. But what an explorer he was and the most modest man that ever travelled the Himalaya.[6]

Attempts to climb Everest continued in the 1930s, as did the inspiration Kellas gave to many of the participants in that endeavour. One of the leading lights in that epoch was Eric Shipton, who in the enforced calm of the wartime years felt that one lesson in particular given by Kellas' experience had been forgotten. Criticising the increasing tendency towards large, industrialised expeditions, Shipton wrote, putting Kellas amongst the greatest of the Himalayan pioneers;

> But the sad thing was that the lessons taught by the great pioneers – Longstaff, Conway, Kellas, Godwin-Austin, Freshfield, the Shlagin-tweits – who had achieved so much by the simple but hardy application of their art, were forgotten or ignored.[7]

Hardly less important in Himalayan circles at that time was Frank Smythe, who must rank as one of Kellas' most fervent admirers. In his book *The Kangchenjunga Adventure* (1930) Smythe acknowledges the importance of Kellas' exploratory work in the region surrounding this Himalayan giant, and the book is full of praise for Kellas, amounting almost to a paen at times. (Smythe failed to climb Kangchenjunga, but did on that expedition take part in the first ascent of Jonsong Peak, which Kellas had previously attempted.)

Of all the mountaineers in the Kangchenjunga district, and for that matter in the Himalayas, Dr A.M. Kellas' name will stand pre-eminent...

As one who has humbly followed in his footsteps on the Jonsong Peak, I can safely say that from the technical point of view of route-finding and mountaineering Dr Kellas will stand out as the greatest pioneer of Himalayan mountaineering...

Eastwards of the Jonsong La is a nameless peak of 22,160ft, and the Langpo peak, 22,700ft which was climbed by Dr Kellas. It was but one of the many great ascents that he made in this district... When the history of the Golden Age of Himalayan exploration comes to be written, Dr Kellas' name will take a high place in the select little list of early mountaineers.[8]

The next year, 1931, with Shipton, Smythe took part in the first ascent of Kamet, the mountain Kellas had been so near ascending in 1920. In his *Kamet Conquered* (1932) Smythe talks of Kellas and Meade's attempt as being one which was well capable of succeeding, but which failed due to difficulties encountered with equipment and porters;

I believe that his (Kellas') experiences on the many other Himalayan peaks that he had previously ascended had taught him the value of slow upward progression at great altitudes. Meade and Slingsby both suffered from the effects of altitude, but Kellas and Morshead were not seriously inconvenienced, and, had it not been for difficulties other than those of the actual mountain and its height, they might have reached the summit.[9]

Even as late as 1950, when he published his wonderful book *This, My Voyage*, Tom Longstaff, whose pioneering achievements in the Himalaya including the ascent of Trisul constituted a formidable mountaineering CV, was prepared to cede pride of place to Kellas in that illustrious band of pioneers in the Greater Ranges. He wrote that Kellas's death at Kampa Dzong;

was a severe loss to Himalayan mountaineering: he had done more high climbing than any other man, and this with the sole assistance of Bhotias and Sherpas whom he had himself trained... (he) was a mountaineer of the utmost courage and resolution.[10]

But it would be a mistake to regard Kellas as a mere local hero amongst what could be the rather Anglo (despite Kellas' Scottishness) – centric world of the British mountaineering establishment. As we saw previously, even before his death he was recognised as such an expert in high altitude physiology that he was invited to give a paper to the International Alpine Congress held in Monaco in 1920. However, it was in Germany that Kellas was to become a super-hero, a development that was to lead to Kellas' name being applied to an actual Himalayan peak.

Kellas Mania in Germany appears to have started with an article published in the *Deutsche Alpenzeitung* the year after his death. It was written by Walther Flaig and is entitled 'Tantalus.' Anyone who thinks that the extreme, subjective, overblown style in mountaineering writing as invented in the 1980s, should read this article. It contains almost no concrete information about Kellas, or on the Everest Expedition of 1921, instead it is largely a work of fantasy which elevates Kellas into a sort of demi-God, at utter variance with the real Alec from Aberdeen. Here is a typical extract;

> Half of his life had been filled with longing for the Mountain of Gods. Since he had seen the first ice dome rising into the blue sky, since he had measured his strength against sharply pointed rocky ridges in a joyful struggle, since he had taken many a walk along icy edges and breezy snow cornices, and since he had experienced the many, many great wonders of the mountainous world – since that time it had been his desire's ultimate goal to reach the as yet unclimbed peak of the highest mountain on earth...
>
> His hopes came true!
>
> He – Dr Kellas – was among the chosen ones, who were sent by the English Alpine Club as the most courageous and daring people in order to conquer the highest peak of the Himalaya, the mountain of the world...
>
> Two friends climb a massive mountain, a vassal of the Mother-Goddess, in order to find a vantage point. Kellas laughs: What does he want with a vantage point? The highest peak itself is what he wants – and he storms uphill, towards her...
>
> Kellas is shaking with joy all his desires are close to fulfillment.
>
> But the Goddess is furious and sends an evil ghost. The next day a painful disease runs rampant through his intestines and weakens his

proud strength. No medicine can help. His powerful body declines...

Brutal, painful thoughts torture his mind; the black birds of insanity flutter around him... The evening comes. The shadows of the night fill the valleys. Once more the sun collects all its gleaming splendour and crowns the summit of the world with a lavish glow. As the last red shimmer ascends from the head of the Godess Mother into the high blue night, the man's soul flies up into the realm of the blessed, to the one for who he has died.[11]

From this beginning the Kellas Myth in Germany grew. Whilst Mallory had named an Everest outlier as Kellas Rock Peak in honour of the man he knew for so short a time, the International Kangchenjunga expedition in 1930 under Professor GO Dyhrenfurth went one better and named a more imposing mountain in north-west Sikkim as Kellas Peak (6,680m) – still unclimbed as of autumn 2009 when one of the authors of this book was part of an unsuccessful attempt to ascend it.

Famed German mountaineer and expedition leader Paul Bauer was later to co-author an article with Peter Aufschneiter in a volume edited by Theodor Herzog entitled *Der Kampf um die Weltberge* (The Struggle for the World's Great Mountains), which was equally admiring of Kellas as had been Flaig, though this time the authors based themselves on more reliable sources. It is clear from reading their accounts both of Kellas' climbs in Sikkim and in the Garhwal, that the authors had studied Kellas' own versions of these expeditions. The authors comment;

One of the most unusual characters amongst Himalayan climbers was Dr A.M. Kellas who, mostly

KELLAS PEAK.
Lower than Kellas Rock Peak near Everest but, unlike the latter, still unclimbed.
Named by the admiring members of the 1930 Kangchenjunga expedition in honour of a Kellas, a man they recognised as a great Himalayan mountaineer and explorer.
(Frank Smythe, courtesy of The Smythe Estate)

on his own, accompanied only by his small group of porters, was able to achieve a whole series of successes.

As well as his actual ascents in Sikkim, Bauer and Aufschneiter cite as Kellas' further achievements his discovery and use of local Sherpas as mountaineers and his work on acclimatization to which they attribute the lack of effect of altitude upon Morshead and Kellas on Kamet, adding;

> As a result of this slow adjustment, the altitude did not have any effect on them. He and his companion could have made it to the summit, but they only advanced a little further than Meade's Col, because the porters refused to go any further.[12]

But even then German admiration for Kellas was not exhausted. In 1935 Paul Geissler contributed an article to the *Deutschen Alpenzeitung* lamenting – somewhat inaccurately – that Kellas had been forgotten in Germany, the land where he had gained his PhD. But in every other respect this is the most accurate and exhaustive study of Kellas that had yet been published, and remained so till the publication of this book. Geissler examined almost every scrap which had been published relevant to Kellas to that date, either by him or about him. Had this article ever been translated into English it might have prevented Kellas slipping out of the historical picture in the way he did. But (though Geissler's article shows no mark of this) by 1935 the influence of Nazi ideology on German mountaineering writing was so great that there was somewhat of a general repugnance against its productions outside of its homeland. Geissler pays tribute to all of Kellas' mountaineering and scientific achievements and insights, and specifically (given the German obsession at this time with Kangchenjunga) states that (though possibly somewhat unfairly in the light of what we have discussed above);

> Kellas, through his travels and research, paved the way like no other man for the three Kangchenjunga expeditions. But in the books by Bauer and Dyhrenfurth, one searches in vain for words worthy of this genius.[13]

Kellas' reputation continued to shine brighter in the German-speaking world than the English-speaking one throughout the 1950s. In GO Dyhrenfurth's 1955 book *To the Third Pole: The History of the High Himalaya* (originally in German as *Zum Dritten Pol*), discussion of Kellas' work

Deutsche Alpenzeitung
1935   30. Jahrgang

Alexander M. Kellas, ein Pionier des Himalaja

Von Paul Geißler

In dem Ringen um die Eroberung des Everest sind die ersten Junitage von schicksalhafter Bedeutung gewesen: am 1. Juni 1933 wurde Smythe sei seinem letzten so erfolgversprechenden Vorstoß gegen den Gipfel zur Umkehr gezwungen, am 8. Juni 1924 traten Mallory und Irvine den Gang an, von dem sie nicht mehr zurückkehren sollten, und der 5. Juni 1921 ist der Todestag eines Mannes, der als eines der hervorragendsten Mitglieder zur Teilnahme am ersten Angriff auf den Everest ausersehen, während des Anmarsches zum höchsten Gipfel der Welt plötzlich dahingerafft wurde, so daß er sein Ziel nur aus der Ferne schauen konnte: Dr. Alexander Kellas. Einer der vielseitigsten Kenner des Himalaja, ist er außerhalb der Grenzen seiner Heimat so gut wie unbekannt geblieben. Auch in Deutschland nahm man von der Nachricht von seinem tragischen Ende kaum Notiz, obwohl er einen Teil seiner wissenschaftlichen Ausbildung an einer deutschen Universität genossen und an ihr sich auch den deutschen Doktortitel erworben hat. Auch hat er wie kein anderer den drei Kantscherpeditionen durch seine Fahrten und Forschungen die Wege geebnet, und doch sucht man in den Büchern von Bauer und Dyhrenfurth vergebens nach einem Wort, das seiner Bedeutung gerecht würde. Wohl hat ihm die Internationale Himalaja-Expedition 1930 an der vornehmlichsten Stätte seiner Wirksamkeit ein Denkmal gesetzt, indem sie einen von ihm zuerst betretenen Hochsattel und einige markante Punkte im Umkreis des Jongsong Peak nach ihm benannt hat (Kellas Saddle, Kellas Peak, Kellas Corner), und auch die Everestmänner haben einen Gipfel im nördlichen Teil des Everestmassivs „Kellas Peak" getauft. Da es aber den Gepflogenheiten der indischen Landesvermessung widerspricht, Geländepunkte nach Personen zu benennen, so

haben diese Bezeichnungen keinen Eingang in die offiziellen Himalajakarten gefunden. Seine wissenschaftlichen Forschungen und seine Erschließertätigkeit sind von anderen weitergeführt worden; so ist sein Name in der alpinen Welt bald in Vergessenheit geraten. In dem jüngst erschienenen, von Theodor Herzog herausgegebenen Buche „Der Kampf um die Weltberge" sind Kellas' wichtigste Himalajafahrten zum ersten Male zusammenhängend geschildert worden; im übrigen wird sein Name in der neueren Himalajaliteratur — von den englischen Darstellungen abgesehen — meist eben gerade erwähnt; eine Vorstellung von ihm als Mensch und Bergsteiger und seiner Stellung in der Erschließungsgeschichte des Himalaja besteht kaum. Bei der ungewöhnlichen Zurückhaltung und fast übertriebenen Bescheidenheit des Mannes ist das übrigens verständlich. Dem wollen diese Zeilen abhelfen und auf Grund seiner spärlichen zum Teil schwer erreichbaren Veröffentlichungen ein Lebensbild und eine Würdigung dieses ebenso großen wie eigenartigen Bergsteigers und Forschers bieten.

Das äußere Leben von Alexander Mitchell Kellas verlief in ruhigen Bahnen. Am 21. Juni 1868 wurde er in Aberdeen als Sohn eines Beamten der dortigen Marinebehörde geboren. Nach Abschluß seiner Schulbildung studierte er in Edinburgh und London Chemie und Physik, bestand 1892 das Examen als Bachelor of Science und erwarb sich den naturwissenschaftlichen Doktorgrad. Anschließend war er drei Jahre lang Assistent des berühmten englischen Chemikers und Nobelpreisträgers Sir William Ramsay. 1895 ging er nach Heidelberg, wo er seine naturwissenschaftlichen Studien fortsetzte und sie 1897 mit der Promotion abschloß. Nach der Rückkehr nach England übernahm er eine chemische Professur an der

Middlesex Hospital Medical School in London, an der ein anderer namhafter Führerloser und Himalajamann, George Finch, in gleicher Eigenschaft wirkte. Dies Amt versah er über 20 Jahre lang, bis ihn 1919 schwere Arbeit zwang, der Lehrtätigkeit vorläufig zu entsagen und in seiner schottischen Vaterstadt Erholung zu suchen. Am 5. Juni 1921 starb er bei Kampa Dzong in Tibet auf dem Anmarsch zur Erkundung des Everest.

Ursprünglich war Kellas reiner Physiker und Chemiker. Seine berufliche Tätigkeit an einem großen Krankenhause stellte die Verbindung zur Physiologie und Medizin her und gab seinen wissenschaftlichen Studien eine besondere Richtung: er widmete sich nun der Erforschung physikalisch-chemischer Einflüsse auf den menschlichen Körper. Eine Frucht dieser Studien waren die beiden besonders für Medizinstudenten bestimmten einführenden Lehrbücher der Chemie (1906 und 1910). Vornehmlich befaßte er sich mit der Frage der atmosphärischen Einwirkung auf den Organismus, einem Problemkreis, in den die Anpassung an die dünne Luft der großen Höhen, die dadurch bedingte Veränderung des Blutes, die Höhenkrankheit u. ä. hineingehören. Die Klärung dieser Fragen bedurfte vieler Versuche, die er sowohl im Laboratorium wie praktisch an seiner eigenen Person in der freien Natur vornahm. Bald war er die anerkannte Größe auf diesem Gebiete. Seine Leistungen für die Wissenschaft wären noch größer gewesen, wenn er sein Amt als Lehrer nicht so ernst genommen hätte; für seine Studenten, vor allem die Zurückgebliebenen, war er immer da und gab sich unendliche Mühe, ihnen über ihre Schwierigkeiten hinwegzuhelfen. Während des Weltkrieges machte sich das englische Luftfahrtministerium seine Kenntnisse und Erfahrungen zunutze; sie waren für den

Mitteln eine kleine Expedition nach seiner Weise auszurüsten, ohne fremde und offizielle Unterstützung in Anspruch nehmen zu müssen. Er unternahm seine Fahrten aus eigener Initiative, organisierte sie allein und bestritt auch ihre Kosten. Die ihm zur Verfügung stehende Zeit — die Ferien zwischen den beiden Studiensemestern des Jahres — reichte aus, um trotz der langen Hin- und Rückreise in den indischen Bergen etwas zu leisten, das sich lohnte.

Doch so erfolgreich Kellas' ganzes Wirken war, es blieb Vorbereitung. Die Verwirklichung seiner höchsten bergsteigerischen und wohl auch Lebensziele, vor allem das Mitwirken an der Eroberung des höchsten Gipfels der Erde, hat er nicht mehr erlebt. Für die Everest-Mannschaft war sein Ausfall ein Verlust, der sich nicht ersetzen ließ. Als die Everest-Stürmer zum dritten Male geschlagen und mit schweren Wunden heimgekehrt waren, gab Noel ein Urteil

ab, das uns heute allzu optimistisch erscheint, das aber hier zum Schlusse angeführt werden darf, weil es zeigt, wie Kellas von seinen Zeitgenossen eingeschätzt wurde: „Wäre Kellas nicht gestorben, so wäre, glaube ich, der Everest jetzt erobert, und zwar durch nichts als die Verbindung von Kellas' Himalajakenntnissen und -erfahrungen und Mallorys vorwärtsstürmendem Kampfgeist. Kellas und Mallory waren das ideale Paar, das den Weg zum Gipfel finden mußte."

Schriftenverzeichnis

(Von Kellas' Schriften sind nur die alpin und biographisch wichtigen angeführt)

1. Kellas, A. M.: Lebenslauf. In: Kellas: Über die Esterifizierungsgeschwindigkeit der monosubstituierten Benzoësäuren...(Dissert. Heidelberg, 1897), 52.

2. The late Dr. Kellas' early Expeditions to the Himalaya. Alpine Journal 34 (1921/22), 408—414.

3. Kellas, A. M.: Mountaineering in Sikkim and Garhwal. Ebd. 26 (1912), 52—54.

4. —, The Mountains of Northern Sikkim and Garhwal. Ebd. 26 (1912), 113 bis 142.

5. —, Dasselbe. [Überarbeitet.] Geograph. Journal 40 (1912), 241—263.

6. —, A fourth Visit to the Sikkim Himalaya, with ascent of the Kangchenjhau. Alp. J. 27 (1913), 125 bis 153.

7. —, W. H. Shockley: Mountain Sickness. Geogr. J. 40 (1912), 654—655; 41 (1913), 76—77.

8. —, A Consideration of the possibility of ascending the loftier Himalaya. Ebd. 49 (1917), 26—48. (Auszug daraus: Alp. J. 31 (1917), 134—138).

9. —, The Possibility of aerial reconnaissance in the Himalaya. Ebd. 51 (1918), 374—389.

10. —, The Nomenclature of Himalaya Peaks. Ebd. 52 (1918), 272—274.

11. —, [The Approaches to Mount Everest.] Ebd. 53 (1919), 305—306.

12. —, J. S. Haldone, E. L. Kennaway: Experiments on acclimatisation to reduced atmospheric pressure. J. of Physiology 53 (1919/20), 181—206.

13. —, H. T. Morshead: Dr. Kellas' Expedition to Kamet in 1920. Alp. J. 33 (1920/21), 312—319.

14. —, — Expedition to Kamet. Geogr. J. 57 (1921), 124—130; 213—219.

15. —, Sur les Possibilités de faire l'ascension du Mont Everest. Congrès de l'Alpinisme, Monaco 1920, Comptes-rendus (Paris 1921), T. 1, 451—521.

16. Collie, J. N.: The Range north of Mt. Everest as seen from near the Kang La. Alp. J. 33 (1920/21), 303 bis 305.

17. Noel, J. B. L.: Dr. Kellas's plan. In: Noel: Through Tibet to Everest (London 1927), 87—91.

18. Tobin, H. W.: Exploration and climbing in the Sikkim Himalaya. Himalayan J. 2 (1930), 1—12.

19. —, Lama Anden. Ebd. 6 (1934), 157.

20. Aufschnaiter, P., P. Bauer: Himalaja und Karakorum. In: Der Kampf um die Weltberge, hrsg. von Th. Herzog (München 1934), 131—134; 136; 162.

21. Flaig, W.: Tantalus. Deutsche Alpen-Zeitung 18 (1922), 53—55. [Reine Phantasie.]

22. Nachrufe auf Kellas: Geogr. J. 58 (1921), 73—75. Nature (London) 107 (1921), 560—561. Cairngorm Club J. 1921, 128—130. Scottish Mountaineering Club J. 16 (1921/23), 74—76 (von G. W.). Alpine J. 34 (1921/22), 145—147 (von J. N. Collie. Mit Portr.). Middlesex Hospital J. 22 (1921), 66—69 (von J. N. Collie).

GEISSLER *DAZ* ARTICLE FIRST AND LAST PAGE.
Those without German and the ability to read Gothic script, will surely take our word for the fact that this was the fullest, and most fullsome, account of Alexander Kellas' mountaineering career published until the appearance of the present work.

in the Himalaya is prefaced by glowing words such as 'the great, solitary pioneer of the Himalaya' (p.9) and 'that great Himalayan pioneer' (p.98). In fact, Dyhrenfurth fairly falls over himself in praise of Kellas, stating that Kellas 'climbed alone' to the summits of Pauhunri, Chumiumo, and Kangchenjhau (p.9). However, Kellas was, of course, accompanied on all of these successful climbs by his favorite Himalayan travelling and climbing companions – the Sherpas. Whether this was an ethnocentric statement by Dyhrenfurth or merely an oversight is not known, but in his own writings Kellas never hesitated to give full credit to his Sherpa companions.

After the war came the Golden Age of Himalayan Mountaineering, starting with the ascent of Mount Everest in 1953. Kellas largely disappears from the picture, or more accurately he is relegated to a far distant Himalayan horizon. This contrasts with the fate of Mallory, who remains iconic as Mallory of Everest. It is likely that the latter's death with Irvine, high on Mount Everest – and the mystery long associated with their fate – fitted in with the heroic and romantic images of the Golden Age. This was not the case with the rather more squalid dysenteric demise of Alec Kellas on the bleak Tibetan plains at Kampa Dzong – whilst he was still out of sight of the actual mountain. But there is more to it than this. Mallory was mainstream English upper middle class Alpine Club material, and young and good-looking. Kellas by comparison was a middle-aged awkward provincial who had not gone to the right school and University and who was of undistinguished, unprepossessing appearance. If Mallory was the equivalent of the silent screen heart-throb of the 1920s, Rudolf Valentino, Kellas was – unfortunately – more in the Charlie Chaplin mould.

Whatever the reasons might be, it is hard to find much reference to Alexander Kellas' contribution to the ultimate success of Himalayan mountaineering from the 1950s through to the 1980s. John Hunt's *The Ascent of Everest* makes no mention of Kellas, but then it can be said that this is an expedition story and no more. However Bill Murray also wrote *The Story of Everest* in that same year of 1953, a book which provided a broader historical backcloth to the 1953 ascent. Murray gives fellow Scotsman Kellas five brief mentions, three of which are simply mentions of his death. The other two are interesting, stating that 'Kellas had done more high altitude climbing than any man alive' and noting of the area around Everest that 'few knew the country better than he (Bruce); Kellas perhaps was one.'[14] Comments so brief as to be almost missable – one would have thought such (well-merited) claims merited a little elaboration from Murray.

And if he slides to the edge of the Everest picture, Alec falls over the Kangchenjunga precipice altogether. Charles Evans' *Kangchenjunga, The Untrodden Peak* (1956) does note some of the early explorations of that mountain, including the one by Raeburn – whilst not mentioning the rather more extensive travels in the region by Kellas over a much longer period. The Germans might recognise Kellas as a Kangchenjunga pioneer – the British who climbed it did not appear to do so.

By 1981, when Walt Unsworth published his *Everest*, Kellas had moved a bit further into the foreground. Unsworth praises Kellas as follows 'in terms of Himalayan experience he was the greatest of them all'[15] and gives an outline of his climbs, his importance in relationship to the Sherpas, and his oxygen work. But as he was still relying on the original, sometimes not wholly accurate, obituaries of Kellas' death and on a study of some, but far from all, of Kellas' writings, Unsworth's account does Alec somewhat less than justice.

The re-discovery and re-evaluation of Kellas' role in Himalayan mountaineering owes more than anything to the interest and researches of high altitude physiologist John B West in the 1980s. Although published mainly in limited circulation scientific journals, West's series of articles on Kellas, and his subsequent re-publishing of some of Kellas' own writings, led to a wider appreciation of the man and his legacy, which was further consolidated by his history of high-altitude physiology, *High Life* in 1998, where West states that,

> As a result of [these] numerous expeditions to the Himalayas, Kellas probably knew more about the physical difficulties of getting to Mt. Everest than anybody else. This was one of the reasons why he was invited to join the 1921 Everest reconnaissance expedition. However, not only was he more knowledgeable than anyone else about the geography of the Everest region, he had also given more thought to the physiological challenges posed by the immense altitude of Everest. This combination of exploratory experience and physiological analysis of extreme altitude made him unique.[16]

In addition John West assiduously collected papers and unpublished materials on Kellas and carried out a worldwide correspondence with people such as the aged Geissler and with surviving members of the Kellas family, searching for further information. Though prevented by other obligations from taking his work on Kellas on to fruition, it is no exaggeration to say that the authors of this book stand on West's shoulders and that we could not have completed the work without the benefit if his initial endeavours.

The situation now is that the general histories of Himalayan or Everest mountaineering do give more place to Alec Kellas and his contribution. For example in 2003 Michael Ward's monumental *Everest; A Thousand Years of Exploration* outlined Kellas' mountaineering achievements and was additionally able to contextualise and evaluate Kellas's paper 'A consideration of the possibility of climbing Mt. Everest' which had been published two years before through the offices of John West, noting its 'many correct predictions' and lamenting that 'Kellas' extraordinary prescience was ignored by the Everest expeditions of the 1920s and 1930s.'[17]

The increasingly international spread of Kellas reputation was demonstrated in 2006, when on the 75th anniversary of the ascent of Kamet, Meher Mehta, the Vice President of the Himalayan Club spoke of Kellas scientific papers and his work on Kamet as;

> key catalysts in driving scientific thinking into climbing big peaks. His studies included the physiology of acclimatization in relationship to important variables like altitude, barometric pressures, alveolar PO2, arterial oxygen saturation, maximum oxygen consumption, and ascent rates at different altitudes. He had concluded that Mt. Everest could be ascended by men of extreme physical and mental constitution without supplementary oxygen if the physical difficulties of the mountain were not too great.[18]

And in 2008 there appeared the substantial volume, *Fallen Giants: A History of Himalayan Mountaineering from the Age of Empire to the Age of Extremes*, where the authors talk of Kellas variously as 'inexhaustible', 'ubiquitous' and 'incomparable',

> ... an unassuming chemist whose remarkable (and remarkably unsung) climbing career in the years before the First World war is inseperably bound up with the history of Everest and of high-altitude physiology...
>
> He was the first to think systematically and seriously about the effects of high altitude and diminished atmospheric pressure on human physiology. He wrote very little however, drew little attention to himself, and thus has fallen into ill-deserved obscurity.[19]

However, though putting Kellas back on the radar, these more recent accounts mentioned above remain very general ones, and lack the detailed description of his life and mountaineering which alone would allow us to evaluate his true position in the honourable line of Himalayan pioneers, and to answer the question – Did this still largely unknown man deserve

EVEREST MEMORIAL AT RONGBUK.
The memorial, constructed in 1924 sums up what we try to say in this book. Kellas is commemorated at Rongbuk in the company of the Sherpas who died in 1922 and 1924, and in that of the illustrious Mallory and Irvine. He deserves his pole position. (Beetham carved the memorial tablets, which have subsequently been looted). (Courtesy of Bentley-Beetham Collection, Durham University)

his position on the memorial at the Rongbuk Glacier beside – indeed, above – the almost household names of Mallory and Irvine?

Let us consider his claim to be so honoured.

At the time of his death in 1921, Kellas had not only spent more time above 20,000ft than any man alive, but had also climbed more summits above that figure than any one else, including ascending the highest peak climbed to that date, Pauhunri. That alone would make him a candidate for the position of greatest mountaineer of his day. Had he lived – or had better luck – it is perfectly feasible that he could have climbed Jonsong Peak, Kamet and possibly Kabru before they were actually conquered.

He was thus a great mountaineer.

Kellas' explorations in the region of Kangchenjunga give him a claim, recognised by the German parties between the wars, but subsequently over-looked, to have prepared the ground for the initial attacks on the mountain and its subsequent conquest. In addition, due to his explorations, mapping and photography he was, at the time of his death, more knowledgeable about Everest and its approaches than any man alive, and his work paved the way for the Expeditions of the 1920s.

He was thus a great explorer.

More than anyone else at the time, Alexander Kellas recognised the unique qualities of the Sherpas, and himself personally training up selected men, was unique in carrying out almost all of his exploration with only Sherpas for company, not simply as porters but as climbing companions. That Sherpa Tenzing stood on Everest with Edmund Hillary in 1953 is a wonderful vindication of Alec's faith in the Sherpas. In addition, travelling in small groups, using local resources, Kellas is an unsung pioneer of low impact mountaineering.

He was thus a great logistician and planner.

Kellas was a pioneering high altitude physiologist, virtually *the* pioneer of mountaineering high altitude physiology. He carried out ground-breaking work in the area of the impact of diminished oxygen on the body and of ways of combating this. It is not fanciful to argue that had Kellas lived, and carried on his work on oxygen, Everest would have been climbed earlier than it was. Further, Kellas' studies led him to believe that, though himself an advocate of oxygen, Everest could be climbed without it. This view was not just a rabbit plucked from a hopeful hat, but was based on scientific study. When Messner and Habeler stood on the summit of Everest 25 years after its first ascent they vindicated, as Tenzing had done in 1953, one of Alec's greatest insights. Indeed Messner and Habler's progress over the last 1,000ft was almost exactly what Kellas had predicted a superbly fit human being would be able to accomplish.[20]

He was thus a great high altitude mountaineering physiologist.

Therefore, it is beyond doubt that Alexander Mitchell Kellas merited his place on the Rongbuk memorial along with Mallory and Irvine, indeed that he merited pride of place. We need also remind ourselves that he was commemorated there in the further company of Lhakpa, Narbu, Pasang, Pema, Sange, Temba, Dorge, Shamsar and Manbahadur. These nine were Sherpas killed on the 1922 and 1924 Everest expeditions. Alec would have been proud to have been recognised in such a roll of honour. One imagines he would also have been pleased had he been able to know that his prediction that one day a man would stand on the summit of Everest without the use of supplementary oxygen had been vindicated. And from what we know of Kellas it is reasonable to state that he in all probability would have been equally – or indeed more – pleased to know that one of the duo to first climb the mountain was a Sherpa.

That anyone could achieve in Himalayan mountaineering what Kellas did in so short a time is remarkable. That this was accomplished by a man with Kellas' psychological issues, is little short of amazing. The time has surely come for Alexander Mitchell Kellas to be recognised as what he indisputably was, that is – one of the greatest Himalayan mountaineers of all.

NOTES

1   The only possible exception to this consensus on Kellas might be seen in the comments of Aleister Crowley who denounced the early Everest expeditions, including that of 1921. Crowley was a great believer in the 'rush' for the summit and likened acclimatization to the illusion that gradually reducing an animal's feed would mean that eventually it would be able to live on nothing. Kellas must therefore presumably be included in Crowley's wrath when the latter stated, 'We may therefore leave 'acclimatization' to the mentally defective heroes of the Everest expeditions of 1921 and 1922.' *The Confessions of Aleister Crowley*, p.320.

2   'Obituary', *Alpine Journal*, (1921) 34, pp.145–7.

3   'Obituary', *Nature* (1921), 107, pp.560–1.

4   'Obituary', *Geographical Journal* (1921), 58 pp.73–5.

5   'Obituary', *Cairngorm Club Journal* (1921), pp.128–9.

6   'Obituary', *Scottish Mountaineering Club Journal* (1921), No. 16, pp.74–6 – and elsewhere, see Bibliography.
    Alpine Journal, (1921), Vol. 34, No. 223, (1921), pp.145, 146–7.
    Through Tibet to Everest, JBL Noel (1927), pp.87–8, p.111. Noel's strong feeling for Kellas was reflected in the fact that he kept up some contact with the family after Alec's death. For example, as a member of the 1924 Everest Expedition, Noel sent a post card from Everest base camp to James Kellas, Alec's half-brother, who was at that time living in retirement at Balmacassie outside Aberdeen.
    The Epic of Mount Everest, (1926), Francis Younghusband, pp.30–31.
    Himalayan Wanderer, CG Bruce (1934), pp.296–7.

7   *Upon that Mountain*, Eric Shipton, (1943), p.137. Much the same views – and similar admiration for Kellas – were expressed by Tilman's often comrade-in-arms, Bill Tillman.

8   *The Kangchenjunga Adventure*, Frank Smythe, p.28, 30, 335.

9   *Kamet Conquered*, Frank Smythe, p.25 Meade and Slingby were climbers who had made attempts on Kamet previous to that of Kellas and Morshead.

10 *This, My Voyage*, Tom Longstaff (1950), p.152, 153. Though it is worth noting that much of this book was complied from journals written by Longstaff many years before when Kellas' reputation was high, and his comments are not representative of how Alec was generally seen in 1950, when he was all but forgotten.

11 'Tantalus', *Deutsche Alpenzeitung* 18, (1922) pp.53–55. Amongst Flaig's fanciful ramblings are several references to the Vedas and other Indian Mythology, elements which were later to feed into the irrationalist philosophy of much Nazi-inspired German mountaineering of the 1930s.

12 'Himalaja und Karakorum', P Aufschneiter, P Bauer, in *Der Kampf um Die Weltberge,* herg. Th. Herzog, (1934), p.131, 162.

13 'Alexander M. Kellas, ein Pioneer des Himalaja', Paul Geissler *Deutsche Alpenzeitung* 30, (1935), pp.103–110, p.103. Interestingly in his extensive Bibliography on p.310 Geissler mentions Flaig's article 'Tantalus' from the DAV of 1922 (footnote 10), dismissing it as *Reine Phantasie* (Pure Fantasy.)

14 *The Story of Everest*, Bill Murray (1953), p.5, p.47. On a personal note, one of the authors of this book grew up in Aberdeen and was part of the mountain scene in the 1960s. Whilst we devoured mountain literature the name of Alexander Kellas was totally unknown to us, and that in a town where local heroes normally loom larger than national and international ones. It was not until the lead up to 50th anniversary of the Everest ascent of 1953 that I [IRM] personally became aware of Kellas' existence.

15 Walt Unsworth *Everest*, 1981 p.38.

16 John B West, *High Life* (1998), p.170. For West's numerous other publications, see the bibliography.

17 Michael Ward, *Everest; A Thousand Years of Exploration*, (2003), p.31. Like West, Ward was a high altitude physiologist, a breed which has served Alec Kellas' heritage better than has the mountaineering community *per se*.

18 'The Lure of Kamet', Meher Meta, in *Kamet Commemorative Souvenir*, (2006). p.7.

19 *Fallen Giants* (2008), Maurice Isserman and Stewart Weaver, p.78.
20 Just what this achievement cost can be seen by reading Peter Habeler's *Everest: Impossible Victory* (1979). Though Messner is most often associated with this achievement, Habeler appears to have weathered the climb the better of the two, although he also was on the verge of collapse at the summit. Interestingly, though Habeler's book confirmed Kellas' predictions from over half a century before, it does not mention him.

Appendix

HIGH ALTITUDE MEDICINE & BIOLOGY
Volume 2, Number 3, 2001
Mary Ann Liebert, Inc.

A Consideration of the Possibility of Ascending Mount Everest

ALEXANDER M. KELLAS

Formerly Lecturer in Chemistry,
Middlesex Hospital Medical School, London

INTRODUCTION

PHYSICAL DIFFICULTIES:

1 Routes of Access
2 Time of year for ascent
3 Physical difficulties

PHYSIOLOGICAL DIFFICULTIES:

1 Consideration of Balloon and Aeroplane ascents
2 Experiments in air chambers
3 Consideration of observations and experiments of physiologists and mountaineers at sea level and altitudes up to 20,000ft.
4 Mountain sickness
   Definition–symptoms–causation
   Possibility of avoidance–
   Mountain Lassitude
5 The process of acclimatisation to altitude
   a Increase of oxygen pressure in the alveolar air
   b Increase of red corpuscles and haemoglobin
   c Excretion of oxygen by the alveolar epithelium
   d Increase of the frequency and depth of breathing
   e More rapid circulation of the blood at high altitudes during moderate exercise

General conclusions from physiological data

Variation of barometric pressure with altitude

Relationship of alveolar oxygen pressure to altitude

Alveolar oxygen pressure at the summits of various mountains, including
    Mt. Everest

Limits of permanent acclimatization to high altitudes

Rate of ascent at high altitudes

Method of ascent

CONCLUSIONS

NOTES

EDITORS NOTES

*This manuscript was given to the secretary of the Alpine Club in London
by Kellas in March 1920 and has been in their archives since 1923. It is
published by permission of the Alpine Club and one of Kellas's nephews, A.
R. H. Kellas.*

Introduction

AT THE COMMENCEMENT of this century, three geographical achievements of primary interest and importance were unaccomplished, namely
the conquest of the immediate North and South polar areas, and the
exploration of that group of mountains between Nepal and Tibet which
contain Mt. Everest, the loftiest tri-angulated summit on the earth's
surface. Both the North and South poles having now been reached, the
geographical survey of the Mt. Everest group remains, and will probably
be undertaken in the near future. To us, as mountaineers, this survey is
of peculiar interest, because an attempt to reach the summit of Mt.
Everest will presumably be made at the same time, and it is with the
possibility of such an ascent that we are concerned at present.

The first problem for consideration might be stated as follows:-
Could a man in first rate training ascend to the summit of Mt. Everest
(Tibetan Chomo-Langmo) 8,882m (29,141ft)[1] above sea level *without
adventitious aids*.

Such a problem has often been discussed, and the answer given has
usually been in the negative, in fact as lately as 1874 it was supposed
that 21,500ft or thereby represented the maximum height attainable. In
that year a well known mountaineer, President of the British Alpine
Club[2] in connection with a tour in S. America, wrote as follows:- 'I
could not repress a strange feeling as I looked at Tupungato (21,550ft)
and Aconcagua (23,080ft) and reflected that endless successions of men
must in all probability be for ever debarred from their lofty crests.'

'Those who, like Major Godwin-Austen, have had all the advantages
of experience and acclimatisation to aid them in attacks upon the higher
Himalaya agree that 21,500ft is near the limit at which man ceases to
be capable of the slightest further exertion.'

This quotation is made, not in the vaguest degree to discredit the
opinions of observers of the front rank, but merely to indicate a transi-
tory phase of thought, reached before sufficient scientific experiments
had been carried out to justify any conclusion.

Alpine opinion has altered considerably since 1874, but a leading
British daily paper[3] recently had an article on the subject, in which they
decisively reached the conclusion that an ascent of Mt. Everest, even
when aided with oxygen, was impossible.

In the following paper, I hope to be able to show that the ascent is possible even without adventitious aids, provided that the physical difficulties of the mountain are not excessive, and that the ascent should be possible if oxygen be used, even if the mountain might be classed as difficult from the climbing point of view.

The difficulties of ascending the loftier Himalaya must be considered from two aspects, firstly those due to physical obstructions, and secondly those due to the necessity for physiological adaptation.

Physical Difficulties

These might be discussed from the points of view of (1) access to Mt. Everest, (2) time of year for ascent, and (3) actual physical difficulties of the mountain.

I ROUTES OF ACCESS

As regards access, the mountain has so far never been visited by white men, and it is unlikely that any mortal has reached an altitude of even 20,000ft (6,096 m) upon it. Although in the main Himalaya Range, and regarded as the culminating summit of the whole System for the past 70 years, political difficulties have prevented access, because the mountain lies between Tibet and Nepal, countries so far practically closed to Europeans. The nearest route would be through Nepal, but as it is likely that access will be more readily granted through Tibet, only routes through the latter country need be considered.

The base from which a start should be made would be either Darjeeling or Siliguri, and the length of the route would be approximately 300 miles. A good pony track leads northwards through Sikhim up the valley off the Teesta River for about 140 miles, passing Gangtok and Lachen. Proceeding due North from Gyamtshona, where the Teesta Valley bends to the East, one would cross the Tibetan frontier by two easy passes, the Koru La (16,900ft, 5,121m) and the Sepu La (17,200ft)[a]. Twelve miles (approx.) would bring one to Kampa Dzong, an important village of S. Tibet, whence the route would lie N.W. to Kanjoonglabran, where the Phungtu Chu, the westerly branch of the Arun River, may be crossed by a hiderope bridge. The Arun River is the only serious obstacle to reaching Mt. Everest by this route. The photographs show the rope bridge, and the smoothly flowing Phungtu Chu near the crossing. Further South, where the Arun River cuts its way through the main Himalayan chain, its fall and velocity greatly increase and crossing becomes difficult.

From Kanjoonglabran[3a], the route turns sharply to the South, along the Arun to Kharta, passing the village of Pharuk. Kharta is situated about 25 miles to the N.E. of Mt. Everest, and two ways of accessing would thence be available. The shortest would proceed first westwards, and then S.W. over a lofty pass called the Langma La, which brings one to the N.E. glacier flowing from Mt. Everest. Panoramic photographs of the view from the Southern slopes of the pass show that the scenery of the Mt. Everest group is of a very high order.

If access were granted only through Tibet, the above is probably the best route, but it is worth noting that there is a variant, which would save over 40 miles. From Kampa Dzong one would proceed about due W. to Kharta, passing the village of Saar, and crossing by the Tok Tok La, the range which runs N. and S. and connects the main Himalaya with a parallel range to the North.

A third route which is about the same in length as that first described would proceed S. from Saar over the Nila La (about 17,000ft) to Tashirak, near which Nepal is entered. Some distance beyond Tashirak the route turns S.W. and reaches the Arun River at Hatia, where a crossing can be effected. From Haitia, Mt. Everest can be attained along a westerly affluent of the Arun River or via Kharta. A modification of this route was recently described by Major JB Noel[4].

Of the routes through Nepal, it might merely be mentioned that from Khanwa Ghat on the Kosi River, Mt. Everest is only about 110 miles distant in a direct line, and it would be possible to proceed N. along the Arun River to Hatia, and thence to Mt. Everest-probably about 160 miles.

All the above modes of access would lead to the E. face of the mountain, but the W. face could be reached either from Kampa Dzong via Kanjoolglabran, Dingri and the Pangu La, or from Khanwa Ghat by the Sun-Kosi and Dudh- Kosi Rivers. The map [FIG.1] gives a general idea of the nature of these routes.

2 TIME OF YEAR FOR AN ASCENT

With regard to time of year possible for an ascent, it must be pointed out that as Mt. Everest is in the main Himalayan Chain, climbing would hardly be possible during the Monsoon, which lasts as a rule from the middle of June to the end of August: fresh snow may during this period fall on the mountain every day. Perhaps the best times for an ascent would be either from mid April to mid June, or from mid August to mid October.

3 PHYSICAL DIFFICULTIES

So far as can be said from examination at a distance, Mt. Everest can be ascended by the E. face and the N.E. arete. A few photographs show the relationships of the mountain to surrounding peaks, notably Makalu (often mistaken for Everest), and the valley of the Arun River. In the Himalaya, photographs are apt to mislead if taken from a distance. For example, mistakes have also been made in the representation of the mountain from the E., well exemplified by the photograph from Chunjerma in E. Nepal, which shows a peak as part of Everest, which is really about 10 miles to the N.E.[5]

The photographs shown appear to indicate that the physical difficulties are not insuperable, and one might therefore say that the main difficulty in climbing Mt. Everest without adventitious aids would depend upon the possibility of adaptation of the body to the great height, that is to say would be of a physiological order.

Before leaving the consideration of the physical difficulties, a few photographs of other lofty summits of the Himalaya might be shown to indicate that Mt. Everest from the climbing point of the view is probably easier than any known mountains above 26,500ft in height. The photographs of the E., W., and S. faces of Kangchenjunga, K_2 in the Karakorum, and the N. and S. faces of Nanga Parbat indicate that these summits present mountaineering difficulties of a far greater order.

Physiological Difficulties

The physiological difficulties are undoubtedly great and essentially depend upon the diminished supply of oxygen. In order to explain how the body adapts itself to this deficiency, a little must be said regarding the process of respiration, which will be more fully discussed later.

During respiration an important cycle of operations takes place. Air is drawn into the lungs during inspiration, and at expiration is expelled,

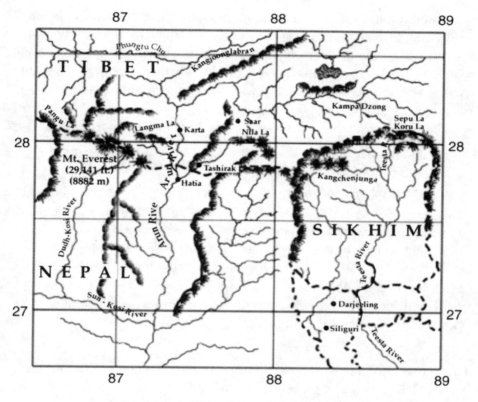

FIG.1 Map of Sikkim, Eastern Nepal and S. Tibet

the process occurring 12 to 18 times per minute during resting conditions at sea level. The air consists chiefly of two gases, oxygen and nitrogen, the latter having no intrinsic physiological significance.

The body is kept alive by oxygen taken up by the blood from the air in the ultimate ramifications of the lungs-the alveoli. The violet substance in blood called haemoglobin combines with the oxygen to form red oxyhaemoglobin which gives up oxygen to the tissues. How absolutely fundamental respiration is in maintaining life may be grasped when it is stated that unconsciousness would ensue in about three quarters of a minute if an indifferent gas like pure nitrogen were breathed, the body being at rest. Death would follow in a few minutes unless oxygen were supplied. The body cannot store oxygen beyond the small quantity remaining in the lungs, when the breath is held as in diving.

At the summit of Mt. Everest, the pressure of the atmosphere is only about one third of that at sea level, so that if equal volumes of air were breathed only about one third of the oxygen corresponding to sea level would be available, and one has to consider whether the body can adapt itself to the altered conditions, so as to oxygenate the blood satisfactorily, not only at rest, but while climbing.

The problem might be attacked by the four following methods:

1. By consideration of the physiological effects recorded during high balloon and aeroplane ascents.

2. By correlation of the results obtained in air chambers at sub-atmospheric oxygen pressures.

3. By evaluation of observations and experiments of physiologists and mountaineers at sea level, and moderate altitudes-up to 20,000ft. This involves a discussion of mountain sickness.

4. By consideration of the effects of Alpine ascents above 20,000ft. which requires consideration of the limits of permanent acclimatisation to high altitudes.

1a BALLOON ASCENTS

Two classic ascents are of special importance in this connection, namely that of Glaisher[6] and Coxwell from Wolverhampton in 1862, and that of Tissandier and two companions from Paris in 1875.

In Glaisher and Coxwell's ascent, Glaisher became paralysed and then insensible. Coxwell, unable to raise his hands, seized the valve rope in his teeth, and managed to open the valve before almost losing consciousness. Fortunately Coxwell's action gradually stopped the ascent of the balloon, which undoubtedly saved their lives. Glaisher claimed that the balloon rose to 37,000ft., but the height has been recalculated as 29,500ft (8,992m).

Tissandier's[7] ascent to about 28,220ft (8,600m) with two companions (Sivel and Croce-Spinelli) was not so fortunate. Although provided with oxygen, the three men were paralysed before they could raise the tubes of the oxygen reservoirs to their lips. A few sentences from Tissandier's graphic narrative give a good idea of the condition.

'J'arrive à l'heure fatale où nous allions être saisis par la terrible influence de la dépression atmosphérique ... Vers 7,500 métres, l'état d'engourdissement où l'on se trouve est extraordinaire. Le corps et l'esprit s'affaiblissent peu à peu, graduellement, insensiblement, sans qu'on en ait conscience. On ne souffre en aucune façon, au contraire. On éprouve une joie intérieure, et comme un effet de ce rayonnment de lumière qui vous inonde. On devient indifferent; on ne pense plus ni à la situation périlleuse ni au danger; on monte et on est heureux de monter. Le vertige des hautes régions n'est pas un vain mot. Mais autant que je puis en juger par mes impressions personelles, ce vertige apparait au dernier moment; il précède immédiatement l'anéantissement, subit, inattendu, irrésistible.'

When he recovered consciousness his two companions were dead and the ballon in rapid descent.

The conclusion from these balloon ascents must inevitably be that an ascent of Mt. Everest without adventitious aids would be quite impossible if the physiological conditions of mountaineers and balloonists are analogous, more especially as the climber would require far more oxygen than the balloonist. Their conditions are not comparable, however, as the mountaineer would be acclimatised to high altitude, which, as will be shown later, is of fundamental importance, whereas the balloonist is not acclimatised.

In many more recent balloon ascents oxygen has been used with success. In 1898 Berson and Spencer ascended from London to 27,500ft, and in 1901 Berson and Suring[8] ascended from Berlin to about 35,500ft, an actual barometric reading corresponding to 34,500ft being made before both men, notwithstanding oxygen inhalations, became unconscious. The significance of the effect of oxygen in connection with the ascent of Mt. Everest is obvious.

1b AEROPLANES

The physiological effects observed in aeroplanes correspond to those in balloons. Aerial pilots generally find considerable physiological difficulties if they ascend much above 20,000ft without using oxygen, and some start using it at 18,000ft or lower. The highest recorded ascent approx. 36,000ft (10,973m) was made with the use of oxygen.

2 EXPERIMENTS IN AIR CHAMBERS

Considering pressure alone, it might at the outset be stated that considerable variations of pressure, eg, increase up to four atmospheres pressure, or diminution to a fourth of an atmosphere hardly affect the body. Provided that decompression be not too rapid, one might say that moderate variations of pressure are innocuous. Recent experiments show for example that one can reduce pressure to 360mm[b], corresponding to 21,000ft (6,401m) in from 5 to 10 minutes without the slightest evil effects, a result of importance to airmen. If, however, decompression be very rapid, bubbles of gas, chiefly nitrogen, are apt to be liberated in the blood with very serious results. Caisson illness depends upon this fact. It is, as already indicated, alteration of the available amount of oxygen which causes serious results, and this alone need be fully considered.

Two types of experiments are worth studying:

A   Experiments in which the pressure of the air breathed was diminished

    a   Single experiments. Acclimatisation impossible.
    b   Connected Series of Experiments. Acclimatisation possible.

B   Experiments in which the oxygen percentage in the air breathed was slowly reduced.

A *Experiments where pressure is diminished*. (a) **Single experiments**. For various reasons experiments of this type are of greater importance from our point of view, as being more comparable with the conditions of the mountaineer at high altitudes[c].

Professor Mosso[9] in a typical experiment lowered the pressure in an airchamber to 310mm corresponding to 25,000ft, at 150C[d]. 'His mental faculties became blunted, he experienced difficulty in reading his watch, was twice unable to count his pulse, his handwriting altered, and his memory weakened.' Cases of fainting in airchambers at pressures corresponding to moderate heights (e.g. 356mm, 21,000ft) have been recorded. These results have been regarded as typical, but Haldane has recently (1919) proved that certain individuals are only slightly affected, at a pressure corresponding to 25,000ft for a short period of time.

In considering the results of experiments in airchambers, Prof. Starling[10] states that the lowest limit at which life is possible corresponds to the tension in the alveoli of 27 to 30mm, which is distinctly above that calculated for Mt. Everest. It is almost certain, however, that experiment will indicate that somewhat lower alveolar pressures of oxygen can be tolerated.

Single experiments in air chambers are not comparable with ascents in the Himalaya for the reason already stated, namely that the subjects in airchambers under such conditions cannot become acclimatised to the low pressure, whereas the mountaineer can.

(b) **Connected series of experiments**. Haldane recently proved that partial acclimatisation is possible in airchambers, and that a considerable amount of physical and mental work could be carried out at 312 mm corresponding to 25,000ft (7,620m).

From this series of experiments[11], when on consecutive days several hours were spent in an airchamber at pressures corresponding to approximately 11,600, 16,000, 21,000, and 25,000ft, it seems possible that the ascent of Mt. Everest could be effected without adventitious aids, provided the physical difficulties were not very great.

Prolonged experiments in airchambers at low pressures in many cases cause illness with symptoms exactly similar to those observed in the so-called mountain sickness.

In air enriched with oxygen Paul Bert, one of the first experimenters in this field, successfully withstood a pressure of 240mm which corresponds to nearly 32,000ft. The best results were obtained with a mixture of oxygen and carbon dioxide; and Aggazzotti actually breathed such a mixture at a pressure of 120 mm for some time[e]. This pressure corresponds to approximately 50,000ft above sea level. Dr G Regnier[12] found that the mixture mentioned was of value in mountain sickness.

B *Alteration of percentage of oxygen in the air breathed.* On reducing the percentage of oxygen in the inspired air below the value at sea level (20.96 per cent), little effect is produced until the percentage is 12 to 14, and then the breathing becomes deeper. Haldane[13] states that 'marked symptoms of mental incapacity are also present. Simple observations or calculations become impossible.' Consciousness is usually lost when the percentage of oxygen in the air breathed sinks to between ten and seven per cent, but Dr Schneider[14] has recently pointed out in connection with tests of aeroplane pilots that a few individuals can 'endure, at least for brief periods, as low as six per cent of oxygen corresponding to 31,000ft.'

Considering the whole series of single experiments in airchambers one might state that the ascent of Mt. Everest would be impossible without adventitious aids agreeing with the observations of balloonists. Schneider's results can hardly be evaluated in this connection, but as already mentioned Haldane's connected series of experiments seems favourable.

3 CONSIDERATION OF OBSERVATIONS AND REQUIREMENTS OF PHYSIOLOGISTS AND MOUNTAINEERS AT SEA LEVEL AND ALTITUDES UP TO 20,000FT

The researches carried out by Bert[15], Haldane, Barcroft, Zuntz, Mosso, Hasselbalch, Sundstroem and their respective coadjutors are of special importance. Between them, they have clearly explained the phenomena connected with that debateable subject called mountain sickness, and have indicated how it might be avoided. Mountain sickness was until recently supposed to be one of the main dangers of mountaineering at high altitudes, and a brief summary regarding the incidence and causation must be given, although the subject can only be superficially treated in a paper of this type.

4 MOUNTAIN SICKNESS

Definition of mountain sickness. Dr Hepburn had stated that the expression 'mountain altitude sickness' is only justified when we have proved that there is a definite disorder, which may accompany muscular exertion at high altitudes, and 'which cannot occur under other conditions'[16] must be pointed out however that if, for any reason, sickness occurred earlier on mountains that under similar conditions at sea level the designation is justified.

Dr Longstaff[17] defines mountain sickness as symptoms of illness or distress primarily produced by the ascent of mountains, whether due directly to reduced atmospheric pressure, or to some other cause or causes.

For reasons which will appear during the discussion of the subject, one would prefer to define mountain sickness as *symptoms of illness or distress on mountains caused directly or indirectly by deficiency of oxygen.*

Symptoms of mountain sickness. The symptoms described have been of an extraordinary varied character. Using Hepburn's systematic method of classification, the more important might be summarized as follows, but it must be understood that only a few symptoms may appear in a particular case.

1 *General Symptoms*: General malaise: lassitude.
2 *Respiratory Symptoms*: Accelerated respiration and breathlessness on moderate exertion. Periodic or Cheyne Stokes respiration.

3 *Circulatory Symptoms*: During illness pulse rate may rise to 120 or upwards. Cyanosis of lips, ears, etc., especially on exertion.

4 *Nervous Symptoms*: Acute headache, giddiness, diminution of intellectual powers, eg, memory weakened. Fainting (Syncope).

5 *Symptoms due to disturbance of alimentary tract*: Lack of or diminished appetite; Indigestion; Nausea and Vomiting.

6 *Muscular Symptoms*: Fatigue of the limbs, especially the lower limbs, and decreased capacity for muscular work.

Clinton Dent[18], Prof. Clifford Allbutt[19], and Prof. Roy[20] discuss other symptoms, but space prevents adequate consideration. The bleeding at mucous surfaces mentioned by mountaineers of the 18th and 19th centuries (de Saussure, v. Humboldt, v. Tschudi:- and the Schlagintweits[81]) has been observed so rarely recently that it may be neglected, but Waddell[21] mentions cases of noses bleeding on the Donkia La (18,000ft).

Incidence of mountain sickness. The incidence of mountain sickness merits careful consideration, as erroneous ideas seem to have been widely accepted. It has been stated to occur on ranges of any elevation from Grampians to Himalaya, but evidence will be adduced to show that in the case of normal trained healthy individuals it could hardly occur below 7,000ft unless under exceptional conditions when fatigue would be the main factor.

The following general statements, which have been made by various authors merit consideration:

1 The height at which an attack begins varies greatly with different individuals.

2 It varies with the same individual at different times.

3 The altitude of incidence varies with different continents.

4 The incidence varies within narrow areas of the same region.

5 Natives of high mountain regions, e.g. Andes and Himalaya, are often less immune than white men visiting the regions.

As regards the first general statement, Zuntz[22], who has studied the matter very carefully, following v. Schrotter[23] summarizes as follows:

'Some quite healthy individuals are attacked at 3,000m (9,843ft), and the majority between 3,000 and 4,000m (13,124ft). Very few are immune above 4,000m, but there are exceptional men, who can climb to 5,000m, or even 6,000m (19,686ft) without being seriously affected.'

While it cannot be denied that individuals do seem to differ considerably as regards incidence, it is obvious that above statement has no real importance, when it can be proved that the same individual may belong to any of the classes mentioned, depending on his state of training. For example, one well known climber, a President of the British Alpine Club, has stated that he has been attacked at 3,000, 8,000, 11,000, and 18,000ft but has been immune on difficult ascents at 19,000 and 21,000ft Whymper and two first rate guides (JA and L Carrel) were simultaneously attacked on Chimborazo at 16,664ft and were afterwards unaffected on many ascents of from 19,000 to 21,000ft. Many other examples might be given.

Zuntz has also pointed out that mountain sickness seems to vary greatly in incidence with locality. He observes that it is met with at 3,000m in the Alps and Caucasus, at 4,000m in the Andes, and at 5,000m in the Himalaya.

This statement would be difficult of explanation if true, since the composition of the atmosphere is practically uniform, except with regard to relative humidity, but it can only be considered a vague generality, expressing the chances of acclimatisation. As indicated later, if untrained individuals can rapidly alter their altitude mountain sickness may be produced, but if the alteration be slow acclimatisation prevents incidence. Hooker[24] for example states that he never suffered when riding even when at 18,300ft in the Himalaya, (where the traveller by road generally takes at least a week to reach 15,000ft), but he suffered when climbing on foot.

More important because more difficult of explanation is the fourth statement, that mountain sickness varies within certain narrow areas. Two general statements have been made in this connection.

1 It has been repeatedly affirmed by travellers and natives of the Himalaya and Andes that passes of about the same height in the same region differ greatly as regards incidence of mountain sickness. For example v. Tschudi[25] states that it is incident with great severity in some districts of Peru, 'while in others of higher altitude it is scarcely perceptible.'

2 It has also been generally assumed that one is more liable to be

attacked when climbing in gullies and on snow, than on open ridges and rock.

Many quotations might be given regarding this latter statement. De Saussure[26] in describing the early unsuccessful attempts on Mont Blanc says that in 1783 two chamois hunters ascended by a series of rock aretes to within 2,500ft of the summit, and that 'the air on those slopes was so easy and light that there was no fear of that kind of suffocation felt in the valley of snow, which extended from the mountain of La Cote' at a lower elevation, which had defeated another attempt during the same year.

In 1831 Boussingault[27] wrote in connection with his attempt on Chimborazo, 'A hauteur égale, je crois avoir remarqué que l'on respire plus difficilement sur la neige, que lorsque l'on se trouve sur un rocher.'

Conway[28] in connection with the ascent of Pioneer Peak remarks that on the peak they felt much worse on slopes than on the arete, in fact they had difficulty in restraining themselves from taking to the cornice.

Thomas[29] on the contrary found climbing on rocks more difficult than on snow, suggesting that the heated rocks caused rarefaction of the air, agreeing with Zurbriggen, a guide of quite exceptional ability and experience, who told Prof. Mosso that he suffered more on bare mountains than on snow or ice.

Probably all these vague statements are capable of simple explanation. It seems unnecessary to invoke ionisation of the air due to radioactivity of the minerals present in certain mountain regions, a theory due to Zuntz. Intense electrical disturbances, which would produce ionisation seem to have little effect on the incidence of mountain sickness, but Mosso cites examples of an apparent influence, perhaps psychic in origin.

The true explanation of the above contradictory statements regarding incidence of mountain sickness is probably much simpler, but may depend upon several factors, all of which would require to be considered in any particular case:

a   Nature of the ground, eg, whether snow or rock, and whether easy or difficult.
b   Presence or absence of wind.
c   Possible deficiency or alteration of diet as compared with normal.
d   Weather.

As indicated above, it is generally assumed that snow, especially melting snow under a hot sun, is far more likely to cause trouble than rock, and a ravine or gully with stagnant air is more likely to produce mountain sickness than an open ridge, where currents of air usually circulate.

In the first connection it has been suggested by Prof. Roy that melting snow will dissolve a large quantity of oxygen from stagnant air. In 1830, Boussingault had however already carried out a series of experiments, which seemed to show that only the air in the pores of the snow contained less oxygen than normal, and further experiments could easily be made.

It is far more likely that the climber is influenced by the intense reverberation of the sun's rays from the snow, by the stagnancy of the air allowing respired air to mix with inhaled air, and by the promotion of shallow respiration. The beneficial effect of air in motion is known to anyone who has occupied an inner cabin provided with an electric fan in a hot climate.

In the second connection, the benefit of a moderate breeze is undoubted, and appears to act by directly raising the alveolar oxygen pressure and other ways. Airmen probably benefit in this way as their speed creates a breeze. Freshfield[30] cites an opposite example on Elbruz, and the writer has found a breeze on snow at 23,000ft to make climbing comparatively easy. A very cold wind is not helpful.

In the case of high passes in the Himalaya or Andes, where mountain sickness has frequently been observed, the steepness and nature of the surface (eg loose scree) of the last few thousand feet would have a considerable effect. Fatigue might be produced, which, as will be indicated presently, is a potent cause of mountain sickness.

Another factor of importance would be the chance of modification of diet owing to difficulties of transport of fuel causing food to be either uncooked or badly cooked. Natives are notoriously improvident and thoughtless in this connection, and indigestion or want of food may have a considerable effect in accelerating an attack, especially if loads are being carried. Colonel Waddell[31] states for example that cases of mountain sickness on the Jeylap La (14,000ft) and other passes during the British Expedition to Tibet in 1904 were often due to indigestion from imperfect cooking of food, arising partly from hurry, but chiefly from insufficient fuel, and the lowered boiling point of water.

Finally the weather might have an effect by altering the difficulty of the route, lowering vitality, and promoting fatigue. The weather in certain Andean districts is exceptionally inhospitable.

Taking all of the above factors into consideration, one must come to the conclusion that any variable incidence of mountain sickness at approximately equal altitudes of narrow areas can probably be readily explained.

(5)[f] As regards the incidence of mountain sickness in the case of natives of high mountain regions, Humboldt[32] seems to have first stated that they were less resistent than white men. In connection with his attempt on Chimborazo, he states that the Indians with one exception abandoned them at an altitude of 15,600ft. 'Prayers and threats were alike vain; they declared that they were suffering much more than we.' Other Andean travellers, e.g. Bouguer, have seemed to corroborate this statement.

Travellers in the Himalaya, eg Dr and Mrs Bullock Workman, Dr Longstaff and Sven Hedin have made similar statements regarding natives indigenous to from 8,000 to 14,000ft, but Longstaff has also given reasons for their peculiar anomaly. He points out that the natives are as a rule carrying loads, which makes a great difference, and also that white men have usually more and better food than the natives. Longstaff's observations agree with those of the author, who has never observed a single case of mountain sickness in the case of picked trained natives climbing with him without loads in several expeditions up to over 23,000ft where clothing and food were carefully supervised.

Before going on to consider the causation of this baffling illness, a discussion of the incidence in a few specific cases at different altitudes may suggest reasons.

The most important general fact to note in this connection is that the incidence is very common if untrained individuals rapidly alter their altitude either by railway (or other means of transport) or by climbing. One of the best series of observations on the incidence of mountain sickness was carried out on Pikes Peak, Colorado (14,109ft) by Haldane and co-workers in 1911. Pikes Peak has a cogwheel railway to its summit, upon which there is a small hotel. The difference of incidence on an ascent when work was done, and fatigue might be expected, and an ascent by railway is very striking. Haldane summarizes as follows:

'Among the numerous visitors who came up by train and stayed only about three quarters of an hour, the most marked and almost universal symptoms was blueness of lips, cheeks etc., accompanied by great hyperpnoea (i.e. deep breathing) on exertion. As a rule there was no marked discomfort, but some persons became very miserable and faint, and actual fainting was observed occasionally as well as vomiting. One press representative who came to 'interview' us, became so alarmingly blue and faint that we gave him oxygen, which revived him at once, and immediately restored his colour and spirits. He continued all right for a few minutes, and then again became blue and faint, and was again revived by oxygen, after which he hurried into a descending train.

Among those who walked up, or came on donkeys, the symptoms were much more general and severe. The blueness was more marked, and nausea, vomiting, headache and fainting, were extremely common. Many persons walked or rode up during the night to see the sunrise, especially on Sunday morning, and the scene in the restaurant and on the platform outside can only be likened to that on the deck or in the cabin of a cross-channel steamer during rough weather.' And this occurred at 14,100ft!

Mental effects were also observed, as was to be expected, for the brain seems particularly sensitive to a deficiency of oxygen. Many visitors were inclined to be unreasonable, the symptoms being similar to those of alcoholic poisoning, and a Deputy Sheriff is therefore stationed at Summit House during the summer.

This psychic effect is apparently not confined to those unacclimatised to altitude. Miss FitzGerald[33], one of Haldane's collaborators, who independently carried out observations at many high mining camps in Colorado, states that the nervousness of the people, both men and women, was very apparent, especially above 7,000ft, and adds: 'The miners and others were fully conscious of this nervous tension, and attributed to this impulsive actions mentioned as common in mining communities at these altitudes.' At the same time it must be noted that the Tibetans, Nepalese and Bhutias resident at high altitudes do not seem to show similar symptoms of nerve tension, and as the altitudes considered are far below these for permanent acclimatisation, more data is required.

It might be observed however that there are many references to transient mental distress. Dr Saussure mentions 'an indescribable uneasiness,' Mumm[34] and Cheetham[35] both give interesting descriptions of profound mental depression; while Dr de Filippi and Dr Hans Meyer[36] describe another form of the malady. Dr Guglielminetti[37] states that 'one of the most curious results of mountain sickness was the annihilation of the will, and the complete indifference to ourselves and others' indicating a similarity with sea sickness.

Barcroft's[38] comments are of special interest, but space only permits quotation of the following note: 'At Col D'Olen (10,000ft) I have heard two clever and distinguished physiologists pause to discuss whether or not 4 times 8 made 32,' which reminds one of Mosso's statement that a Professor of Botany gradually forgot the names of plants as he ascended, but remembered them again as he descended.

In spite of such remarkable statements regarding comparatively low altitudes, psychic effects above 20,000ft are rarely mentioned, and these will be referred to later.

In the case of the visitors to Pikes Peak, the alteration of level would as a rule be 8,000 to 9,000ft, and similar cases of mountain sickness have been observed on other ascents where considerable change of height can be attained in a short period of time, for example on the Oroya Railway by which in about nine hours one can be taken from Lima (500ft) to Yanamina (15,732ft). Longstaff states that mountain sickness is not uncommon during ascents of Fusiyama (12,375ft), and the Peak of Teneriffe (12,200ft), both easy walks.

In the Alps the alterations of level in the case of the Rigi, Stanserhorn, Pilatus and Gorner Grat Railways are not so great as those mentioned above, and the final heights attained are also much less, so that mountain sickness is comparatively rare, but on the new Jungfrau Railway one would expect to meet with cases.

One can deduce from the above summary of known facts that mountain sickness is often met with if altitude is rapidly altered, especially by untrained tourists.

Causation of mountain sickness. One should now be able to indicate that these facts agree with the definition given, namely that mountain sickness depends upon deficiency of oxygen.

According to Jourdanet, d'Acosta[39] in 1590 was the first to definitely describe the symptoms as a definite illness. A few of the earlier reasons assigned to explain the symptoms are quaint and interesting.

The Jesuit Johannes Grueber[40] who crossed the Himalaya is 1661 assigned the blame to poisonous weeds, and others supposed minerals to have an effect, while MM Huc[41] and Gabet, who entered Tibet from China suggested carbon dioxide, but Desideri[42], an Italian priest who visited Lhasaa in 1715, arrived at a correct conclusion arguing as follows:

'Many people believe that the discomfort one experiences arises from the exhalation from certain minerals, but as no unmistakeable traces of such minerals have been found hitherto, I rather think that the unpleasant symptoms are due to the thin sharp air.'

Gerard[43] in 1817 similarly pointed out that the symptoms occurred where there was no vegetation so that 'the noxious qualities of a poisonous plant' could not be the cause.

In connection with Andean exploration, Bouguer and v. Tschudi may be mentioned. Bouguer[44], who remained encamped on the summit of the rock of Pinchincha (14,500ft) for three weeks in 1740, makes many interesting comments on mountain sickness, which he considered due to fatigue and cold, and not to the air.

v. Tschudi, who travelled in Peru about 1847, states that mountain sickness is called veta which means a 'lode' or soroche (signifying iron Pyrites) and is ascribed to the exhalation of metals, especially antimony.

By 1878 the real cause of mountain sickness had been deduced, and proved to be deficiency of oxygen. Jourdanet[45] elaborated the theoretical argument, and Prof. Paul Bert by a systematic series of experiments on men and animals 'had proved the theorem conclusively.'

Bert's experiments were carried out under different pressure, and using various mixtures of oxygen, nitrogen, and other gases. He showed clearly that symptoms similar to mountain sickness were produced when the partial pressure of oxygen in the mixture breathed fell below a certain value.

Two other theories have subsequently been proposed, firstly Prof. Angelo Mosso's 'Acapnia' theory, and secondly the mechanical theory of Dr Kronecker[46]. Space prevents discussion of these theories, and it might merely be stated that Mosso regards diminution of the carbon dioxide in the blood as the cause, and Kronecker states that 'mountain sickness depends not upon deficiency of oxygen in the air, but on circulatory disturbances in the lungs produced by the diminished air pressure.'

The researches of Haldane, Barcroft, and Zuntz seem to have proved these theories to be incorrect, but in connection with the 'acapnia' theory it is worth noting that recent American work[47] had indicated that the washing out of carbon dioxide from the blood by rapid breathing may cause an 'alkalosis' or abnormal alkaline condition, which might produce mountain sickness, and Sundstroem[48] has found this condition present in one case. As a rule the removal of carbon dioxide is caused by deficiency of oxygen, which would primarily be the cause of the rapid breathing. It is possible however that the alkalosia is merely transient under certain conditions and that a following acidosis would be present in some cases of mountain sickness. The carbon dioxide might be sub-normal for the conditions in each case, agreeing with Mosso's statement. Further work is required before the relationship between blood reaction and mountain sickness is definitely elucidated.

While deficiency of oxygen must be regarded as the primary cause of true mountain sickness, which alters the condition of the blood causing an alkalosis (or acidosis), the onset is promoted by several secondary factors of which the following are the chief: (I) Inadequate training, (II) Fatigue, (III) Diet, (IV) Want of acclimatisation to altitude, (V) Psychic effects, (VI) Temperature, (VII) Light effect, (VIII) Bad weather, (IX) Want of sleep, (X) Physical Defects. A few notes might be made with regard to each of above factors.

I **Inadequate training**. Mountaineering is one of the more strenuous forms of sport. For the individual of average weight the ascent 1,000ft per hour on a mountain means the expenditure of about 1/10 Horse power of energy. To keep up such an expenditure without disturbing the normal balance of the body is only easy for the individual in good training. In the case of the untrained, the rapid accumulation of fatigue products upsets the body's equilibrium, and some of the symptoms mentioned may result. Over 40 years ago Emile Javelle[49] noted that 'novices who begin by a big excursion have frequently to pay tribute.'

The main difference between the trained and the untrained men depends upon many factors. The condition known as 'Health' is not a static, but is a dynamic state of complicated balance. Training means the tuning up of all the complexly related systems of the body to a condition of maximum resiliency, a numerous series of waste products being eliminated during the process. Some of these have slowly been accumulating in certain types of cells owing to work done, or are eddying in stagnant backwaters, where they clog the capacity for muscular and mental exertion.

In the case of the average towns dweller, the resiliency is small, and strenuous exertion over an extended period will cause bad effects even at sea level. In the case of the trained man, on the contrary, the excellent inter-relationship of the different systems of the body means that work is done with the minimum production of unnecessary heat, that is to say, there is little waste of energy. Not only so, but the muscular co-ordinations of the man trained to mountain climbing are so arranged as to give exceptional efficiency, which may mean a considerable gain. Hueppe worked out a series of determinations, using towns dwellers and an Alpine porter as subjects, with the result that the efficiency of the porter as regards work performed was about 100 per cent above that of the untrained man. Dr Gruber[50] and Prof. Kronecker confirmed the increase of efficiency during training by another series of experiments on work done in the ascent of the Cathedral Tower of Berne.

Both researches proved that the trained man requires far less oxygen during an ascent than the untrained.

II **Fatigue.** During exercise as already noted, fatigue products are produced, which tend to upset the body's state of dynamic equilibrium. Even the trained individual may be attacked by mountain sickness in some form if he over-exerts himself, e.g. ascends at 2,000ft per hour when over 10,000ft, which represents about 1/5 HP. It is therefore best to go at a moderate steady pace, as experienced mountaineers well know, and if a slightly trained man is in the party, frequent halts may allow him to accomplish long arduous accents without mountain sickness, because, in the case of healthy people, the body is continually striving to get back to its normal state of balance, as will be discussed later.

III **Diet.** The importance of diet in connection with mountain sickness is well known to all practised mountaineers. While the trained individual can eat a moderate meal of the common foodstuffs at any hour of the day or night, the untrained man should be careful to select the more easily digestible proteins, fats and carbohydrates. A heavy meal might promote mountain sickness, especially above 15,000ft, by inducing cerebral anaemia, and anything causing indigestion at sea level would act similarly. More will be said regarding foodstuffs in connection with acclimatisation to high altitudes, where diet is of special importance. Want of sufficient food might cause mountain sickness by promoting exhaustion.

IV **Want of acclimatisation to altitude.** It has already been pointed out that mountain sickness commonly attacks untrained individuals, who by railway or other means rapidly change altitude, and from what has been said above, it is evident that the untrained man who has ascended by walking say from 5,000 to 14,000ft is sure to be more acutely attacked, than the man who ascends by rail. The reactions to altitude mentioned as occurring on Pikes Peak are quite typical. If however untrained people remained for a few days in the comfortable hotel at the summit, where normal diet and exercise could readily be taken, they became quite well, and able to carry out a nearly normal amount of work. The complex manner by which the body adapts itself to altitude will be discussed later, as it is obviously of great importance.

V **Psychic Effects.** A few notes have already been made in this connection. Under certain conditions psychic effects might be of importance. In the case of a beginner in a dangerous position, temporary splanchnic dilation with cerebral anaemia might start mountain sickness, but this effect seems comparatively rare.

VI **Temperature.** Extreme cold, by reducing the vitality, or excessive heat, by promoting either shallow respiration or by causing panting, might precipitate an attack of mountain sickness, since the former would cause deficient oxygenation, and the latter might promote an exceptional alkalosis of the blood as already indicated.

VII **Light.** The intense snow glare of high altitudes should only have an effect if the spectacles were inadequate.

VIII **Bad Weather,** IX **Want of Sleep,** and X **Physical Defects** might act by causing exhaustion, especially if insufficient food were available. In a few cases the sense of equilibrium may be disturbed by the unusual movements of the semicircular canals of the inner ear.

The first 4 factors mentioned above, Training, Fatigue, Diet, and want of acclimatisation, are the more important secondary causes of mountain sickness, but it must be emphasised that the first three might cause sickness at sea level, and therefore all illness on the mountains is not necessarily real mountain sickness. If however deficiency of oxygen is an appreciable factor it may be so regarded. Dr Pavy[51] for example mentions an opposite case of an athlete who walked 65½ miles at an average speed (including short rests) of 4½ miles per hour, but was obligated to give in after 14 hours 25 mm with symptoms identical to those of acute mountain sickness. If the same amount of exercise had been carried out by the same individual on a mountain, similar illness would have occurred earlier. This fact explains cases on mountains like the Niesen and Faulhorn cited by Dr Kronecker, the sickness in such cases being presumably due to want of training, and being primarily due to fatigue, and secondarily to deficiency of oxygen. At comparatively low levels under 4,000ft surprising distances can be covered in one day. The best known case is that of Dr Wakefield[52], who covered over 85 miles in the English Lake District including many ascents aggregating 25,000ft in 22 hours 7 min.

A few examples from mountaineering literature would perhaps make the above consideration of secondary factors more concrete.

Dr Egli. Sinclair[53] and two companions, sceptical as to the reality of mountain sickness, ascended to the Vallot hut on Mt. Blanc (14,000ft approx.), and remained there 13 days. As Dr Monro[54] puts it, they descended 'sadder, thinner and wiser men,' having suffered from lack of appetite, and other symptoms during the whole of their visit. Dr Egli. Sinclair lost about 14 lbs in weight. This evidently is a case of want of acclimatisation, and perhaps also insufficient training.

In connection with ascents up to 16,000ft one must remember that the pioneers of Mount Blanc, Dr Paccard and Jacques Balmat unroped, without a tent, and probably inadequate food ascended the mountain, and returned with easily avoidable snow blindness as the only evil effect.

In the Duke of the Abruzzi's ascent of Mt. St Elias, 18,090ft the incidence of mountain sickness was quite exceptional, in contradistinction to the experiences of his party in the Karakorum Himalaya, which will be referred to later. On Mt. St Elias, Dr de Filippi[55] states that '6 out of 10 white men suffered, but that was largely due to fatigue and excitement and consequent want of sleep on the preceding night.' Want of acclimatisation would also be a factor.

It has already been pointed out that in Whymper's[56] first ascent of Chimborazo, he and his guides suffered from an acute attack of mountain sickness at 16,664ft, which he describes in his usual graphic manner, beginning as follows: 'When we arrived at 16,664ft, we ourselves were in good condition, which was to be expected, as we had ridden most of the way, but in half an hour I found myself lying on my back along with the Carrels, hors de combat and incapable of making the least exertion.' This was evidently a case of want of acclimatisation, and for various reasons a meal taken immediately before may have been another factor. The experiences of Fitzgerald[57] and Vines on Aconcagua and Young-husband[79] in the Karakoram are also examples where want of acclimatisation had an effect.

It is obvious therefore that acclimatisation to altitude will be of special importance in connection with any attempts on Mt. Everest, and the factors affecting acclimatisation are worth careful consideration, but it might be emphasised before going further that with due precautions, acute mountain sickness may be entirely avoided up to the highest altitude so far attained, namely 24,600ft.

5   THE PROCESS OF ACCLIMATISATION TO ALTITUDE

Many extended experiments in connection with acclimatisation to altitude have been carried out at heights between 12,000 and 15,000ft. The results are unfortunately not in agreement, and space prevents a discussion of the variations. In the case of Haldane's party of four on Pikes Peak (14,109ft), where conditions were peculiarly favourable, all suffered somewhat at first, but acclimatisation had progressed considerably in a few days, although it varied between three and four weeks before the process seemed complete. Their experience was typical as already indicated for Haldane states that 'among healthy persons it appeared to be invariably the case that after a stay of two or more days on the summit, the blueness, headache, nausea, lack of appetite etc. completely disappeared, while the excessive hyperpnoea on exertion became less. It was thus perfectly clear that acclimatisation to the low pressure occurred to a very marked extent.' The difference between the rapid acclimatisation on Pikes Peak, as compared with attempts in the Alps already referred to, indicates the importance of comfort and diet in this connection.

The problem which now has to be solved in connection with Mt. Everest might be stated as follows:- Is it possible to become sufficiently acclimatised to high altitudes to enable one to climb from a camp at 25,500ft or thereby to the summit (29,141ft) in one day? This question can only be answered after a study of the scientific explanation of acclimatisation to moderate altitudes, which has been worked out by Haldane, Barcroft, Zuntz, Mosso, Hasselbalch[58] and their respective co-workers. In order to render the explanation clear, a further note must be made regarding respiration.

During the process of respiration as already noted, the violet substance called Haemoglobin present in the blood cells takes up oxygen from the lungs forming a red compound called oxyhaemoglobin, which is carried to the heart, and then pumped through the arteries to the tissues, where it gives up its oxygen, thus maintaining life, which depends upon the continuity of a series of slow oxidation reactions. The two processes mentioned might be represented as a reversible chemical equation.

$$Hb + O_2 \rightleftharpoons HbO_2$$

In the lungs under a certain pressure of oxygen, which varies with altitudes, oxyhaemoglobin is formed, and in the tissues, where the oxygen pressure is less, oxygen is given up, forming carbon dioxide and other products. It is obvious that a study of the pressure conditions under which haemoglobin respectively takes up and gives up oxygen might help one to understand the physiological difficulties of respiration at high altitudes.

Experiments were carried out by Hüfner, with haemoglobin dissolved in water at blood temperature ($34°C$), and a varying pressure of oxygen, with the following results [Table 1].

To enable these values to be thoroughly understood, consider one pressure, e.g. 60 mm. If a large quantity of air containing oxygen of partial pressure 60 mm be shaken with a small quantity of haemoglobin dissolved in pure water, the haemoglobin takes up oxygen until 92 per cent saturated, that is to say there would be in solution 92 per cent oxyhaemoglobin, and eight per cent of haemoglobin.

If the oxygen pressure be increased, as by adding oxygen, more of that gas will be taken up by the solution, but if the oxygen pressure be diminished, as by adding nitrogen, oxygen will be given off from the oxyhaemoglobin; for example if the pressure of the oxygen were diminished to 10 mm, oxygen would be given up until 50 per cent of haemoglobin remained as oxyhaemoglobin.

The connection between the haemoglobin in water, and the oxygen pressure is best represented not by the figures in Table 1, but by a curve,

TABLE I	
Pressure of Oxygen in millimetres of mercury	Percentage saturation of the haemoglobin with oxygen
10	50
20	71
30	81.7
40	87
50	90
60	92
70	93.5
80	94.5
90	95.5
100	96

which shows graphically the relationship between the two interrelated quantities.

Plotting the pressure of oxygen in millimetres of mercury horizontally, and the percentage saturation of haemoglobin in water vertically, one obtains what is termed the Dissociation Curve of Oxyhaemoglobin in water [FIG.2].

This dissociation curve, worked out by Hüfner, somewhat puzzled physiologists, because even at comparatively low pressures, the haemoglobin is nearly saturated with oxygen. For example, the alveolar oxygen pressure in the lungs at the top of Mt. Blanc (15,780ft) should be nearly 50 mm corresponding to 90 per cent saturation, and at sea level the oxygen pressure is about 102 mm corresponding to a saturation of 96 per cent. The trifling difference of six per cent in saturation for an alteration in altitude of nearly 16,000ft should not cause serious effects, and Bert's explanation that oxygen deficiency was the exciting cause of mountain sickness seemed unintelligible.

The difference was explained when it was discovered that the Dissociation Curve of Haemoglobin in blood is quite different from that of Haemoglobin in water. Many factors affect the action of oxygen on haemoglobin, notably (1) Temperature, (2) Presence of Carbon Dioxide (an acidic body), (3) Presence of other acidic bodies like lactic acid, (4) presence of salts.

With regard to temperature, it is obviously only profitable to consider one temperature, viz. 37°C (99°F), the normal blood temperature.

The substances mentioned are present in blood, and tend to flatten the dissociation curve of haemoglobin. The normal dissociation curve of haemoglobin in blood can be drawn from the following experimental data [Table 2], the pressure of carbon dioxide being taken as 40 mm, the normal pressure at sea level.

These results can be expressed by a curve, the Discussion Curve of Haemoglobin in blood [FIG.3]. For comparison the Dissociation Curve of Haemoglobin in water is given as a dotted curve.

The blood of each individual has a particular characteristic dissociation curve, but the variation is not great, and need not be considered. The accompanying curve [FIG.4] shows graphically the possibility of variation in normal individuals as given by Barcroft.

This normal Dissociation Curve for Haemoglobin in blood is, as already remarked, flatter than that for haemoglobin in water, with the result that the haemoglobin is less saturated for any given pressure of oxygen. For example, the saturation of haemoglobin in water with oxygen at 24 mm oxygen pressure – the calculated alveolar pressure for the top of Mt. Everest – would be 74 per cent, whereas the saturation of haemoglobin in blood with oxygen at the same pressure would be only about 40 per cent.

Variations of the dissociation curve due to carbon dioxide. As the quantity of carbon dioxide in the lungs diminishes with altitude, the

TABLE 2	
Oxygen pressure in millimetres of mercury	*Percentage saturation of the haemoglobin in blood with oxygen*
10	10
20	32
30	57
40	74
50	84
60	90
70	92
80	93.5
90	95
100	96

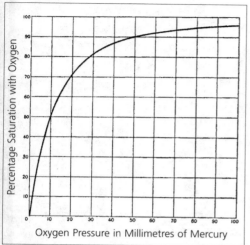

FIG 2. Curve No. 1:
Dissociation Curve of Oxy-Haemoglobin
dissolved in water at 37°C
(Blood Temperature)

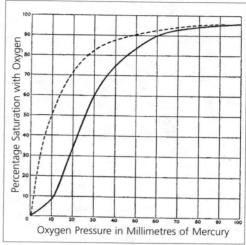

FIG 3. Curve Series No. 2:
Dissociation Curve of Oxy-Haemoglobin in
Blood at 37°C (Blood Temp.). The Dissociation
Curve of Oxy-Haemoglobin in water is given
as a broken line for comparison.

effect of the variation of carbon dioxide from the normal 40 mm present at sea level might seem worth study and expression by a series of curves. It will be sufficient to indicate the curves, without giving the data of the experiments [FIG.5].

From these curves, one might suppose that at high altitudes, as the carbon dioxide diminishes, the dissociation curve would be displaced to the left, and the blood haemoglobin more easily saturated with oxygen, which on superficial consideration might seem advantageous to the climber[58a]. Barcroft however proved by experiments carried out on the Peak of Teneriffe that, although the carbon dioxide in the blood diminished with altitude, yet the resting dissociation curve for any individual was nearly identical with his curve at sea level. This perhaps means that, at rest, the hydrogen ion concentration of the blood (i.e. its acidity or alkalinity) remains nearly constant.

This surprising fact was confirmed by Haldane on Pikes Peak, and the explanation was thought by Barcroft to depend upon an increased acidity (or rather diminished alkalinity) of the blood in such quantity as to exactly compensate for the loss of carbon dioxide, which itself is acidic in character, but this explanation has recently been questioned.

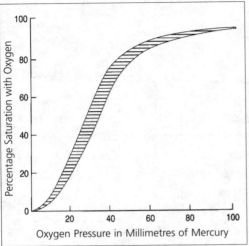

FIG 4. Curve Series No. 3:
Graphic Representation of the Limits
of the Oxy-Haemoglobin Dissociation
Curve for Blood of Normal Individuals.

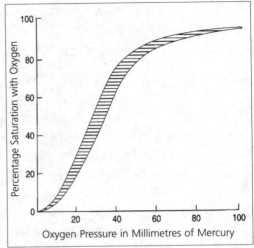

FIG 5. Curve Series No. 4:
Curves showing the effect of different
pressures of Carbon Dioxide (CO_2) in Blood, on
the Dissociation Curve of Oxy-Haemoglobin.
The Normal Curve at sea level (40mm. CO_2)
is given as a continuous line, and the other
curves as broken lines.

This relationship between carbon dioxide and blood acidity is of far more vital importance than might at first sight appear. The *automatic regulation of the process of respiration* at sea level depends primarily upon the carbon dioxide in the blood, the pressure of which is the same as that in the alveoli of the lungs. The carbon dioxide in the blood affects the regulation by acting directly on a nerve tract called the 'respiratory centre' in the medulla oblongata, nerves from which control the muscles of respiration. Normally 12 to 18 respirations occur in a minute with the body quiescent as already noted, but if work is being done, more carbon dioxide is produced, the respiratory centre is more powerfully stimulated, and one breathes more deeply and rapidly, thus supplying the necessary extra oxygen to the tissues.

One can confirm the above explanation by the following simple experiment. If while at rest one breathes rapidly for about a minute – forced breathing – so as to wash the carbon dioxide out of the blood, the respiratory centre ceases to be stimulated, and breathing stops – apnoea until sufficient carbon dioxide is formed to act as an excitant. A few individuals are not so affected, the reason for this being still obscure.

At high altitudes, as mentioned, the quantity of carbon dioxide in the blood is lowered, but the acidity increases (or rather the alkalosis produced by removal of carbon dioxide is diminished correspondingly), and the respiratory centre remains adequately stimulated, but the exact relationships are not yet fully understood.

It follows that there is little danger of the normal acclimatised individual fainting at high altitudes because of apnoea induced by the rapid breathing during climbing, which invariably occurs above 22,000ft. This is of primary importance because an unacclimatised individual in an air-chamber at 310mm corresponding to 25,000ft might faint if he carried out forced breathing, and so induced apnoea.

The effects of diet and exercise on the dissociation curve of oxy-haemoglobin are probably of considerable importance in connection with mountain sickness, but more work is required, and space prevents discussion, except with regard to exercise.

During muscular work there is increased production of acid bodies, such as carbon dioxide and lactic acid. The next curve series shows the effect of adding .025 per cent of lactic acid to blood. It will be observed that the curve is displaced to the right, as on addition of carbon dioxide (curve Series No.5) [FIG.6].

Barcroft and collaborators have carried out experiments where ascents were made under definite conditions, for example from sea level to 1,000 ft on Slieve Foy (Ireland), and from 10,000 to 15,000ft on Monte Rosa. The next curve Series shows the effects of this exercise [FIG.7].

It is evident from these curves that the more severe and continued the exercise, the greater is the displacement of the dissociation curve, and it is obvious too that the displacement could not go on indefinitely without causing physiological disturbances, if exercise requiring a large quantity of oxygen were carried out[58b]. During rest, the dissociation curve tends to return gradually to its normal value, so that adequate halts are important in preventing mountain sickness as already noted.

We are now in a position to grasp the significance of the different factors conditioning acclimatisation to moderate altitudes. These factors are five in number, and might be briefly discussed in the following order. The third factor is at present debatable:

1   The oxygen pressure in the alveolar air rises.

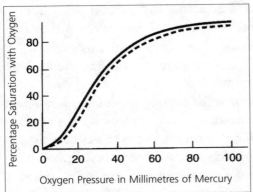

FIG 6. Curve Series No. 5:
Dissociation Curve of Oxy-Haemoglobin in
Blood to which .025 per cent of Lactic Acid
has been added, shown as a broken line.
The Normal Dissociation Curve is given as a
continuous line.

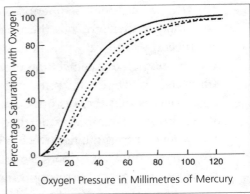

FIG 7. Curve Series No. 6:
The Effect of Exercise upon the Dissociation
Curve. The Curve represented by a dotted line
shows the displacement of the Dissociation
Curve produced by an ascent of 1,000 ft from
sea level in 30 min. The Curve represented by
a broken line shows the change produced by
an ascent from 10,000 to 15,000 ft in 8 hours.
The Normal Dissociation Curve of the same
person at sea level is given as a continuous line
for comparison.

2   The number of red blood corpuscles, and the quantity of haemoglobin in the blood increase in due proportion to each other.

3   There may be actual secretion of oxygen by the lung epithelium,
that the arterial oxygen pressure can be raised above that in the
alveoli.

4   The frequency and depth of breathing may both be increased.

5   The blood stream may circulate more rapidly during exercise at
high altitudes than at sea level.

(a) Increase of oxygen pressure in the alveolar air. The increase of
pressure of oxygen is brought about at altitudes above sea level by the
abnormally small quantity of oxygen causing deeper and more rapid breathing, which lowers the carbon dioxide in the blood causing alkalosis. The
alkali in the blood is then lowered to agree with the remaining carbon
dioxide, other acidic bodies compensating, for the loss of the latter, as
already noted. The diminution of carbon dioxide in the alveolar air means
an increase of oxygen. The acclimatisation may take a few days before
equilibrium is reached, depending upon the altitude, but the major part

of the alteration takes place rapidly in healthy individuals. The gain of alveolar oxygen pressure is considerable, as is shown in the following table [Table 3].

Considering the calculated and observed pressures at 15,000ft the great advantage of the extra 17 mm pressure is evident. On referring to the Dissociation Curve of Haemoglobin in blood, one sees that at 51.4 mm pressure of oxygen the blood would be almost about 80 per cent saturated with that gas, whereas at 35 mm pressure it would only be about 65 per cent saturated. One notes too that the alveolar oxygen pressure corresponding to 25,000ft would only be 7mm if the carbon dioxide pressure remained at 40mm as at sea level, a value far below that which would support life. As many healthy individuals can be rapidly decompressed in airchambers to 25,000ft, this illustrates the astonishing adaptability of the body.

An interesting point in connection with this alteration of the oxygen pressure has been worked out by Barcroft. Many climbers at high altitudes have noted that, even after thorough training, a considerable ascent and return to a lower camp seems advantageous. According to Barcroft the real reason depends upon diminution of alkalinity of the blood (acidosis) produced by climbing at the higher altitude, but this is uncertain. In any case, it means diminution of carbon dioxide, and increase of alveolar oxygen as described, and on descending the lowered carbon dioxide persists

TABLE 3

Table Showing the Variation of Oxygen Pressure on Acclimatisation caused by Alteration of Alveolar Carbon Dioxide Pressure with Altitude

Altitude feet	Atmospheric pressure 15°C	Alveolar Pressure of Oxygen: Calculated for 40mm CO_2 as at sea level	Alveolar Pressure of Oxygen: Either observed or calculated for acclimatisation condition
Sea level	760	102 (approx.)	102 (approx.)
5,000	635	75.1	82.9
10,000	529.5	53.4	67.1
15,000	443.4	35.0	51.4
20,000	367.6	19.1	39.3
25,000	309.5	7.0	28.6
28,225	276	0	25.1

for some time, so that the oxygen pressure at the lower elevation is higher than normal for that altitude.

(b) Increase of red corpuscles and haemoglobin. As first observed, by Viault[59], there is generally as a rule an increase in the number of red blood corpuscles and haemoglobin in the peripheral blood at high altitudes, and this undoubtedly seems to constitute an important factor in connection with acclimatisation to moderate altitudes up to at least 18,500ft. Data above that height are at present meagre, and their significance uncertain. The normal number of peripheral red corpuscles for man[59a] is about 5,000,000 per cubic millimetre at sea level, and values up to over 8,000,000 have been recorded at different altitudes. A few typical determinations might be quoted [Table 4].

The above values seem easy of interpretation. To use a familiar simile, the number of ships available for carrying their precious cargo of oxygen to the tissues is increased, more oxygen cargoes will therefore be despatched in a given time from the lungs, and this may compensate for a diminution in weight of each freight carried.

If, however, the number of corpuscles increases quickly simultaneously with a rapid alteration in altitude, it is almost certain that the blood merely concentrates itself by transudation of part of its plasma (in which corpuscles float) through the capillary walls, into the lymphatic system; this would of course mean an increase in the number of corpuscles per cubic millimetre.

TABLE 4

The Variation of Red Blood Corpuscles with Altitude

Place	Altitude		Red corpuscles
	Metres	Feet	
Sea level	0	0	5,000,000 (approx.)
Zurich	412	1,352	5,752,000
Davos Platz	1,560	5,118	6,551,000
Pikes Peak	4,300	14,109	7,000,000 (approx.)
Andes	4,392	14,410	8,000,000
Taghdumbash	3,200	10,500	6,624,800
Pamir	4,115	13,500	7,402,500
	5,548	18,203	8,320,000

In 1908 the writer carried out a series of experiments in London and Silvaplana, which seemed suggestive. His average corpuscular value in London was approx. 5,400,000. During the journey of about 30 hours duration, (which meant rail to St Moritz, and then drive of four miles) his red corpuscular value rose to approx. 6,200,000, that is to say there was an increase of about 800,000 corpuscles per cubic millimetre, during a rise of about 6,000ft. As it would be difficult to devise anything less stimulating to the corpuscle-manufacturing mechanism of the body than a long railway journey, concentration of the blood must have occurred. The same phenomenon has been noted by other observers and by balloonists.

In several recent researches on the subject however, for example those of Cohrtheim[60], Morawitz[61], Zuntz and Sundstroem, no great increase of corpuscles was found at 7,000 or even at 10,000ft, but one doubts the reality of the acclimatisation in such cases. On Pikes Peak Haldane found the results for different individuals varied greatly, but there was a distinct gradual increase during about a month in each case. The increase of haemoglobin as measured colorimetrically varied between 115 and 154, taking 100 as the normal value for sea level. The corpuscular increase was proportional.

It is assumed that this slow increase probably represents abnormal production of new or slower destruction of old corpuscles than usual; there is a third theory which assumes variation of distribution of corpuscles in the peripheral and deeper blood.

An interesting curve worked out by the manager of a tin mine at Pazna, Bolivia (15,000ft) is worth reproducing from the paper by Haldane on the Pikes Peak observations[G]. It shows that after leaving sea level, the curve of haemoglobin value rose rapidly during four day's journey while ascending to Pazna (this rapid increase being presumably chiefly due to transudation of plasma), and then continued to increase for about 2½ months. The variation was from 94 at sea level to 146 at Pazna after long acclimatisation [FIG.8].

Some observers regard this alteration of corpuscular and haemoglobin value as the chief adaptation to high altitudes, and as already mentioned it is undoubtedly important. Hingston[62], who was engaged in survey work on the Pamir ranges, states that a carrier of his, who seemed inadaptable to high altitudes, had a blood count of only 5,750,000 at 13,300ft, whereas the rest of the party had a value of about 7,000,000. It is worth noting in this connection, however, that Sundstroem gives 7,610,000 as occurring after a month at sea level, and that two of Haldane's party during nearly a month on Pikes Peak (14,109ft) had lower average values than what Hingston considered inadequate, namely 5,530,000 and 5,240,000 respectively, although both were in excellent health, and at a higher level. It is worth mentioning also that the author at a camp at 20,000ft had a blood count of only 6,500,000, and on ascending Pawhunri (23,180ft), and taking his blood count a few hours after return to this camp, it was only 7,200,000. This presumably means that incomplete acclimatisation to the altitude produced a temporary anaemia. Diet and exercise probably affect matters, especially above 20,000ft, and there is considerable individual idiosyncracy as indicated in Table IV. According to Dr Jacot. Guillarmod[80], severe anaemia may occur during indisposition at high altitudes.

(c) Excretion of oxygen by the alveolar epithelium. Two theories have been proposed to explain the passage of oxygen from the alveoli of the lungs to the blood, through the epithelium and capillary walls. One theory supposes that the physical process of diffusion is sufficient to explain the transference, but the other postulates that under certain conditions, e.g. high altitudes, or hard physical work, the cells of the lung epithelium secrete oxygen from the alveoli, and pass it on to the blood in the capillaries. According to the first theory, the oxygen pressure in the alveoli would always be greater than the arterial oxygen pressure, but according to the second, the arterial oxygen pressure might be higher or lower than the alveolar.

Haldane's party on Pikes Peak found that the arterial oxygen pressure in acclimatised subjects was invariably far greater than the alvelolar pressure (35mm above or more), whereas in newcomers it was about the same, and they regard the secretory action of the lung epithelium to be one of the most important means of adaptation to high altitudes. If secretion actually occurs, its value at high altitudes must be considerable, but Krogh[63] and other physiologists oppose the theory, so that further confirmation is required. Haldane's recent acclimatisation experiments in airchambers seem to confirm the theory.

(d) Increase of the frequency and depth of breathing. During exercise at

high altitude, there is no doubt that this method of compensation is an important one. M. Vallot[64], who has carried out many experiments near the summit of Mt. Blanc, writes as follows:

'Par quel méchanisme d'accommodation les habitants de hautes régions du globe peuvent-ils s'habituer à l'air raréfié des grandes altitudes? Là encore mes experiences peuvent donner la clé du mystére. Trois journées d'habitation au sommet du Mont Blanc ont suffi pour modifier entièrement le regime de ma respiration; le dernier jour, ma capacité pulmonaire avait notablement augmenté, et mesurait 2500 (au lieu de 1000 c.c.); le nombre des inspirations était de 17 par minute, au lieu de 14 dans la plaine.'

The following table [Table 5], reduced from a series of results obtained in the Pikes Peak expedition, gives a few figures for reference, and clearly shows the nature of this form of compensation to altitude.

It will be observed that there is a great increase in the volume of the

TABLE 5						
				At 37°c, moist & prevailing barometer		Vol.
Place	Conditions	Bar. pressure	Breaths per min.	Litres breathed per min.	Cubic centimetres per breath	breathed 0°c & 760mm dry	Ratio to sea level as unity (volumes)
Oxford	At rest, standing	752	17.1	10.4	612	8.5	1.4
Pikes Peak	do. do.	459	20.8	14.9	726	7.1	
Oxford	3 miles per hour	747	16.2	24.8	1,535	20.1	1.6
Pikes Peak	do. do.	460	24.4	38.8	1,595	18.6	
Oxford	4 miles per hour	749	18.2	37.3	2,064	30.3	1.5
Pikes Peak	do. do.	459	24.1	57.0	2,369	27.2	
Oxford	5 miles per hour	756	18.5	46.5	2,524	38.2	2.4
Pikes Peak	do. do.	461	35.9	110.2	3,085	52.9	
Pikes Peak	Gradient of 1 in 4	459	47.8	108.4	2,295	51.7	2.3

air breathed on Pikes Peak as compared with sea level, the ratio being 1.6 to 1 for 3 miles per hour, (instead of 1.7 to 1 as required by the relative pressures,) which agrees with M. Vallot. At 5 miles per hour, however, and on a steep gradient, the ratio has become so high, that care would be required or mountain sickness might supervene.

It must be pointed out too, that the above figures do not agree with those of other observers. Mosso states that an average of 6 persons gave a volume ration of 1.17 for the Margherita hut of Monte Rosa (14,965ft), taking the volume at sea level as unity, instead of 1.8 to 1 which would correspond to the relative pressures, but the low ratio presumably means imperfect acclimatisation.

Drs A & J Loewy and L Zuntz[65] found that the rate of respiration and respiratory volume increased at first, but during a stay at the Gnifetti Hut on Monte Rosa (11,965ft), they afterwards gradually decreased.

(e) More rapid circulation of the blood at high altitudes during moderate exercise. On Pikes Peak, the pulse rate at rest was generally considerably accelerated for the first few days, but after acclimatisation reverted to a little above normal.

On moderate exercise however, the pulse rate rose to a much greater extent than at sea level. This would be beneficial if the rate were not very rapid, (say beyond 120).

Allowing for difference in conditions, these results agree with determinations in airchambers, where the pulse rate is practically invariably quickened at low pressures, but usually after some time tends to revert towards normal. Two examples in airchambers might be given, which show that the individual variation is great, and this is also true on the mountains, where similar values are met with, but more data are required in this latter case.

Pressure	Pulse rate for short period	Pressure	Pulse rate for short period
720	64	760	72
650	72	360	85
424	84	312	95

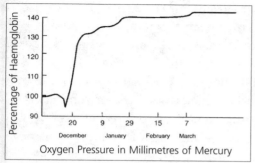

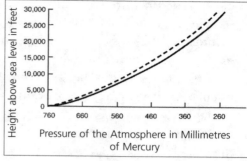

FIG 8. Curve Series No. 7:
Curves showing the variation of Haemoglobin Value during three consecutive months, the first of which was spent at sea level, one week was then spent between sea level and 15,000 ft, and the remaining 7 weeks at 15,000 ft. 100 Per Cent Haemoglobin is taken as the normal value for sea-level.

FIG 9. Curve Series No. 8:
Normal Pressure Curves. Curves showing the variation of Atmospheric Pressure with Altitude, when the pressure at sea-level is normal. Curve for 0°C is broken. Curve for Temp. of 15°C is continuous.

General Conclusion from Physiological Data

There seems to be no doubt that (a) the rise of alveolar oxygen pressure, (b) the diminution in the alveolar carbon dioxide pressure, and corresponding decrease in acidity of the blood, and (c) the increase in the quantity of haemoglobin and red corpuscles are of great value in promoting acclimatisation. If confirmed, the secretion of oxygen by the lung epithelium will doubtless be further studied, and might yield useful information.

While one must keep in view that personal idiosyncracy in the case of each person is considerable, much more work must be carried out at high altitudes before exact evaluation of the different factors conditioning acclimatisation can be made, but all above considerations are valuable, as enabling one to form approximate conclusions.

One might, however, work out the essentials of the problem under consideration in another way. If one could determine the relative strain under which the body has to undergo adaptation at different altitudes, the approximate difficulties of an advance above 25,000ft can be computed.

The strain can be gauged by consideration of the relative capacities for saturation of the blood at different heights under the respective alveolar pressures, which would obtain after acclimatisation. A connected series of these curves will show the theoretical relative difficulties of ascent at high altitudes.

The first curves (Series No. 8) [FIG.9] show the alteration of normal barometric pressure with altitude. Two variants of the curves are given, so as to indicate the considerable effect of mean temperature of the air-column. To make the relationships more concrete, the pressures at a few of the chief summits of the different continents are indicated.

The values might be given in a table [Table 6], along with the calculated alveolar oxygen pressures for acclimatisation at their summits, as the latter are required in drawing other curves[h]. From recent experiments (Haldane) it is probable that in the case of the loftier mountains, the calculated values are 2 or 3mm too low.

The curve shows that the variation of pressure with increase of altitude becomes relatively smaller as one ascends, a factor of advantage to the climber. From sea level at 0°c one only has to ascend 34.6ft to alter the pressure of the atmosphere by 1mm, but at 29,000ft one would have to climb 104.5ft to alter the pressure to the same extent.

The second curve [FIG.10] expresses the relationship of the alveolar oxygen pressure to altitude. This curve indicated that while the oxygen in the atmosphere diminishes to one third at the top of Mt. Everest, the

TABLE 6

| Mountain | Height | | Barometric Pressure | | Alveolar oxygen pressure calculated |
	Feet	Metres	0°C millimetres	15°C millimetres	
Mount Everest	29,141	8,882	251.0	266.9	236
Kangchenjunga	28,225	8,603	259.9	275.8	25.0
Nanga Parbat	26,620	8,114	276.3	292.2	27.8
Kamet	25,447	7,756	288.9	304.7	29.4
Aconcagua	23,080	7,035	316.1	331.8	33.6
Denali	20,400	6,187	351.3	366.6	39.2
Kilima 'Njaro	19,321	5,889	364.7	379.7	41.2
Mt. Elbruz	18,465	5,628	376.4	391.2	43.3
Mt. Ararat	16,969				
Mt. Blanc	15,785	4,811	417.2	431.0	49.5
Aorangi (Mt. Cook)					
Fusi Yama approx.	12,349	3,764	475.3	487.8	58.9
Gorner Grat	10,290	3,136	514.0	524.0	65.0
Mt. Kosciusko	7,328	2,236	575.0	584.0	73.5
Rigi	5,905	1,800	606.0	613.0	78.4
Ben Nevis	4,406	1,343	642.0	649.0	83.6
Scafell Pike	3,210	978.4	673.0	677.0	88.7
Sea Level	0	0	760	760	102.5

available oxygen, as shown by the calculated alveolar oxygen pressure (24mm) diminishes to less than a fourth of that at sea level (102.5mm approx). This, of course, tells heavily against the climber, but, as already observed, 24mm is probably too low.

The relative capabilities of the different alveolar oxygen pressures at the heights mentioned to saturate the blood is well indicated by plotting the heights of the mountains on the Dissociation curve of Oxyhaemo-globin in blood, as to show the alveolar oxygen pressures at their summits [FIG.11]. This curve is very suggestive, in fact from the climbers point of view, it is most important of all those considered.

The curve shows that the strain on the climber is nearly negligible up to 10,000ft, and at about 15,000ft becomes appreciable, but one must pass above 20,000ft before the steepening of the curve indicates that the mountaineer will have to adapt himself carefully to his aerial environment. At 23,000ft the curve is getting much steeper, and the climber will obviously be put on his mettle above 25,000ft for the curve then attains its greater inclination. Every thousand feet still higher must mean considerably increased difficulty, and the climber near the summit of Mt. Everest

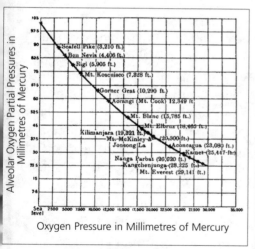

FIG 10. Curve Series No. 9:
Curve showing the variation of Alveolar Oxygen Pressure with Altitude.

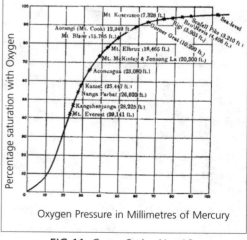

FIG 11. Curve Series No. 10:
Dissociation Curve of Oxy-Haemoglobin in Blood with the heights of a few notable mountains plotted so as to show the saturation of the Blood with Oxygen corresponding to the alveolar oxygen pressures at their summits.

will probably be near his last reserves in the way of acclimatisation and strength, if ascending without adventitious aids.

The different factors conditioning acclimatisation to high altitudes have now been fully considered, but there remains a problem which so far has not been worked out, namely the limits of permanent acclimatisation to high altitudes, that is to say, what is the maximum height at which one could live without steadily losing strength.

Limits of Permanent Acclimatisation to High Altitudes

The experiences of most mountaineers, who have climbed above 20,000ft seem to indicate that there is a distinct depreciation of strength above that altitude, and after a time a diminished appetite, which would inevitably tend towards loss of weight, lowered vitality and anaemia.

As already pointed out mountain sickness does not seem to be a necessary concomitant of climbing at any altitude so far reached, but 'mountain lassitude' is undoubtedly almost invariably experienced above 20,000ft indicating depreciation of vitality.

The reports of the different observers however are not in agreement as the following quotations show.

General Bruce[66], who has done more climbing in the Himalaya than anyone, makes the following significant comment, 'Although one thoroughly enjoys climbs of 22,000ft and over after they have been accomplished, I don't think anyone will truthfully say that he is quite happy at over 20,000ft. This refers more especially to climbing, as one can be quite happy when at rest if conditions are favourable up to 25,000ft at least.'

Whymper by careful walking tests at sea level and at Quito (10,170ft) found a depreciation of strength of eight per cent, the respective results being 11mm, 4 sec. and 11mm 58 sec. as averages for one mile. Whymper comments upon these results as follows. 'As regards myself, it appeared to me conclusive that a marked effect was produced, and an effect of a kind which I had never suspected at corresponding altitudes in the Alps, where there was no possibility of applying a similar test.'

Sir Martin Conway[67] agrees with Whymper that there is considerable depreciation of strength at such altitudes as La Paz (12,300ft) and his guides (Maquignaz and Pellissier) were emphatic regarding lowered capacity for work at 14,000 to 15,000, which agrees with de Saussure.

Dr Longstaff has decisive ideas in this connection and writes 'I am personally convinced that the mountaineer will gain no advantage by a prolonged residence at high altitudes. The more he is accustomed to breathe and climb at low pressures, the better for his chance of accomplishing very high ascents, but once he has begun his final attack on a peak, let him pass as few nights as possible at pressures of half an atmosphere (19,000ft) and less.' Dr Longstaff then mentions 15,000ft as his limit for complete acclimatisation, but this is probably somewhatlow[67a]. Dr de Filippi[68] in connection with the Duke of the Abruzzi's Himalayan expedition writes 'After living for nearly two months above 17,000ft, 7 Europeans spent nine days at a height of more than 20,700ft during which time four of them camped for the night at 21,673 and 22,843ft and this without even the incon-venience of sleeplessness.' Dr de Filippi goes on to point out that there was a decrease in appetite, but the process was slow. Mummery[69] after his experiences on Nanga Parbat wrote: 'There is no doubt the air affects us when we get beyond 18,000ft.'

Clinton Dent has indicated that workmen engaged in constructing a railway tunnel at 15,645ft in Peru could do full work after acclimatisation, but Mosso points out that at a lower altitude on Monte Rosa the men levelling the rock for the Regina Margherita hut (14,953ft) did not suffer at all during the first days, but afterwards when they felt fatigued they experienced such distress that they declined to continue at any price. This latter case is instructive, the explanation probably being that the men overworked themselves for the elevation. When the body's equilibrium is seriously upset at high altitudes, the normal state is re-attained with much greater difficulty than at sea level, that is to say the physiological condition even at 15,000ft is more labile than at sea level, as Sundstroem and others have remarked.

Dr and Mrs Bullock Workman[70] who have had great experience in the Himalaya suggest that in camps above 20,000ft want of sleep may cause difficulty. Among the Nun Kun Mountains of E. Kashmir, they had three high camps at 19,000ft, 20,632ft, and 21,300ft respectively, and make the following comment regarding five days climbing.

'We were conscious of a distinct decline in strength during the last two days, and after six consecutive days of hard work and five sleepless nights, everyone felt an irresistible desire to relieve the tension by a descent to a lower level.'

In many cases the mountain lassitude may become acute, and must then be regarded as a type of mountain sickness.

Hooker, for example, described this condition as one where the climber felt as if he had 'a pound of lead on each knee cap, two pounds in the pit of the stomach, and a hoop of iron around the head.'

Conway mentions a severe attack as affecting his party on Illimani, writing as follows:

Pellissier (one of the guides) who was physically the strongest of us, when sent off to fill a small bucket with water from a rivulet 100 yards away, found it necessary to rest four or five times in that little distance. Yet the altitude was only 16,500ft.

Judging from experience, and evaluating all the above extracts, probably the limit of permanent acclimatisation lies between 16,000 and 20,000ft, depending upon the comfort of the camp and the diet available.

The depreciation of strength is probably chiefly due to the fact that the most suitable diets for high altitudes have still to be worked out. The ordinary foodstuffs presumably yield metabolites which do not oxidise readily enough for the available supply of oxygen, and their circulation in the blood may have an effect on respiration and power of doing work. If so, the depreciation in strength might be overcome by intermittent use of oxygen.

Space does not permit of a discussion of the diets suitable for high altitudes[71] but a few points might be noted. Firstly, easily digested foodstuffs should be specially tested, along with such auxiliary foodstuffs as sanatogen, plasmon, Benger's food etc. Secondly, the antis-corbutic value of the different aliments available must be noted, and special attention should be paid to those mysterious food adjuvants, the vitamines. For example, preserved lemon juice is a good anti-scorbutic, but preserved lime-juice has negligible value in that connection; tinned meats seem to have no actiscorbutic value, but tinned acid fruits (e.g. tinned tomatoes) have. Germinated pulses and cereals are both anti-scorbutic and anti-beri-beri in character, the latter property being also possessed by eggs, fresh or dried.

Above 20,000ft (6,096m), the physiological condition is so labile that far greater care must be taken as regards diet, avoidance of chill etc. In testing airmen Schneider found that even trivial indisposition such as 'a cold, indigestion, late hours or worry, reduced the resistance temporarily by many thousand feet.'

Since there is distinct depreciation of strength above 20,000ft, as might be expected from curve series No. 10, one has to consider how far the mountain lassitude will affect the rate of climbing between 25,000 and 29,000ft.

Rate of Ascent at High Altitudes

To standardise rate of climbing is difficult, but probably 1,000 ft per hour at the height of Mt. Blanc (15,780ft) might be taken as a fair speed on a mountain of moderate difficulty. On Mt. Ararat, Bryce[72] ascended at the rate of 830ft per hour for the last 5,000ft. Freshfield's[73] party on Elbruz (18,465ft) climbed the last 2,500ft at the rate of 550ft per hour. Collie's[74] party on Diamirai Peak (19,000ft) ascended between 6,000 and 7,000ft at about 1,000ft per hour, while Whymper, on his second ascent of Chimborazo (20,517ft), averaged 900ft per hour from 17,280 to 19,400ft. Longstaff's[75] party on Trisul (23,450ft) climbed the last 6,000ft in ten hours or at the rate of about 600ft per hour, agreeing approximately with observations of the author on similar mountains.

There is only one dissentient as regards diminution of strength at high altitudes, namely Graham[76], who claimed to have ascended Kabru (24,020ft), and to have observed no depreciation of rate of climbing. While not attacking Graham's veracity, which is quite unimpeachable, he was almost certainly mistaken in the mountain he ascended, and his conclusions cannot be accepted.

If steps have to be cut or in deep snow, or if the party be not thoroughly acclimatised the speed would be much less. For example the Duke of the Abruzzi's party on Bride Peak averaged 200ft per hour in deep snow towards 24,600ft, which is similar to that of Rubenson and Aas[77] on Kabru (24,000ft) when steps had to be cut. Belmore Brown and Parker because of want of acclimatisation and defective food supply averaged 400ft per hr at 18,000ft on Denali.

From the above series of results, one might say that the rate of ascent at 23,000ft should be about 600ft per hour on an easy mountain. From this value, a very rough approximation of the rate of ascent at 29,000ft might be computed in various ways.

One might for example determine the rate from the saturation of the blood with oxygen corresponding to the alveolar oxygen pressure. This theoretical saturation – which, for many reasons, would not be the real saturation for the higher altitudes – is roughly 80 per cent at 16,000ft, 60 per cent at 23,000ft and 40 per cent at 29,000ft. If there be a fall of 40 per cent in the rate of climbing due to a loss of 20 per cent of blood saturation, then the rate of climbing near the top of Mt. Everest would be 600–(40 per cent of 600), equals 360ft per hour.

One might check the above result by calculating in another way from the alveolar oxygen pressures, taking into consideration the actual quantity of oxygen required by the body when climbing at 29,000ft which would make the calculation more concrete.

To make this method of calculation quite clear, the results of a series of experiments carried out by Haldane and co-workers on Pikes Peak and at Oxford might be given, showing the respiratory exchange (the ratio of oxygen taken up to carbon dioxide produced), and also the respiratory quotient (the ratio of the latter to the former) [Table 7].

The table shows that at sea level, the minimum quantity of oxygen required by the body per minute at rest is 237 c.c. and on Pikes Peak 248 c.c., while at rest standing the respective values are 330 and 345 c.c.

At four miles per hour, equal quantities of oxygen are taken up at sea level and on Pikes Peak, namely roughly 1,600 c.c., disagreeing with a

---

TABLE 7

The Respiratory Exchange, and Respiratory Quotients under Stated Conditions at Oxford and on Pikes Peak (14,109 ft.)

Conditions	Oxford Vol. calculated to 0°C & 760 mm			Pikes Peak Vol. calculated to 0°C & 760 mm		
	Vol. of oxygen taken up per min.	Vol. of CO2 produced per min.	Respiratory quotient	Vol. of oxygen taken up per min.	Vol. of CO2 produced per min.	Respiratory quotient
1 At rest in bed	237	197	0.83	248	206	0.83
2 standing still (erect)	330	266	.81	345	285	.83
3 Walking 2 miles per hour	780	662	.85	785	666	.85
4 Walking 3 miles per hour	1,065	922	.87	103	922	.89
5 Walking 4 miles per hour	1,595	1398	.88	1,557	1,438	.92
6 Walking 5 miles per hour	2,474	2,329	.94	2,113	2,208	1.045
7 Ascending gradient (1 in 4)	–	–	–	1,940	2,238	1.152

statement of Zuntz. One might consider four miles per hour as corresponding to 1,000ft per hour at 16,000ft. In any case 2,000 c.c. of oxygen
would be ample, corresponding to the requirements of nearly five miles
per hour on level ground.

One might then calculate what volume would be taken up under
similar conditions at 23,000 and 29,000ft respectively by assuming them
proportional to their relative alveolar oxygen pressures. From the volume
one would have to subtract at least 345 c.c. – or allowing for lowered
temperature, preferably a minimum of 400 to 450 c.c. – before calculating the rate of climbing from the volumes of oxygen available. The following table [Table 8] shows the results.

The values calculated seem to indicate that at 29,000ft on
moderately easy ground, a man in good training might expect to be able
to climb at from 300 to 350ft per hour[l]. It might be argued that if steps
had to be cut, or in deep soft snow, the pace might be reduced to under
200ft per hour, but against this one must point out that on good hard
snow in the early morning it is possible to climb at 1,000ft per hour up
to at least 21,000ft. The above values seem to clearly indicate that the
ascent should be possible from a camp above 25,000ft, but it would
mean an early start, say 4.30am which indicates that specially warm
footgear would be required. Preferably the highest camp should be at
say 25,500ft[J], and the exact method of procedure, taking into consideration all the essential factors already summarized would be as follows:

Method of Ascent

From a base camp at say 17,000ft at which one would remain a few
days so as to be thoroughly acclimatised, one would push up camps to
20,500, 23,500 and 25,500ft, from the latter of which the attempt on the
summit would be made. It might be possible to ascend from 25,500ft to
the summit, and retreat to the camp at 23,500ft or lower in one day.
Careful attention would obviously have to be paid to equipment. Small,
double-walled tents might be used above 20,500ft, and the camps
should either be on rock or in deep hollows dug out of the snow, so as
to obviate difficulties regarding wind. It must be noted however that the
wind has only about one third of the lifting power at 29,000ft, which it
possesses at sea level ($f = 1/2 \ mv^2$), but that a very cold wind may rapidly
reduce vitality unless protection is adequate.

TABLE 8

Calculation of Rate of Ascent at 29,000ft. From the Amount of Oxygen Required while Walking at 4 and 5 miles Per Hour Respectively at Sea Level

Energy	Altitude feet	Alveolar oxygen pressure	Oxygen absorbed per minute calculated at 0°c and 760mm	Oxygen available for climbing after substration of 400 cc. as a constant factor for vital	Rate of climbing
Energy used	16,000	49.5	2000 c.c.	1600 c.c.	1,000
corresponds to	23,000	33.0	1333	933	584
5 miles per hour at sea level	29,000	24.0	970	570	356
Energy used	16,000	49.5	1600 c.c.	1200 c.c.	1,000
corresponds to	23,000	33.0	1068	668	557
4 miles per hour at sea level	29,000	24.0	776	376	313

If defeated on the first attempt, the climber might retreat to a rest camp at say 14,000ft, well below the limits for permanent acclimatisation, and after a few days again advance to the attack, the higher camps being left standing, and if defeated a second time repeat if necessary as long as weather and time allowed.

Since the preceding considerations seem to clearly indicate that Mt. Everest could be climbed by an individual of excellent physical and mental constitution in first-rate training[78a] without adventitious aids, the ascent using oxygen should be comparatively easy. In Haldane's experiments at the Lister Institute in April 1919 it was found that a light oxygen cylinder fitted up by the Royal Air Force Technical Dept. which could give a supply of oxygen for five hours using one Litre per minute allowed moderately hard work to be carried out at a pressure of 312 mm corresponding to 25,000ft as already indicated.

The ascent of Mount Everest, more especially without adventitious aids, would be a notable human achievement. Scientific work of great value might at the same time be carried out, in connection with geodosy, geology, meteorology, magnetism, and electricity. In connection with the last named the shadow effect of the Great Himalaya range upon wireless telegraphic and telephonic waves would be of interest.

According to the tradition the youth of the Gael in the first century of this era tested their physical fitness on the arete of Scuir-na-Gillean[k], and perchance in the distant future young men in India may test their courage on the world's loftiest summit.

Conclusions

1 The physical difficulties against the ascent of Mount Everest are not insuperable, provided that access be allowed through Nepal or Tibet.

2 Consideration of observations by aeroplane or balloon seem to indicate that the ascent of Mt. Everest would be impossible without the use of oxygen.

3 Single experiments in airchambers also seem to show that the ascent would be impossible without oxygen, but a recent series of acclimatisation experiments indicates that the ascent might be possible without adventitious aids.

4 Mountain sickness primarily depends upon deficiency of oxygen, which causes either an alkalosis or acidosis of the blood depending upon conditions, but an alka-losis may be more generally present in acute attacks.

5 Numerous secondary factors, especially want of training, fatigue, improper diet, and want of acclimatisation, may prompt an acute attack of mountain sickness.

6 Mountain sickness is not a necessary concomitant of climbing up to the highest altitudes so far attained, but the physiological condition is more labile at high altitudes, and 'Mountain lassitude' has a variable effect above the limits of permanent acclimatisation (17,000 to 20,000ft).

7 The process of acclimatisation to high altitudes depends upon the following factors:
   a Increase of oxygen pressure in the alveolar air
   b Increase of red corpuscles and haemoglobin
   c Secretion of oxygen by alveolar epithelium
   d Increase of frequency and depth of breathing
   e More rapid circulation of the blood at high altitudes

8 A study of the variation of alveolar oxygen pressure with altitude indicates that Mt. Everest could probably be climbed.

9   A study of the dissociation curves for oxyhaemoglobin indicates that the ascent of Mt. Everest should be possible.

10 The limits of permanent acclimatisation being taken as 17,000 to 20,000ft–provided suitable diets are employed–Mt. Everest could be climbed from a camp at say 25,500ft.

11 The rate of ascent would be about 300ft per hour at 29,000ft on moderately easy ground.

12 General Conclusion. Mount Everest could be ascended by a man of *excellent physical and mental constitution in first rate training*, without adventitious aids if the physical difficulties of the mountain are not too great, and with the use of oxygen even if the mountain may be classed as difficult from the climbing point of view.

NOTES

1   Col. Burrard's corrected value is given. The High Peaks of Asia. Burrard and Hayden [Burrard SG, and Hayden HH (1907–1908). Sketch of the Geography and Geology of Himalaya Mountains and Tibet, Part I: The High Peaks of Asia, Supt., Govt. Print., Calcutta, India; Reprinted by Gian Publications, Delhi, 1980. In this edition dated 1907–1908, the height of Mount Everest is given as 29,002ft. This was apparently changed to 29,141ft in a later edition.]

2   Hinchliff. 'Over the sea and far away.' [Hinchliff T.W. (1876). Over the Sea and Far Away, Longmans Green, London.]

3   *Daily Mail* [It has not been possible to find this article.]

3a This is not a village. [As Kellas notes earlier, it is the site of a bridge across the Phungtu Chu river.]

4   Major JB Noel. Geog. Journal. May 1919. [Noel JB (1919). A journey to Tashirak in southern Tibet, and the eastern approaches to Mount Everest. Geogr. J. 53:289–308.]

5   Given in both 'Round Kanchenjunga' (Freshfield) and Western Himalaya (Dr de Filippi). [Freshfield DW (1903). Round Kanchenjunga; A Narrative of Mountain Travel and Exploration, E Arnold, London; Filippi F de (1912). Karakoram and Western Himalaya, Constable, London.]

6   Glaisher. Travels in the Air. 1871. [Glaisher J., Flammarion C., de Fonvielle W., and Tissandier G. (1871). Travels in the Air, JB Lippincott Company, Philadelphia.]

7   Tissandier. Journal. 'La Nature.' May 1875. (Also given in Prof. Paul

Bert's La Pression Barometrique, 1878.) [Tissandier G (1875). Le voyage à grande hauteur du ballon 'Le Zenith.' La Nature (Paris) 3:337–344; Bert P (1878). La Pression Barométrique, Masson, Paris; English translation by MA and FA Hitchcock. College Book Company, Columbus, Ohio, 1943; reprinted by the Undersea Medical Society, Bethesda, MD, 1978.]

8   Berson and Suring. 'Illustrierte aeronautische Mittelungen' 1901. [The balloon ascent to an altitude of 10,500m was described in Berson A and Süring R (1901), Ein Ballonaufsteig bis 10,500m. Deutsche Ztg. Luftsch. 5:117–119.]

9   Prof. Angelo Mosso. Life of Man in the High Alps. [Mosso A (1898). Life of Man on the High Alps, T Fisher Unwin, London.]

10   Prof. Starling. Physiology. p.1226 [Starling EH (1912). Principles of Human Physiology, Lea & Febiger, Philadelphia, p.1226.]

11   Haldane, Kellas, and Kennaway. Journal of Physiology 1919. [Haldane JS, Kellas AM, and Kennaway EL (1919)]. Experiments on acclimatisation to reduced atmospheric pressure. J Physiol. (London) 53: 181–206.]

12   Dr G Regnier. Le Mal de Montagne. Etude experimentelle–faites aux observations du Mont Blanc. [Regnier G. (1911). Le Mal de Montagne: Étude Experimentale Faite aux Observations du Mont-Blanc, Jules Rousset, Paris.]

13   Haldane. General Pathology. Pembrey and Ritchie. p.455. [Haldane, JS (1913). Respiration, in Text-Book of General Pathology, Pembrey MS, and Ritchie J eds., Arnold, London, pp.432–497.]

14   Journal of the American Medical Association. 1918. (Oct. 26). [Schneider E.C. (1918). Medical studies in aviation. II. Physiologic observations and methods. J. Am. Med. Assoc. 71:1384–1389.]

15   Prof. Paul Bert. 'La Pression Barométrique.' 1878. [Bert P (1878). La Pression Barométrique, Masson, Paris; English translation by MA and FA Hitchcock. College Book Company, Columbus, OH, 1943; Reprinted by the Undersea Medical Society, Bethesda, MD, 1978.]

16   Dr Hepburn. *Alpine Journal.* Vol. xx and xxi. [Hepburn ML (1901). The influence of high altitudes in mountaineering. *Alpine Journal* 20: 368–393; Hepburn ML (1902). Some reasons why the science of altitude-illness is still in its infancy. Alpine Journal 21:161–179.]

17   Dr Longstaff. Mountain Sickness. 1906. [Longstaff TG (1906). Mountain Sickness and Its Probable Causes, Spottiswoode, London.]

18   Clinton Dent. Geographical Journal. 1893. [Dent, C (1893) Physiological effects of high altitudes. Geogr. J 1:46–48.]

19 Clifford Allbutt. System of Medicine. Vol. III. p. 456. [Allbutt, C. (1908). Mountain-sickness. In Allbutt C, and Rolleston HD, eds. A System of Medicine, Vol.III. Macmillan and Co., Ltd., London, pp. 243–252; Kellas gives a different page number perhaps because he used another edition.]

20 Prof. Roy. Mountain Sickness (Appendix. Conway. W. Himalaya). [Roy CS (1894). Mountain sickness. In: Climbing and Exploration in the Karakoram-Himalayas, Containing Scientific Reports. WM Conway, ed. TF Unwin, London, pp.109–127.]

21 Col. Waddell. Among the Himalaya. [Waddell LA (1900). Among the Himalayas, 2nd ed., A Constable and Co., Westminster

22 Zuntz, Loewy, Muffler and Caspari. Höhenklima und Bergwanderungen. Berlin 1906. [Zuntz N, Loewy A, Muller F, and Caspari W (1906). Höhenklima und Bergwanderungen in ihrer Wirkung auf den Menschen, Bong, Berlin.]

23 H v. Schrotter. Zur Kenntniss der Bergkrankheit 1899. [Schrotter, H von (1899). Zur Kenntnis der Bergkankheit, Wilhelm Braumuller, Wien, Leipzig.]

24 Sir JD Hooker. Himalayan Journals. [Hooker JD (1854). Himalayan Journals; or, Notes of a Naturalist in Bengal, The Sikkim and Nepal Himalayas, The Khasia Mountains, &c. J Murray, London; reprinted by Natraj Publishers, Dehra Dun, India, 1999, 2 volumes.]

25 Dr JJ von Tschudi. Peru. 'Reiseskizzen.' 1838–1842. [Tschudi, JJ von (1846). Peru Reiseskizzen aus den Jahren 1838–1842, Scheitlin und Zollikofer, St Gallen.]

26 HB de Saussure. Voyages dans les Alpes. [de Saussure H.-B. (1786). Voyages dans les Alpes, Chez Barde, Manget et Compagnie, Geneva.]

27 Boussingault and Hall. Gay Lussac's Ann. de Chimie et de Physiologie. [It has not been possible to find this article.]

28 Sir Martin Conway. Climbing in the Karakoram Himalaya. [Conway WM (1894). Climbing and Exploration in the Karakoram-Himalayas, TF Unwin, London.]

29 Thomas. Mountaineering in the Rockies. Alp. Journ. 1894. [Thomas P.W. (1894). Alpine notes: Rocky mountain sickness. Alpine J 17:140–141.]

30 DW Freshfield. Geog. Journ. 1917, p.47. [Freshfield DW (1917). A consideration of the possibility of ascending the loftier Himalaya–discussion. Geogr. J 49:46–48.]

31 Col. Waddell. Lhassa and its mysteries. [Waddell LA (1905). Lhasa and Its Mysteries, 5th ed., J Murray, London, 1905; Cosmo Publications, Delhi, India, 1996.]

[32] A v. Humboldt. Kleinere Schriften. [Humboldt A von (1853). Kleinere Schriften, J.G. Cotta'scher Verlag, Stuttgart, Tubingen.]

[33] Miss Fitzgerald. Phil. Trans. Royal Soc. v. 203. p.351. [FitzGerald MP (1913). The changes in the breathing and the blood at various altitudes. Phil. Trans. R. Soc. Lond. Ser. B 203:351–371.]

[34] AL Mumm. Five months in the Himalaya. [Mumm AL (1909). Five Months in the Himalaya, Edward Arnold, London.]

[35] JF Cheetham. *Alpine Journal* III. p.137. [Cheetham JF (1867). The Tibetan route from Simla to Srinágar; notes of a Himalayan ramble in the summer and autumn of 1859. *Alpine Journal* 3:118–153.]

[36] Dr Hans Meyer. In den Hoch Anden von Ecuador. p.388. [Meyer H (1907). In den Hoch-Anden von Ecuador: Chimborazo, Cotopaxi etc. Reisen und Studien, Reimer, Berlin.]

[37] Dr Guglielminetti. Trois semaines au Mont Blanc. L'Echo des Alpes. 1894. [Guglielminetti E. (1894). Trois semaines au Mont Blanc. L'Echo des Alpes 2: 133–147.]

[38] J Barcroft. 'Respiratory Function of the Blood.' [Barcroft J (1914). The Respiratory Function of the Blood, University Press, Cambridge.]

[39] G di Acosta. 'Historia naturale a morales della India.' Italian Tran. 1596. [Original edition is Acosta I. de (1590), Historia Natural y Moral de las Indias, Iuan de Leon, Seville.]

[40] Johannes Grueber. Travels from China to Europe. 1661. [Grueber J. (1750). Reisen von China nach Europa im Jahre 1661, durch den Jesuiten, Johann Gruber. In: Allgemeine Historie der Reisen zu Wasser und Lande, Bey Arkstee und Merkus, Leipzig]

[41] ER Huc. 'Souvenirs d'un voyage dans la Tartare, le Thibet, et la Chine.' [Huc E-R (1878). Souvenirs d'un Voyage dans la Tartarie, le Thibet, et la Chine Pendant les Annees 1844, 1845 et 1846, 6th ed.; Gaume, Paris translated by Hazlitt W (1898). Travels in Tartary, Thibet, and China during the years 1844–1846, Office of the National Illustrated Library, London; reprinted (1987) Dover Publications, New York]

[42] PI Desideri. 'Il Tibet.' 1715–1721. [Desideri I (1904). Il Tibet, Roma, Societa Geografica Italiana.]

[43] Gerard. Account of Koonawur. [Gerard A (1841). Account of Koonawur, J Madden & Co. London; reprinted (1993) Indus Publ., New Delhi]

[44] P Bouguer. Le figure de la terre determinee. [Bouguer, P (1749). La Figure de la Terre, Determinée par les Observations de Messieurs Bouguer, & de la Condamine, de l'Académie Royale des Sciences, envoyés par ordre du Roy au Pérou, pour observer aux environs de l'Equateur; Avec une

Relation abregée de ce Voyage, qui contient la description du Pays dans lequel les Opérations ont été faites. C-A Jombert, Paris]

45 D Jourdanet. Influence de la Pression de l'air sur la vie de l'homme. 1876. [Jourdanet D (1875). Influence de la pression de l'air sur la vie de l'homme. Climats d'altitude et climats de de montagne, Masson, Paris.]

46 Dr Kronecker. Die Bergkrankheit. [Kronecker H (1903). Die Bergkrankheit, Urban & Schwearzenberg, Berlin.]

47 Henderson and Haggard. Journ. of Biol. Chem. v. 33. 1918. [Henderson Y, and Haggard HW (1918). Respiratory regulation of the CO_2 capacity of the blood. III. The effects of excessive pulmonary ventilation. J. Biol. Chem. 33:355–3634

48 Sundstroem ES, Studies on the adaptation of man to high altitudes. (8 papers.) Univ. of California Publications. 1919. [Sundstroem ES (1919). Studies on the adaptation of man to higher altitudes. I. Effect of high altitudes on pulse, body temperature, blood pressure, respiration rate, output of urine, and loss of energy in feces. Univ. Calif. Publ. Physiol. 5:71–86; Sundstroem ES (1919). Studies on the adaptation of man to higher altitudes. II. Effect of high altitudes on protein metabolism. Univ. Calif. Publ. Physiol. 5:87–104; Sundstroem ES (1919). Studies on the adaptation of man to higher altitudes. III. Effect of high altitudes on iron metabolism. Univ. Calif. Publ. Physiol. 5:105–112; Sundstroem ES (1919). Studies on the adaptation of man to higher altitudes. IV. Effects of high altitude on the carbon dioxide content and the hydrogen ion concentration of the blood. Univ. Calif. Publ. Physiol. 5:113–120; Sundstroem ES (1919). Studies on the adaptation of man to higher altitudes. V. Effect of high altitudes on salt metabolism with special reference to the mechanism of maintaining the acid-base equilibrium of the body. Univ. Calif. Publ. Physiol. 5:121–132; Sundstroem ES (1919). Studies on the adaptation of man to higher altitudes. VI. Effect of high altitudes on the number of erythrocytes. Univ. Calif. Publ. Physiol. 5:133–148; Sundstroem ES (1919). Studies on the adaptation of man to higher altitudes. VII. Effect of high altitudes on the size of the erythrocytes. Univ. Calif. Publ. Physiol. 5:149–157; Sundstroem ES (1919). Studies on the adaptation of man to higher altitudes. VIII. Effect of high altitudes on the morphology of red and white blood corpuscles. Univ. Calif. Publ. Physiol. 5:159–165.]

49 Emile Javelle. 'Souvenirs d'un alpiniste.' [Javelle E (1906). Souvenirs d'un Alpiniste, 4th ed., Payot, Lausanne.]

[50] Max Gruber. Ueber der Einfluss der Uebung auf den Stoffwechsel. 1888. [There is no record of an article by Gruber with this title. Kellas was probably referring to the following article: Gruber M (1891). Ueber den Einfluss der Uebung auf den Gaswechsel, Zeitschrift fur Biologie 28:466–491.]

[51] Dr Pavy. The Lancet. 1876. [Pavy FW (1876). The effect of prolonged muscular exercise upon the urine in relation to the source of muscular power, Lancet 2:741–743, 815–818, 848–850, 887–889.]

[52] G Abraham. The Complete Mountaineer. [Abraham GD (1908). The Complete Mountaineer, 2nd ed., Methuen & Co., London; 2nd ed., there is also a 3rd ed. (1923).]

[53] Dr Egli. Sinclair. Sur le mal de montagne. Annales de l'observatoire meteorologique de Mont Blanc. [EgliSinclair (1893). Sur le mal de montagne. Annales de Observatoire Météorologique, Physique et Glaciaire du Mont Blanc 1:109–130.]

[54] Dr Monro. *Alpine Journal*. Vol. XVI. [Monro CG (1893). Mountain sickness. Alpine J. 16:446–455.]

[55] Dr de Filippi. Ascent of Mt. St Elias, (1897) [Filippi F.d. (1900). The Ascent of Mount St Elias by HRH Prince Luigi Amedeo di Savoia, Duke of the Abruzzi, FA Stokes Co., New York.]

[56] E Whymper. The Great Andes of the Equator. [Whymper E (1891–1892). Travels Amongst the Great Andes of the Equator, Murray, London; reprinted (1972) by Charles Knight, London.]

[57] Fitzgerald. The Highest Andes. [Fitzgerald EA (1899). The Highest Andes, a Record of the First Ascent of Aconcagua and Tupungato in Argentina, and the Exploration of the Surrounding Valleys, Methuen & Co., London]

[58] Hasselbalch. Experimental physiology of high altitudes. Biochem. Zeitschr. 68, 74, etc. [Kellas is apparently referring to the series of articles by Hasselbalch that were published in this journal.]

[58a] It would not be entirely so, as carbon dioxide aids the dissociation of oxy-haemoglobin.

[58b] Both Hasselbalch and Kennaway have brought forward evidence to show that diminished production of ammonia and also a smaller excretion of acid occur at low pressures, so that the liver and kidneys take an important part in the regulation of the hydrogen ion constant of the blood.

[59] Viault. Comptes rendus CXI. 1890. p.917. [Viault F (1890). Sur l'augmentation considerable de nombre des globules rouges dans le

sang chez les habitants des hauts plateaux de l'Amérique du Sud. C. R. Hebd. Seances Acad. Sci. 111:917–918; translation in Viault F. (1981). On the large increase in the number of red cells in the blood of the inhabitants of the high plateaus of South America. In: High Altitude Physiology, JB West, ed., Hutchinson Ross Publishing Company, Stroudsburg, PA, pp. 333–334]

59a The average value for woman is less, (about 4,500,000), but there is a compensation in alveolar oxygen pressure, which is higher than in men at all altitudes. The relationships are already given by Miss FitzGerald.

60 Cohnheim, Kreglinger, Tolber and Weber. Zeitsch. f. Physiol. Chemie LXXVIII. 1912. [Cohnheim O, Kreglinger G, Tobler L, and Weber OH (1912). Zur Physiologie des Wassers und des Kochsalzes. Zeitsch. f. Physiol. Chemie 78:62–88.]

61 Morawitz and Masing. Deutsche Med. Wochenschr. 1910. No. 8. [Morawitz P (1910). Höhenklima und Blutregeneration, Deutsche Medizinische Wochenschrift 36:389–390.]

62 Indian Survey Reports. 1913 [Hingston RWG (1914). Blood observations at high altitudes and some conclusions drawn from this enquiry in relation to mountain distress. In: Records of the Survey of India, Volume VI: Completion of the Link Connecting the Triangulations of India and Russia 1913, SG Burrard, ed. Dehra Dun, Office of the Trigonometrical Survey, pp. 88–91.]

63 Krogh. The Respiratory Exchange of Animals and Man. [Krogh A (1916). The Respiratory Exchange of Animals and Man, Longmans, Green and Co., London]

64 Vallot. *Alpine Journal.* Vol. XIV. p.34. [The correct citation of this article is: Vallot J (1887). Trois jours au Mont Blanc, Annuaire du Club Alpin Français, pp.13–40.]

65 Drs A and J Loewy and L Zuntz. Pflugers Archiv. Bd. 66. p.477. [Loewy A, Loewy J, and Zuntz L (1897). Ueber den Einfluss der verdünnten Luft und des Höhenklimas auf den Menschen, Pflugers Arch. 66:477–538.]

66 General Bruce. Twenty years in the Himalaya. [Bruce CG (1910). Twenty Years in the Himalaya, E Arnold, London]

67 Sir Martin Conway. The Bolivian Andes. [Conway M (1901). The Bolivian Andes; A Record of Climbing & Exploration in the Cordillera Real in the Years 1898 and 1900, Harper & Brothers, New York, London]

67a The highest village in the world, which presumably would be below the limit of permanent acclimatisation is Thok Djalank, Tibet, 16,340ft

(4980m) [It has not been possible to identify this village. According to people in Lhasa who are studying high altitude, the highest village in Tibet with permanent inhabitants at the present time is Ma-Rong at 5067m]

68 Dr de Filippi. Karakoram and Western Himalaya. 1909. [Filippi F.d. (1912). Karakoram and Western Himalaya, Constable, London.]

69 AF Mummery. My climbs in the Alps and Caucasus (with Lettore Porisho). [Mummery AF (1908). My Climbs in the Alps and Caucasus, 2nd ed, T Fisher Unwin, London. The reference to Lettore Porisho is obscure.]

70 Dr and Mrs Bullock Workman. Peaks and Glaciers of Nun Kun. [Workman FB, and Workman WH (1909). Peaks and Glaciers of Nun Kun; A Record of Pioneer-Exploration and Mountaineering in the Punjab Himalaya, Constable and Company Ltd., London]

71 cf. The Mountains of N. Sikhim and Garhwal. Geog. Journ. Sept. 1912. [Kellas AM (1912). The mountains of northern Sikkim and Garhwal, Geogr. J 40:241–263.]

72 Bryce. Ararat and Transcaucasia. [Bryce J (1896). Transcaucasia and Ararat, Being Notes of a Vacation Tour in the Autumn of 1876, 4th ed. Macmillan and Co. London Ltd.]

73 DW Freshfield. The Exploration of the Caucasus. [Freshfield DW (1902). The Exploration of the Caucasus, 2d ed., E. Arnold, London, 2 vols.]

74 Prof. Collie. Mountaineering in the Himalaya and other Mountain Ranges. [Collie JN (1902). Climbing on the Himalaya and Other Mountain Ranges, D Douglas, Edinburgh]

75 Dr Longstaff. Alpine Club Journal. [Longstaff TG (1908). Mountaineering in Garhwal, 24:107–133.]

76 Graham. Good Words. 1885. [Graham WW (1885). Up the Himalayas, Good Words 26:18–23, 97–105, 172–178.]

77 Rubenson and Aas. Alpine Club Journal. xxiv. p.313. [Rubenson CW (1908). Kabru in 1907, Alpine J. 24: 310–321.]

78 Belmore Brown and Parker. The Conquest of Mt. McKinley (Denali). [Belmore B. (1913). The Conquest of Mount McKinley; The Story of Three Expeditions through the Alaskan Wilderness to Mount McKinley, North America's Highest and Most Inaccessible Mountain, GP Putnam's Sons. London]

78a Individuals of this type are probably rarely met with.

79 Younghusband. The Heart of a Continent. P. 224. [Younghusband F.E. (1904). The Heart of a Continent: A Narrative of Travels in Manchuria,

Across the Gobi Desert, Through the Himalayas, the Pamirs, and Hunza, 1884–1894, 4th ed., J Murray, London]

80 Dr J Jacot Guillarmod. Six mois clans l'Himalaya. [Jacot-Guillarmod J (1904). Six Mois dans l'Himalaya, le Karakorum et l'Hindu-Kush; Voyages et Explorations aux Plus Hautes Montagnes du Monde, W Sandoz, Neuchatel]

81 HA and R v. Schlagintweit. Reisen in Indien und Huchasien. 1869. They also mention cases of epilepsy. [Schlagintweit-Sakünlünski H von, Schlagintweit A von, and Schlagintweit R von (1869–1880). Reisen in Indien und Hochasien, H Costenoble, Jena, 4 vols.]

EDITOR'S NOTES

a It is interesting that although Kellas recommends this pony track through Sikkim following the valley off the Teesta River, the first Everest reconnaissance expedition in the spring of 1921 only a year later chose a different route. They crossed from Sikkim into Tibet over the Jelep La and then trekked up the Chumbi valley, eventually turning west to Kampa Dzong. It is also interesting that Kellas mentions Kampa Dzong on several occasions and shows it in Fig. 1, and this in fact is where he was buried in 1921.

b Here and subsequently 'mm' stands for mmHg.

c When Kellas refers to experiments 'being more comparable with the conditions of the mountaineer at high altitudes,' he is referring to what he calls connected series of experiments, not single experiments.

d When Kellas refers to a pressure of 310 mmHg 'corresponding to 25,000ft at 15°C' he is referring to the mean temperature of the air column up to 25,000ft. The relationship was described by Zuntz et al. (reference 22, pp.37–39) and was also used by FitzGerald (reference 33).

e A number of papers by Aggazzotti have been searched for reference to this observation without success.

f Kellas jumps from heading (2) to (5) without amplifying headings (3) or (4).

g For Fig. 8, Kellas redrew the curve in figure 20 on page 316 of the paper by Douglas CG, Haldane JS, Henderson Y, and Schneider EC (1913), Physiological observations made on Pike's Peak, Colorado, with special reference to adaptation to low barometric pressures, Phil. Trans. R. Soc. Lond. Ser. B 203:185–381, where the actual data are give on p. 317.

h Table VI and Fig. 9 and 10 were previously published in Kellas AM

(1917) A consideration of the possibility of ascending the loftier Himalaya. Geogr. J. 49:26–47.

[i] This predicted climbing rate is very close to that of Messner and Habeler during the first ascent of Everest without supplementary oxygen in 1978.

[j] This is close to the altitude of the highest camp used by Messner and Habeler, which was on the South Col at 26,2000ft (7986m). However, in fairness it should be added that the first ascents of Everest used much higher final camps.

[k] This is a splendid hill in the Cuillin Ridge in Skye with a very fine ridge. Another spelling is Sgurr nan Gillean.

[l] The first part of each footnote is a copy of the handwritten footnote in the manuscript. The second part in brackets is an editorial addition.

Bibliography

PAPERS AND MANUSCRIPTS
Aberdeen City Archives
Alpine Club Archives
Kellas Family Papers
National Library of Scotland (T Graham Brown Collection)
National Archives, Kew (Medical Research Committee Archives)
Royal Geographical Society Archives
Scottish Mountaineering Club Archives
University College London Archives.

JOURNALS AND NEWSPAPERS
Aberdeen Grammar School Magazine
Alpine Journal
Cairngorm Club Journal
Deutsche Alpenzeitung
Geographical Journal
High Altitude Medicine and Biology
Himalayan Journal
Journal of Applied Physiology
Middlesex College Hospital Journal
Modern Asian Studies
Press and Journal (Aberdeen)
Proceedings of the Royal Society
Scottish Mountaineering Club Journal
The Times

BOOKS
Allen, Charles, *Duel in the Snows* (2004)
Anon. *Aberdeen Grammar School Roll of Pupils 1795–1919* (n.d.)
Bauer, P and Aufschneiter, P, *Der Kampf um die Weltgebirge* (1934)
Braham, Trevor, *When The Alps Cast their Spell* (2004)
Burton, John Hill, *The Cairngorm Mountains* (1864)
Carter, Ian, *Farm Life in Northeast Scotland 1840–1914* (1979)
Collie, JN, *A Century of Chemistry at University College* (1927)
Crowley, Aleister, *Confessions* (1977 edn.)
Evans, Charles, *Kangchenjunga, The Untrodden Peak* (1956)
Fraser, WH and Lee, CH, (eds.) *Aberdeen 1800–2000: A New History* (2000)

Freshfield, Douglas, *Round Kangchenjunga* (1903)

Goedecke, Richard, *The Alpine 4000m Peaks* (2006 edn.)

Goodman, Martin, *Suffer and Survive* (2007)

Grey, Affleck, *The Big Grey Man of Ben MacDhui* (1974)

Habeler, Peter, *Everest, Impossible Victory* (English edn. 1979).

Hankinson, Alan, *The First Tigers* (1972)

Harte, Negley and North, John, *The World of UCL, 1829–1990* (1991 edn.)

Howard-Bury, CK, *Mount Everest, the Reconnaissance* (1922)

Hunt, John, *The Ascent of Everest* (1953)

Isserman, Maurice and Weaver, Stewart, *Fallen Giants; A History of Himalayan Mountaineering* (2008)

Kellas, Alexander M, *Introduction to Practical Chemistry* (1909)
  Introduction to Practical Organic Chemistry (1910)
  A Manual of Practical Inorganic Chemistry (1910)

MacGillivray, William, *Natural History of Deeside* (1855)

Meade, CF, *Approach to the Hills* (1940)

Mill, Christine, *Norman Collie; A Life in Two Worlds* (1987)

Mitchell, Ian R, *Scotland's Mountains before the Mountaineers* (1998)

Mumm, AL, *Five Months in the Himalaya* (1909)

Murray, Bill, *The Story of Everest* (1953)

Murray, Shiela, *The Cairngorm Club 1887–1987* (1987)

Noel, JBL, *Through Tibet to Everest* (1927)

Noel, Sandra, *Everest Pioneer: The Photographs of Captain John Noel* (2003)

Robertson, D, *George Mallory* (1969)

Robinson, DH, *The Dangerous Sky: a history of aviation medicine* (1973)

Sale, R, *Mapping the Himalayas: Michael Ward and the Pundit legacy.* (2009)

Sale, R and Rodway, G, *Everest and Conquest in the Himalaya* (2011)

Schlagintweit, R and A, *Results of a Scientific Mission to India and High Asia 1854–58* (1866)

Shipton, Eric, *Upon that Mountain* (1943)

Smith, JS and Stevenson, D, *Aberdeen in the Nineteenth Century* (1988)

Smythe, Frank, *Kangchenjunga Adventure* (1930)
  Kamet Conquered (1932)

Travers, Morris, *The Discovery of the Rare Gases* (1928)
  A Life of Sir William Ramsay (1956)

Unsworth, Walt, *Everest* (1981 edn.)

Victoria, Queen, *Leaves from the Journal of our Life in the Highlands* (1868)

Ward, Michael, *Everest: a Thousand Years of Exploration* (2003)

West, John B, *High Life: a History of High Altitude Medicine and Exploration* (1998)

Younghusband, Francis, *The Epic of Mount Everest* (1926)

ARTICLES

Carrington, Michael, 'Officers, Gentlemen and Thieves; the Looting of Monasteries during the 1903/4 Younghusband Mission to Tibet', *Modern Asian Studies* 1 (2003) pp.81–109.

Flaig, W, 'Tantalus', *Deutsche Alpenzeitung*, 18 (1922) pp.53–5.

Geissler, Paul, 'Alexander Kellas, ein Pioneer des Himalaja', *Deutsche Alpenzeitung*, 30 (1935), pp.103–10.

Kellas, Alexander M, Obituaries,

    Aberdeen Free Press, June 10, 1921.

    Aberdeen Grammar School Magazine, 24, June 1921, No. 3, pp.142–3

    Alpine Journal, Vol. 34 No. 223, pp.145–7.

    Cairngorm Club Journal, Vol. 10. No.57, pp.128–30.

    Geographical Journal, Vol. 58 (1921), pp.73–5.

    Middlesex Hospital Journal, Vol. 21, No. 7, pp.66–9

    Nature, June 1921 pp.560–1

    Scottish Mountaineering Club Journal, Vol.16, No. 92 (1921), pp.74–6.

'A Consideration of Possibility of Ascending the Loftier Himalaya', *Geographical Journal* 49, No. 1, pp.26–46.

'A Consideration of the Possibility of Ascending Mount Everest', *High Altitude Medicine and Biology* Vol. 2, No. 3 (2001), pp.427–61.

'A Fourth Visit to the Sikkim Himalaya, with an ascent of the Kangchenjhau', *Alpine Journal* (1913),Vol. 27, pp.125–53.

'Camping out among the Cairngorms', *Cairngorm Club Journal*, Vol. 1 No. 3 pp.176–7.

'Expedition to Kamet', *Geographical Journal* Vol. 57, (1921), pp.124–30.

'Is Argon contained in Vegetable or Animal Substances?' *Proceedings of the Royal Society*, Vol. 57, pp.490–92.

'On the percentage of Argon in atmospheric and respired Air,' *Proceedings of the Royal Society*, Vol. 59, pp.67–8.

'The late Dr Kellas' Early Expeditions to the Himalaya', *Alpine Journal*, Vol. 34, No. 225, pp.408–12.

'The Mountains of Northern Sikkim and Garhwal', *Geographical Journal* Vol. 40, No. 3, (1912) pp.241–60.

'The Nomenclature of Himalaya Peaks', *Geographical Journal* (1918), Vol. 52, No. 4, pp.272–4.

'The Possibility of Aerial reconnaissance in the Himalaya', *Geographical Journal*, Vol. 51 (1918), pp.374–389.

'Uber die Esterifizierungsgeschwinidchkeit der monosubstituierten Benoesauren und die Verseifungsgeschwindichkeit inhrer Ester', *Zeitschrift fur Physikalischen Chemie*, Vol. 24, No. 2, pp.221–252.

(with JS Haldane and El Kennaway) 'Experiments on acclimitization to reduced atmospheric pressure', *Journal of Physiology* (1919/20), pp.181–206.

Mason, K, 'Exploration and Climbing in the Sikkim Himalaya', *Himalayan Journal*, 9, (1937) pp.167–71.

Meher, Meta, 'The Lure of Kamet', in *Kamet Commemorative Souvenir*, (2006).

Rodway, George, 'Alexander M. Kellas, Everest Forerunner', in *Scottish Mountaineering Club Journal* (2005), Vol. 34, No.196, pp.13–20.

'Prelude to Everest: Alexander M. Kellas and the 1920 High Altitude Scientific Expedition to Kamet', *High Altitude Medicine and Biology* 5, (2004), pp.364–79.

Rubenson, CW, 'Kabru in 1907', *Alpine Journal* Vol. 24, (1908) pp.310–21.

'An Ascent of Kabru', *Alpine Journal* 24 (1908) pp.63–7.

Scott, Douglas, 'Alexander Mitchell Kellas', *Dictionary of National Biography* Vol. 31 (2004) pp.93–4.

West, JB and 'A.M. Kellas. Pioneer Himalayan Physiologist Mountaineer', *Alpine Journal* 94 pp.207–13.

'Alexander M Kellas and the Physiological Challenge of Mount Everest', *Journal of Applied Physiology*, 63 (1987), pp.3–11.

Chronology

1868	Born at Regents Quay, Aberdeen
1878	Kellas family moves to Carden Place in city's west end
1881–84	Attends Aberdeen Grammar School
1885	First big trip (with brother Henry) to Cairngorm Mountains
1887–9	Attends Heriot Watt College, Edinburgh
1889	Second big trip to Cairngorm Mountains with Henry Kellas
1892	Graduates in chemistry at University College London
	Subsequently works on inert gas research in Professor Ramsay's team
1895	Trip with Norman Collie and others to Ben Nevis
1897	Joins Scottish Mountaineering Club
1897	Graduates PhD in Heidelberg, Germany
1899	Moves to Middlesex College Hospital to teach chemistry
1899	Climbs the Breithorn in the Valais Alps
1900	Climbs Finsteraarhorn in the Bernese Alps
1901	Climbs Galdhoppigen, Norway
1905	Climbs Mont Blanc with brother Henry
1907	First visit to Sikkim, also visits Pir Panchal mountains, western India
1909	Second visit to Sikkim, ascends Langpo Peak
1911	Third visit to Sikkim, ascends Sentinel Peak, Pauhunri and Chomiumo. Kellas (unwittingly) breaks the world summit altitude record when climbing Pauhunri (23,375ft, 7,125m)
	Makes an initial visit to Kamet, Garhwal
	Admitted to Alpine Club
1912	Fourth visit to Sikkim, climbs Kangchenjhau
1914	Visits India, Kamet region and other locations, eg Nanga Parbat
1914–18	Works during World War I at Middlesex College Hospital
1919	Breakdown in health, returns to Carden Place, Aberdeen
1920	Writes paper for Monaco Alpine Congress on 'Possibility of Ascending Mt. Everest'
	Attempts Kamet with Morshead, reaches Meade's Col. Carries out oxygen experiments. Winters in Sikkim

1921	Climbs Narsing in Sikkim, explores Kabru glacier.
	Joins First Everest Reconnaissance, dies at Kampa Dzong
1953	Hillary and Tenzing become the first to reach the summit of Everest
1978	Habeler and Messner first to reach summit of Everest without oxygen

Index

Some other books published by **LUATH** PRESS

Mountain Days and Bothy Nights

Dave Brown & Ian R Mitchell
ISBN 978 1906307 83 7 PBK £7.50

This classic 'bothy book' celebrates everything there is to hillwalking; the people who do it, the stories they tell and the places they sleep, where bothies came from, the legendary walkers, the mountain craftsmen and the Goretex and gaiters brigade – and the best and the worst of the dosses, howffs and bothies of the Scottish hills.

This new edition brings a bit of mountaineering history to the modern Munro bagger. The climbers dossing down under the corries of Lochnagar may have changed in dress, politics and equipment, but the mountains and the stories are timeless.

Dave Brown and Ian R Mitchell won the Boardman Tasker Prize for Mountain Literature in 1991 for *A View from the Ridge*, the sequel to *Mountain Days & Bothy Nights*.

Scotland's Mountains before the Mountaineers

Ian R Mitchell
ISBN 978 0946487 39 4 PBK £9.99

In this ground breaking book, Ian R Mitchell tells the story of explorations and ascents in the Scottish Highlands in the days before mountaineering became a popular sport – when Jacobites, bandits, poachers and illicit distillers traditionally used the mountain as sanctuary.

Scotland's Mountains before the Mountaineers is divided into four Highland regions, with a map of each region showing key summits. While not designed primarily as a guide, it is nevertheless a useful handbook for walkers and climbers. Based on a wealth of new research, this book offers a fresh perspective that will fascinate climbers and mountaineers, and anyone interested in the history of mountaineering, cartography, the evolution of the landscape and the social history of the Scottish highlands.

This is a book which every hill-goer, whatever their interests, should own, one of a rare breed offering new delights from hard worn research.
HAMISH BROWN, TGO *Magazine*

The Ultimate Guide to the Munros Volume 1: Southern Highlands

Ralph Storer

ISBN 978 1906307 57 8 PBK £14.99

From the pen of a dedicated Munros bagger comes *The Ultimate Guide* to everything you've wished the other books had told you before you set off. The lowdown on the state of the path, advice on avoiding bogs and tricky situations, tips on how to determine which bump is actually the summit in misty weather... this is the only guide to the Munros you'll ever need.

This comprehensive rucksack guide features:

- Detailed descriptions of all practicable ascent routes up all the Munros and Tops in the region
- Easy to follow quality and difficulty ratings
- Annotated colour photographs and OS maps
- The history of each Munro and Top
- Notes on technical difficulties, foul-weather concerns, winter conditions and scenery

Volume 2: Central Highlands South and *Volume 3: Central Highlands North* are also now available.

The East Highland Way

Kevin Langan

ISBN 978 1906817 91 6 PBK £9.99

The East Highland Way is a detailed and descriptive guide to the route developed by Kevin Langan in 2007. Beginning in Fort William and culminating in Aviemore, the trail forms a new link route between the northern end of the West Highland Way and the southern end of the Speyside Way. In addition, the route joins with the Great Glen Way at its southern point in Fort William, making this an exciting new challenge for seasoned walkers and amateurs alike. Not only an illustrated route description, Langan also details the plethora of wildlife and historical attractions to be spotted along the way in each section of the walk.

There is a real need for alternative routes and The East Highland Way *offers not only an alternative, but a highly attractive and challenging walk in its own right.*
CAMERON MCNEISH

Luath Press Limited

committed to publishing well written books worth reading

LUATH PRESS takes its name from Robert Burns, whose little collie Luath (*Gael.*, swift or nimble) tripped up Jean Armour at a wedding and gave him the chance to speak to the woman who was to be his wife and the abiding love of his life. Burns called one of 'The Twa Dogs' Luath after Cuchullin's hunting dog in Ossian's *Fingal*. Luath Press was established in 1981 in the heart of Burns country, and now resides a few steps up the road from Burns' first lodgings on Edinburgh's Royal Mile.

Luath offers you distinctive writing with a hint of unexpected pleasures.

Most bookshops in the UK, the US, Canada, Australia, New Zealand and parts of Europe either carry our books in stock or can order them for you. To order direct from us, please send a £sterling cheque, postal order, international money order or your credit card details (number, address of cardholder and expiry date) to us at the address below. Please add post and packing as follows: UK – £1.00 per delivery address; overseas surface mail – £2.50 per delivery address; overseas airmail – £3.50 for the first book to each delivery address, plus £1.00 for each additional book by airmail to the same address. If your order is a gift, we will happily enclose your card or message at no extra charge.

Luath Press Limited
543/2 Castlehill
The Royal Mile
Edinburgh EH1 2ND
Scotland
Telephone: 0131 225 4326 (24 hours)
Fax: 0131 225 4324
email: sales@luath.co.uk
Website: www.luath.co.uk

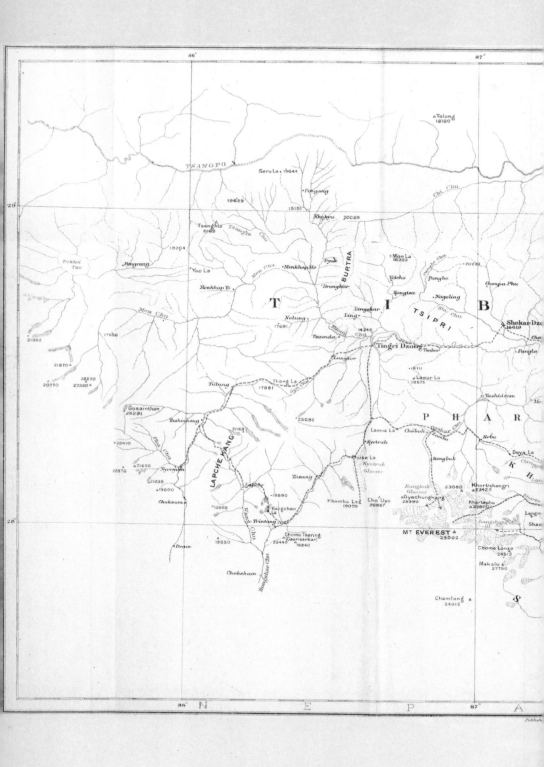